Marxian and Christian Utopianism

Marxian and Christian Utopianism

Toward a Socialist Political Theology

John Joseph Marsden

Monthly Review Press
New York

Library of Congress Cataloging in Publication Data

Marsden, John Joseph.
  Marxian and Christian utopianism: toward a socialist political theology/
John Joseph Marsden.
     p. cm.
  Includes bibliographical references and index.
  ISBN 0-85345-829-4: $33.00. — ISBN 0-85345-832-4 (pbk.): $16.00
   1. Socialism, Christian. 2. Utopian socialism. 3. Communism and
Christianity. 4. Marx, Karl. 1818-1883. I. Title.
HX51.M36 1991
335'.7—dc20   91-15115
                                           CIP

Monthly Review Press
122 West 27th Street
New York, N.Y. 10001

Manufactured in the United States of America

10 9 8 7 6 5 4 3 2 1

For Alis

Contents

Socialism and Christianity have many kinds of concordance, especially in the most important matters. It is good that it is so, both in order to give depth to the avowal of socialism as well as—and perhaps even more important—to give the avowal of Christianity a sign of genuineness, and in such a manner that a new era of Christianity will be indicated, one which will light the way as the light of hope: a new era in which the kingdom of the Son of Man will occur not merely as something "above."

Ernst Bloch, "Man as Possibility"

Preface

Although this book was conceived prior to recent momentous events in Eastern Europe, an exploration of the humanist foundations of Marx's thought has, if anything, acquired even greater relevance. I have used the word "Marxian" specifically in the title as a means of indicating an affinity with the humanism of Marx—developed by thinkers such as Ernst Bloch—rather than the more determinist side of the Marxist tradition.

I would like to express my gratitude to David McLellan, John Heywood Thomas, Vince Drongin, Krishan Kumar, and Karen Judd, who have all given wise counsel and advice. In a study of this kind, however, I must stress that I bear sole responsibility for the views expressed.

Edited versions of Chapters 5 and 9 appeared in *New Blackfriars* and *The Modern Churchman*, respectively, and I am grateful to the editors. An earlier, shortened version of Chapter 6 was given as a lecture at Pittsburgh Theological Seminary, where I benefited from the hospitality of Ronald Stone.

Bishop David Say made possible a period of sabbatical leave at a crucial stage in the preparation. Finally, John Howarth and Chris Pink gave invaluable assistance with the more intricate aspects of word processing.

J.M., 1991

Introduction

The idea of developing a political theology in close association with Marxism is a controversial one. Marx began his work with a critique of religion as a form of alienation, and regarded the rejection of religion as a prerequisite for human emancipation. Christianity, for its part, has often been so preoccupied with other-worldly concerns that it has neglected the task of relating its message to the social and political realm. The aim of this book is to show that when Christianity and Marxism are understood in terms of their utopian content there is a sufficient unity of perspective to justify the construction of a political theology which draws upon a humanist interpretation of Marxism.

In common usage, to describe something as utopian is to condemn it as being unrealizable—the etymology of the word (no place) would seem to confirm this. It was Thomas More who first introduced the word "utopia" from the Greek *ou* and *topos*. However, there was an ambiguity in the meaning More gave to utopia—the poet laureate of the island of Utopia claimed that his country deserved to be called "Eutopia," meaning simply good or ideal place.[1] This highlights the moral content of More's utopia, which was an attempt to consider the social and political implications of the ideals of renaissance humanism. It also indicates a possible understanding of utopia which no longer identifies it with the essentially unrealizable, but defines it as an image of an alternative and ideal world. The distinction is crucial since equating utopia with the unrealizable fulfills a definite ideological function through absolutizing the status quo and thereby affirming the interests of the dominant social group.[2]

Utopianism has its origin in the innate tendency in human beings to desire and strive to create a better world. The utopian drive is a basic impulse and propensity—an anthropological constant.[3] The production of developed literary utopias can be traced back to early Judaic and Classical history. The prophetic and messianic traditions of the Bible are replete with visions and accounts of the utopia which Yahweh will bring, while in Plato's *Republic* we find a description of "the ideal state," a theme taken up by Aristotle.[4] The messianism of the Old Testament merged into the eschatology of Jesus and early Christianity, which despite attempts to suppress it, repeatedly erupted in the millenarianism that has been a constant feature of the Church's history—millenarianism here understood as the belief in a final stage of history, the reign of God's Kingdom on earth, and not just the literal thousand-year period spoken of in the book of Revelation. With the Renaissance, the classical utopia again became influential, and along with the eschatology of Joachim di Fiore and the radical Franciscans, helped give birth to modern utopianism in the West through the work of More and others.[5]

Although some utopias are located in a different place (More), or in the past (the "Golden Age"), the dominant conception which stems from the Judeo-Christian tradition situates utopia in the future—not just any alternative future, but a qualitatively new future, an ideal future, which embodies principles such as justice, peace, and social harmony. The emphasis on total transformation is strongly in evidence in apocalyptic and millenarian sects, with their predictions of the ushering in of an era of universal harmony. In the modern discussion of utopia, Gustav Landauer and Ernst Bloch stress the revolutionary function of utopias—Landauer identifying the way utopias break up stable existing orders. Karl Mannheim also speaks of utopias as tending to shatter the prevailing order of things—though this is only known *post-festum.*[6]

Attempting a definition of utopia is a hazardous task, not least because of the diversity and complexity of the sources. For example, millenarianism, with its emphasis on divine intervention and the extravagance of some of its claims, differs from other forms of utopianism. However, in many respects modern utopianism can be understood as a secularized form of millenarianism, and even where theology may wish to retain a millenarian perspective the need for a process of de-mythologizing is widely accepted. Clearly, if the sense of utopian possibility is not to be damaged, utopia must not be interpreted in absolute terms.[7]

Despite these important qualifications, the various strands within the utopian tradition can be usefully encompassed within a recognizable and workable notion of utopia as *a qualitatively new and ideal future characterized by justice, peace, and a greater harmony.*[8] Moreover, such a definition does have its distinctiveness in that it gives special weight to Jewish and Christian prophetism. It is in Hebrew thought that we have as Paul Tillich puts it, "the real birthplace of a universal historical consciousness."[9] Here we find the idea that history itself has a goal—a definitive break with the cyclical view of history as understood in the ancient world. Here also is the crucial ethical component—the emphasis upon the imperative of *justice.*

Within human history utopian ideas have had a major impact. The ideas and values which utopias enunciate provide a perspective free from the dominant patterns of thinking, and through which the existing situation may be judged. By becoming a catalyst to creative imagination, utopias empower people to transform existing social conditions. They act as a stimulus to critical and revolutionary thinking, making it possible to overcome the inertia and tyranny of the status quo. Zygmunt Bauman correctly points out that utopias have a crucial role in the historical process:

> Utopias relativise the present. One cannot be critical about something that is believed to be an absolute. By exposing the partiality of current reality, by scanning the field of the possible in which the real occupies merely a tiny plot, utopias pave the way for a critical attitude and a critical activity which alone can transform the present predicament of man. The presence of utopia, the ability to think of alternative solutions to the festering problems of the present, may be seen therefore as a necessary condition of historical change.[10]

Inasmuch as the socialism of Marx calls into question the present order, and projects the possibility of a qualitatively new society as an alternative to capitalism, it too can be seen as utopian. Bauman describes the socialist utopia as "the counter-culture of capitalism."[11] Although Marx had his reasons for formally rejecting utopianism, the analysis which occupies the first four chapters of this book seeks to substantiate the case for a utopian reading of his work. This introduction can only in part anticipate the case set out in the main text. The identification of the utopian core in Marx's socialism is not based on isolated references, but established through a consideration of his work in its totality. Central to the argument is an understanding of utopianism which places the human subject at the center. Thus the impersonal determinism of much of later Marxism is decisively rejected. This implies an impoverished view of the human individual, as one who reacts automatically to external stimuli, and who would be a poor subject for sustaining, let alone creating, the society of human freedom.

The perception of the individual as an *active subject,* and of the constitutive role of human consciousness in transforming society, suggests the need for socialism to cultivate utopian aspirations. The vision of a new society nurtures a form of consciousness which calls into question the existing social order, and which is enthused by the prospect for change. Images of the future evoke the desire for their fulfillment, and challenge people to work for their realization. Through their power to inspire, they act like a magnet, drawing people toward the other and better future.

The generation of what William Morris describes as the "ardent desire for socialism" is the prime objective of the socialist cultivation of utopian vision: "Intelligence enough to conceive, courage enough to will, power enough to compel. If our ideas of a new Society are anything more than a dream, these three qualities must animate the due effective majority of the working people; and then, I say, the thing will be done."[12] For socialism to become a reality, it needs its utopia, the images of which cannot be derived solely from the past which is to be transcended, but must also be drawn from the future which is anticipated.

In modern Christian theology, since the rediscovery of eschatology by Weiss and Schweitzer, and with the increased knowledge of Jewish and Christian apocalyptic, it has become widely accepted that Christ's eschatology was radically this-worldly, and that his teaching of the Kingdom of God referred to a reality *within* history.[13] It would be beyond the scope of the present study to include an examination of the New Testament texts themselves. Suffice to say that the case for a millenarian reading of Christian origins has recently been ably demonstrated by Christopher Rowland, who documents the way in which Jesus' conviction about the imminent reign of God on earth was modified by early Christianity. Thus, in the case of Pauline eschatology, Rowland argues that although the belief in future transformation is not abandoned, it no longer has the importance of the quest for personal holiness, as the Christian hope becomes increasingly "internalized and individualized."[14]

The book of Revelation, which was to survive within the Canon, provides eloquent testimony to the persistence of the millenarian perspective. Moreover, although millenarianism within the early Church was forcefully undermined by the identification of the millennium with the Church itself, in Christian history the idea of a third or final stage of history remained influential. Joachim di Fiore's prophecy of the age of the Spirit, the radical sectarians of the Reformation and the dissenters of the English Revolution all kept this interpretation of history alive.

When the utopian content of the original Gospel message is brought to the fore, and with it the will to work for the realization of the Kingdom of God within history itself, and not just transcendentally, the unity of interest and purpose with the Marxist utopia of a society free from injustice and alienation is evident, and justifies the attempt to develop a political theology in union with socialist utopianism. This is not to say that Christianity and Marxism can be simply fused together, but only that in certain vital respects there is a degree of convergence which indicates significant possibilities. For example, a renewed Christianity, through the richness of its imagery and depth of its utopian tradition, along with the social forces it is able to enlist, can bring an added potential to the socialist movement. Marxism in turn helps reinstate and give positive expression to the Christian understanding of the Kingdom of God as an inner-historical reality, and thereby gives it added strength and relevance.

Much of modern social theology in the Western Church has tended to concentrate on the more limited objectives of reform and amelioration within modern capitalist society, preferring to eschew Marxism and to accept the basic legitimacy of the existing social structure. In this way it has in part contributed to the development of what is commonly referred to as "welfare capitalism." However, despite some undoubted material advances, the failure of liberalism and post-war social democracy to bring about a just social and economic order raises the question of whether more fundamental alternatives are needed. With the reemergence of widespread structural unemployment, it has also become increasingly apparent in recent years that changing economic circumstances have eroded the basis of previous consensus policies. Under the impact of less favorable conditions for economic growth the advanced capitalist countries are now no longer committed to the maintenance of full employment, and more aggressive free-market ideologies which seek to undermine existing welfare arrangements have become influential.

It is in this context that the need for a socialist political theology developed in dialogue with Marxist theory, which has as its objective not simply piecemeal reform but real social transformation, becomes a pressing issue. This task is already occupying the attention of theologians in third world countries (whose experience of capitalism has been a good deal less favorable than our own), but comparatively little work has been done in the West. A common charge against recent "liberation theology" has been that it is over-dependent on Marxism and thereby risks compromising the Christian message. However, from the perspective of the present work, the problem with liberation theology is, if anything, that it does not take Marxism sufficiently seriously. The tendency among many of its exponents to make only an instrumental use of the Marxist analysis of society misses the theological import of much of Marx's teaching. The issues raised by Marx's secularized utopianism are in fact of decisive importance for any serious examination of the contemporary relevance of the Kingdom of God, and the significance of

Marxism for theology goes far beyond its use as a convenient tool for the scientific analysis of social structures or the construction of theories of dependence. In saying this, it is assumed that a distinction can, and indeed must, be made between the ideas of Marx and thinkers such as Lenin, Stalin, or Mao. To conflate Marx's work in this way and to regard him as espousing a crude metaphysical materialism hardly constitutes a serious wrestling with the challenge which his ideas represent for Christian theology.[15]

Marxism, like Christianity, has suffered the fate of having its ideas distorted and injustice defended in its name. Existing so-called socialist societies, founded in the most backward and unpropitious circumstances, have done untold damage to the case for socialism. Despite this legacy, in the capitalist societies of the West Marxism has remained a vital intellectual force and has increasingly sought to distinguish itself from the degeneration of socialism elsewhere. The contradictions inherent in the totalitarian societies of the East were readily enough diagnosed. Indeed, for contemporary Marxism the surprising thing about recent events in the communist world is that, even with the contribution to internal cohesion provided by the Cold War, such a crisis did not occur sooner! It is uncertain what kind of political system will emerge from the present mixture of reform and disintegration in the Eastern bloc. The restoration of free market capitalism would seem the likely outcome in a number of countries. Elsewhere the possibilities exist for the development of a renewed and democratic socialism, though the obstacles in economic and cultural terms are formidable.

For these reasons Marxism at the present time is widely seen as discredited. Talk of "post-Marxism" and the triumph of liberal capitalism abounds. However, bourgeois society has not eliminated many of its profound injustices nor its inherent instability. Moreover, while capitalism clearly has not historically exhausted itself, at a future and more advanced stage of its development it could yet provide the material basis for the fulfillment of Marx's utopian vision. To reassert itself Marxism must return to its roots as a humanist form of utopianism and articulate this alternative vision. Theology, too, must respond to the epochal events of our time, which call, not for the abandonment, but for a new assessment of the Christian-Marxist dialogue. This book is offered as a contribution to that project.

The present study has involved work of an essentially interdisciplinary nature, and inevitably there have been certain dilemmas with the organizing of material. The opening chapters are devoted exclusively to establishing the legitimacy of a utopian interpretation of Marxism. This is done through chapters on the early Marx (1), Marx's materialist conception of history (2), and Marx's mature economics (3 and 4). There follows a chapter (5) on the Marxist philosopher Ernst Bloch, whose "messianic Marxism" forms an invaluable bridgehead between Marxism and Christianity and demonstrates the centrality of utopianism for both. The latter part of the book includes chapters on Paul Tillich (6 and 7) and Jürgen Moltmann (8). As preeminent examples of a tradition in modern European theology which gives priority to eschatological themes and dialogue with Marxist theory, the work of these two theologians will be evaluated critically. In the final chapter (9), the idea of constructing a political theology in union with socialist utopianism will be discussed, in the context of considering some of the potential objections and challenges which such a thorough dialogue with Marxism poses.

Although the various chapters stand independently, more than a collection of essays is intended, and utopianism provides the thematic link. It might be considered by some readers that the first part of the book constitutes an unnecessarily long detour, but I bear in mind Paul Tillich's advice: *"The churches ought to acquire an exact knowledge of communism....a true insight into the theoretical foundation of communism."* With some notable exceptions, most theological writing upon Marx suffers from too cursory a knowledge of the subject and much of its criticism is misdirected.[16] The decision to concentrate exclusively on political theory in the opening chapters in fact serves a methodological purpose, since a socialist political theology and the particular issues it raises cannot be adequately articulated in isolation. Central questions such as the atheism inherent in the Marxian vision of the future, and the perceived conflict between socialist utopianism and the Christian doctrine of human nature, are rightly addressed only at the culmination of the present work.

In recent years "political theology" has been associated with particular developments in European theology—most notably the work of Jürgen Moltmann and Johannes Metz, who argue that theology should assume a critical function in relation to the social order and not sacralize existing structures. However, as these thinkers would be the first to acknowledge, all theology is necessarily *political*. In a similar vein one might say that all theology is, or at least should be, *liberation* theology. It is significant in this respect that in its recent declarations the Roman hierarchy has been able to utilize much of the language of the liberation theologians while still opposing their basic ideas. In this general area there is a need for the terminology to made a good deal more specific, and to speak of *socialist political theology* does at least have the virtue of removing some of the ambiguity. The *constructive* task of creating such a theology, if only in outline, would clearly constitute a venture of mammoth proportions, and Chapters 5-9 only make a start in this direction. The project in which I have been engaged is concerned with the preliminary objective of justifying such an endeavor through indicating a productive way in which the dialogue between Marxism and Christianity can be significantly advanced. The centrality accorded to a utopian perspective explains why I have been drawn to the work of Bloch, Tillich, and Moltmann.

Finally, I must add that in relating Marxist utopianism only to Christianity I do not consider the social and political implications of other religious traditions to be withqut relevance, but simply acknowledge that such an enterprise would be beyond my competence. Nor does the fact that I have ignored the non-Marxian heritage within the socialist tradition imply that I dismiss its importance. Even the restricted scope of the present work constitutes a project of potentially enormous proportions. All I can hope to do is to strike out into what is undoubtedly fairly uncharted territory. What is really needed is the impetus of a theological movement committed to wrestling with the questions posed by the serious problems and injustices in contemporary capitalist society, and to the struggle to bring to birth the future which is not-yet.

Chapter 1

Utopian Beginnings: The Early Marx

The idea of a utopian element in Marx's thought is usually dismissed on the basis of Marx's own strictures on utopian socialism, which recur throughout his writings. Closer examination, however, reveals that although his thinking developed in contradistinction to the ideas of the utopian socialists, not only did it have a strong indebtedness to these ideas, but from the outset the structure of his emerging socialist understanding evinced a fundamentally utopian character.

Marx and the Utopian Socialists

The influence on Marx of utopian socialism can be traced back to his childhood. His birthplace, the Rhineland, for a time had fallen under French jurisdiction, and in consequence the ideas and traditions of the French revolution had been introduced into Rhenish culture.[1] In his native Trier, by the 1830s utopian socialism had become the subject of public debate and controversy. The ideas of Fourier were enthusiastically propagated by a city official, Ludwig Gall, and such was the general interest in utopian socialism that the Archbishop felt it necessary to condemn the doctrines of Saint-Simon. We also know that Baron von Westphalen, who took a keen interest in the young Marx's intellectual development, introduced him to the thought of Saint-Simon.[2]

Marx again came into contact with utopian socialism while studying at Berlin, through the poetry of Heinrich Heine and in lectures given by Edward Gans, a liberal Hegelian who lectured in law and had written a book on Saint-Simon.[3] However, it was not until his stay in Paris in 1843-44 that he was to make a really thorough acquaintance with the ideas of the French utopian socialists. In the 1840s Paris was widely acknowledged to be the center of socialist thought and Marx was deeply influenced by this political atmosphere.[4] The two really outstanding figures in the formation of the French socialist tradition had been Saint-Simon and Fourier, whose ideas remained the subject of intense debate long after their deaths in 1825 and 1837, respectively.[5]

The Saint-Simonians, Fourierists, Cabet, and Proudhon could all in varying degrees be classified as utopians, even though their ideas diverged very considerably.[6] It was in this context that Marx developed his own thinking, and it is not difficult to see how ideas such as Saint-Simon's emphasis on the potential of modern productive industry for radically transforming society, and Fourier's invective against the unequal distribution of wealth, would have been extremely important.[7]

When Engels later claimed that Marx's ideas were based on a synthesis of German idealist philosophy, French political theory, and English classical economics, he was rightly acknowledging the extent of Marx's indebtedness to French utopian socialism.[8] However, as Marx developed his own conception of socialism, critically assimilating the various elements of the French socialist tradition, he distanced himself from many of the ideas of the utopian socialists.

Thus already in the *Paris Manuscripts* of 1844 we find certain criticisms of Proudhon, Fourier, Saint-Simon, Cabet, and Villegardelle.[9] By 1846 in *The German Ideology*, Marx, in cooperation with Engels, had formulated his materialist conception of history, and through his analysis of historical development, established a scientific basis for his ideas which contrasted sharply with those of the utopian socialists. Their "systems," we are told, arose at an earlier stage when they "corresponded perfectly to the still underdeveloped consciousness of the proletarians." Marx and Engels now wished to distinguish their own idea of communism: "Communism is for us not a *state of affairs* which is to be established, an *ideal* to which reality will have to adjust itself. We call communism the *real* movement which abolishes the present state of things."[10]

It is in the *Communist Manifesto* of 1848 that we find the first extended discussion of utopian socialism. Here Marx gives a critique of Saint-Simon, Fourier, Owen, and others, whose ideas he again associates with early capitalism, when the bourgeoisie had only just gained the ascendency. In such conditions, since the embryonic proletariat was not yet a recognizable force for emancipation, the utopian socialists had turned their attention to more fantastic schema for social change. Marx considered their appeal to the whole of society, rejection of revolutionary means of change, and fondness for modest experiment to be completely unrealistic. He conceded that, initially, these utopian movements fulfilled a positive and critical function, through their criticism of existing society. Their more or less instinctive response to the social situation and their proposals for the future were of great value, and Marx even acknowledged their works to be "full of the most valuable material for the enlightenment of the working class." However, economic development and the emergence of a more fully developed proletariat made their fantastic projections divorced from the class struggle more of an encumbrance than a positive help.[11]

Thus the reason Marx dismissed the abstract utopias of the utopian socialists was that they were constructed without any consideration of the real forces in society leading to change. However, insofar as Marx did not allow the reticence he inherited from Hegel concerning speculation about the future to preclude projecting the communist future from *existing* conditions, he himself still retained a utopian impulse within his thought. Moreover, his acknowledgement of certain positive elements in the ideas of the utopian socialists shows that he was by no means engaged in a refutation of all utopian ideas.

In their later writings both Marx and Engels occasionally referred to the utopian socialists, and while their comments range from praise to contempt, there are enough favorable citations to suggest that they still valued the heritage of this tradition. For example, in a letter to Kugelmann in 1866, Marx wrote: "In the utopias of a Fourier, an Owen, etc., there is the anticipation and imaginative expression of a new world."[12] In 1870, Engels records his exceedingly high regard for the founders of utopian socialism: "German theoretical socialism will never forget that it stands on the shoulders of Saint-Simon, Fourier and Owen, three men who despite their fantasies and utopianism are to be reckoned among the most significant minds of all time, for they anticipated with genius countless matters whose accuracy we now demonstrate scientifically."[13] Robert Owen was a particular favorite of both Marx and Engels, and Marx paid tribute to him as one of those "really doughty natures who, once having struck out on a revolutionary path, always draw fresh strength from their defeats and become more decisive the longer they swim in the flood tide of history."[14]

Maynard Solomon is therefore justified in his conclusion that "the founding Marxists opposed the schematic programs and universal panaceas of the Utopians but not the revolutionary core of Utopian thought."[15] Despite their strictures, Marx and Engels considered the great social utopias to be precursors of socialism, and recognized that, in part at least, they themselves were building on this achievement.

The Utopian Schema Within Marx's Paris Writings

In the *Paris Manuscripts* of 1844, a selection of notes not intended for publication, Marx formulates a radical critique of capitalism, making a detailed analysis of how human labor is alienated in capitalist society, and expounding his idea of communism. In contrasting his description of alienation under capitalism with an account of future communist society, where human alienation is overcome and there emerges the fully developed individual, Marx presents us with the form which utopianism was to take within the whole of his work. The quality and depth of this analysis sharply distinguishes his work from the more speculative approach of the utopian socialists, and justifies a detailed consideration of the *Manuscripts*, along with an attempt to indicate the importance of the ideas they contain for the rest of his writings.

The *Manuscripts* begin with an extended discussion of economic questions under the headings "Wages of Labour," "Profit of Capital," and "Rent of Land." Marx gives several graphic descriptions of the plight of the worker under capitalism. The worker is reduced "both spiritually and physically to the condition of a machine." In terms of status the worker has become a "commodity and he is fortunate if he can find a buyer."[16] A series of quotations from Schulz, Pecqueur, and Buret describe the worker's pauperization and exploitation, the dehumanizing effect of machinery, and the sheer misery of the factory system. In the section on rent he notes that in the course of history the old feudal lord and serf relationship is exchanged for the impersonal exploitative relationship of capitalist and worker, with the laborer reduced to the status of "an object of speculation."[17]

Marx's general description, then, of the plight of the worker in capitalist society emphasizes the proletarian's dehumanization and subjection to the power of capital. However, although Marx was clearly inspired by a strong moral and humanitarian concern, the extensive quotations he gives from the classical political economists show that his analysis had a definite empirical foundation.[18] As can be seen from his frequent reference to the writings of Schulz, Pecqueur, and Buret, Marx always combined the empirical with the moral. The fact-value distinction which we find in modern positivism would have been quite foreign to him.[19]

The economic section of the Manuscripts is followed by Marx's famous passage on "Alienated Labour," where he gives a detailed conceptual analysis of the worker's condition of alienation. In contrast to the political economists, he makes the wretched and impoverished condition of the worker, which he describes as "a *contemporary* economic fact," the fundamental starting point of his own economic investigations.[20] He identifies four aspects of alienation in capitalist society.

Firstly, workers are alienated from the objects they produce. Marx describes the product of labor as an objectification of labor, but since, with capitalism, objectification appears as "*loss* and as *servitude to the object*, and appropriation as *alienation*," the worker becomes "related to the *product of his labour* as to an *alien* object." Again he writes that the object produced by labor "stands opposed to it as an *alien being*, as a *power independent* of the producer."[21] This alienation from the products of their labor also results in alienation from the "sensuous external world."[22]

Secondly, alienation also arises in the actual process of production. This follows from the fact that if the worker is alienated from the products of labor, then clearly the activity of production must itself be alienating. Thus Marx asks: "How could the worker stand in an alien relationship to the product of his activity if he did not alienate himself in the act of production itself?" In capitalist society labor is external to the worker's essential nature, is forced and not voluntary—an activity belonging to someone else. Marx describes the way in which the worker's activity becomes something alien as "self-alienation."[23]

The third characteristic of alienated labor is that workers are alienated from their species-life. The terms "species-life" and "species-being" that Marx uses are derived from Feuerbach, and indicate that human beings are conscious of themselves not only as individuals but also as members of the species.[24] Marx emphasizes universality and self-consciousness as being the defining human characteristics. By universality he is referring to the way human beings interact with, and make use of, the whole of nature. However, since workers are alienated from the product of their labor and increasingly from the world of nature, as well as in the activity of labor itself, they are therefore also alienated from their species-life.

Explaining what he means by species-being Marx writes: "The practical construction of an *objective world*, the *manipulation* of inorganic nature, is the confirmation of man as a conscious species-being." In contrast, although animals too can produce, they only produce what is necessary for survival, while humans produce universally. Having defined what he understands by true species-being, Marx sets this against the worker's actual conditions: "While, therefore, alienated labour takes away the object of production from man, it also takes away his *species-life*, his real objectivity as a species-being, and changes his advantages over the animals into a disadvantage in so far as his inorganic body, nature, is taken from him."[25]

From the three previous aspects of alienation Marx infers a fourth, namely, that the worker is alienated from other human beings. Beginning with workers' alienation from their species-life Marx asserts: "In general, the statement that man is alienated from his species-life means that each man is alienated from others, and that each of the others is likewise alienated from human life."[26] The point Marx makes is easily understood: if humans must have free interaction with the world of nature, which they shape in coopera- tion with each other, and if this is vitiated under capitalism, then their relation with other people is no longer one of cooperation but of alienation. This alienation from other people also follows directly from the alienation both from the products of labor and in productive activity itself, in that someone else controls the objects produced and the labor process: "The *alien* being to whom labour and the product of labour belong...can only be *man* himself."[27]

The first manuscript unfortunately breaks off uncompleted, and does not follow the analysis of alienated labor with a discussion of unalienated labor. However, precisely such a discussion does occur in Marx's notebook on James Mill, written at this time, and this can help us piece together Marx's ideas. The notebook deals with the dehumanizing effect of money and credit, before considering alienated labor and ends with a description of unalienated labor which we shall quote at length:

> Supposing that we had produced in a human manner; each of us would in his production have doubly affirmed himself and his fellow men. I would have: (1) objectified in my production my individuality and its peculiarity and thus both in my activity enjoyed an individual expression of my life and also in looking at the object have had the individual pleasure of realizing that my personality was objective, visible to the senses and thus a power raised beyond all doubt. (2) In your enjoyment or use of my product I would have had the direct enjoyment of knowing that I had both satisfied a human need by my work and also have objectified the human essence and therefore fashioned for another human being the object that met his need. (3) I would have been for you the mediator between you and the species and thus been acknowledged and felt by you as a completion of your own essence and a necessary part of yourself and have thus realized that I am confirmed both in your thought and in your love. (4) In my expression of my life I would have fashioned your expression of your life, and thus in my own activity have realized my own essence, my human, my communal essence.[28]

This account of unalienated labor complements the idea of species-being found in the first manuscript. Since capitalism suppresses people's essential nature, what is needed is a society organized in a truly human manner which makes possible the full realization of the human essence.[29]

Marx's bitter indictment of capitalism, the analytic penetration and empirical foundation of his critique, and his brief outline of an alternative future unalienated society, constitute more of a breakthrough for utopianism than a departure from it. It was the way Marx was beginning to bring about a synthesis of philosophy, economics, and politics that gave it such profundity when compared with earlier socialist ideas. And yet the heart of this analysis, namely, the preoccupation with the overcoming of alienation, still remained fundamentally utopian.

Marx's analysis of alienated labor must also be considered in close conjunction with the section on "Private Property and Communism" in the third manuscript, where we find his views on the future communist society elaborated as a positive alternative to the alienation experienced in capitalist society. Characteristically, before expounding his own view of communism, Marx attacks the superficiality of the ideas of communism current at the time. He begins by criticizing Proudhon for considering it necessary only to abolish capital, and Fourier and Saint-Simon, who thought all that was needed was to concentrate on particular forms of labor—for Fourier agricultural labor and for Saint-Simon properly organized industrial labor.[30] He then goes on to discuss the first or original form of communism as the generalization of private property. He considers this to be inadequate, since it does not abolish the category of the worker, but merely extends it. This "crude" form of communism, Marx argues, negates human personality in every sphere. With Proudhon clearly in mind, he makes the charge: "The community is only a community of *work* and of *equality of wages* paid out by the communal capital, by the *community* as universal capitalist. The two sides of the relation are raised to a *supposed* universality; *labour* as a condition in which everyone is placed, and *capital* as the acknowledged universality and power of the community."[31] This form of communism, and the other forms to which he briefly alludes, in Marx's view are still contaminated by private property.

Having commented on existing ideas of communism Marx presents his own viewpoint:

> *Communism* is the *positive* abolition of *private property*, of *human self-aliena-*
> *tion*, and thus the real *appropriation* of *human* nature through and for man. It
> is, therefore, the return of man himself as a *social*, i.e., really human, being, a
> complete and conscious return which assimilates all the wealth of previous

development. Communism as fully developed naturalism is humanism and as fully developed humanism is naturalism. It is the *definitive* resolution of the antagonism between man and nature, and between man and man. It is the true solution of the conflict between existence and essence, between objectification and self-affirmation, between freedom and necessity, between individual and species. It is the solution of the riddle of history and knows itself to be this solution.[32]

There can hardly be anything more utopian than the concise outline Marx gives us here of his conception of communism, and his notes continue for several pages on the theme. Rejecting the communism of the utopian socialists, he maintains that communism has its basis in the whole of historical development, and not in isolated historical forms—he mentions here the utopian communism of Cabet and Villegardelle.[33] He repeatedly stresses the social and cooperative character of communist society, along with the union of human beings with nature in such a society.

Also particularly prominent is the description he gives of the fully developed human individual. Private property has resulted in the distortion of all our physical and intellectual senses. Alluding to work by Moses Hess, Marx mentions the alienation of these senses through human possessiveness and the preoccupation with "*having*." But the supersession of private property would liberate all human faculties. Thus Marx's vision of the "whole man" of communist society emerges: "The fully constituted society produces man in all the plenitude of his being, the wealthy man endowed with all the senses, as an enduring reality."[34]

Marx concludes his discussion of communism in language reminiscent of Hegel, describing it as only one stage in the historical process:

> Communism is the phase of negation of the negation and is, consequently, for the next stage of historical development, a real and necessary factor in the emancipation and rehabilitation of man. Communism is the necessary form and the dynamic principle of the immediate future, but communism is not itself the goal of human development—the form of human society.[35]

This seems to contradict his earlier notion of communism as the final stage of history and "the solution to the riddle of history." However, the main point Marx is making is that once communism is firmly established, and society is organized in a truly human way, the ascription "communism" increasingly becomes unnecessary—all that remains is "positive human *self-consciousness*." Thus Marx speaks of how "the *real life* of man is positive and no longer attained through the abolition of private property, through *communism*."[36]

In his understanding of communism Marx was able to go beyond the partial insights of other socialist writers because his whole approach was informed by a much more substantial and elaborate anthropology. His conception of species-being implies humanity's free interaction with the world of nature. This should be a process in which it is the human individual who is the initiator, and who is in control. However, in capitalism this is not the case, and the worker is dominated by external forces. In uncovering this basic human alienation, Marx was convinced that the remedy for this predicament must be equally fundamental and radical, and would require the establishment of fully human social relations and reintegration with the world of nature.

The passage describing communism as "the true solution of the conflict between existence and essence" is, however, far too sweeping. Although communism would markedly change social relationships (and the relationship with the natural world), the notion that it would overcome *all* antagonisms and conflicts is not credible. Personal strife, existential anxiety, disease, and other ills basic to the human condition would still continue to exist under communism.

It is likely in fact that Marx is here presenting us not so much with a literal description of communism, as with an account of communism as a transcendent ideal toward which actually existing communism moves asymptotically. Hence he immediately goes on to write: "Thus the whole historical development, both the *real* genesis of communism (the birth of its empirical existence) and its thinking consciousness, is its comprehended and conscious process of becoming."[37] Yet in the absence of the kind of distinctions in the text which would clarify the intended meaning, it must be said that it would have been much better if he had confined himself to merely predicting the resolution of the major *social* antagonisms, and thus indicated that he had a more modest utopia in mind.

In forming his vision of the "whole man" with renewed and fully developed human faculties, Marx was influenced by the Romantic tradition. Apart from his own reading, his friendship with the poets Heine and Herwegh was no doubt important in this respect.[38] All this may at first seem surprising, since Marx would have clearly poured scorn on romantic notions of a return to some sort of rustic idyll. He would have rejected such reactionary sentiments on the grounds that in primitive conditions scarcity places humans in bondage to nature. The progressive role he assigned to capitalist development shows a definite break with the *weltanschauung* of Romanticism.

However, what he shared with Romanticism was the preoccupation with the fully developed human individual. Marx contended that only a future socialist society could provide the basis for the realization of human freedom to which Romanticism aspired. It should always be remembered that in some respects Romanticism did historically fulfill a positive function, through its criticism of emerging capitalist society.[39] It is perhaps worth noting that Rousseau's notion of an original state of harmony, which had been upset by "civilization" but which could be restored, was not only an important precursor of socialism generally, but also an influence upon Marx.[40]

The publication of the *Paris Manuscripts* in 1932 led to an important reevaluation of Marx and to a renewed interest in the humanist foundations of his thought. It is this humanism which forms the basis of Marx's utopianism, and lies at the heart of both his judgment of capitalist society and his prediction of future communism. Given his intellectual background in classical German philosophy, Marx's humanism should come as no surprise. However, it was not just Feuerbach, or German philosophy in general, that informed and shaped his humanist outlook. The moral outrage we find in the writings of the French socialists, and also in the early critics of capitalism— Schulz, Pecqueur, Buret, and Sismondi—on whom Marx was very dependent, would have also been very important.[41]

Some scholars suggest that Marx quickly abandoned the anthropological perspective of the *Manuscripts*, and that this is clear from his criticisms of "true socialism," which we find in *The German Ideology* and the *Communist Manifesto*. Alfred Schmidt refers to the "abstract and romanticizing anthropology" of the *Manuscripts*, and maintains that Marx "did not completely free himself from Feuerbach's idols 'man' and 'nature', because he lacked an exact knowledge of economic history." It is certainly true that Marx's thought underwent a considerable development after 1844. However, contrary to what Schmidt and others suggest, this did not imply an abandonment of the anthropology we find in the *Manuscripts*, which was already distinguishable from that of Feuerbach.[42] When Marx criticizes "true socialism," it is not his own former position he is rejecting, but the excesses of Grün and Hess, who reduced socialism solely to a moral ideal, regarding love as the foundation of the new society, and completely excluding the notion of class struggle.[43] Marx rightly ridiculed this doctrine, which never made contact with political reality.

The question of whether there is a break between the early and later Marx has been the subject of much controversy, and many leading scholars have postulated such a break.[44] However, since, as we shall see in the following chapters, the central themes of the overcoming of alienation and the full realization of human potential in future communist society recur throughout

Marx's writings, the view cannot be justified, nor can it be claimed that he abandoned his earlier humanist vision.

The persistence of the humanist and the implicitly utopian orientation of Marx's thought does not conflict with the view that Marx accomplished the development of socialism from utopia to science, if we take this to mean that his economic researches and theory of history provided a theoretical basis for the projected future communist society, thus distinguishing his socialism from the utopian socialism of his day. In this limited sense it is true that Marx had broken with utopianism. Understandably, he was reluctant to use the word because of the negative connotations it carried. Nevertheless, despite this formal rejection, utopianism remained an abiding and essential characteristic of his thought.

Chapter 2

History and Utopia:
Marx's Materialist Conception of History

In Marx's *Paris Manuscripts* history is understood as the movement from servitude and alienation to the society of human freedom. However, within this visionary contrast, comparatively little is said about the unfolding of the one form of society into the other. The *Manuscripts* were but a prolegomenon to future work, and in them Marx had only begun the enormous task of integrating the existing socialist tradition with the science of political economy and the heritage of Hegelian idealism. Mapping out the journey of history toward unalienated communist society would require the elaboration of the theory of history which has come to be known as "historical materialism."

Marx himself never used the term "historical materialism" as such. He preferred instead to speak of "the materialist conception of history." Much of what is commonly referred to as "Marxist materialism" in fact stems from later Marxist theoreticians such as Plekhanov, Kautsky, and Lenin—even Engels' work in this particular respect differs markedly from that of Marx.

Attempts to suggest that there exist within Marx's work differing and contradictory views of history are misguided. Issue must therefore be taken with Helmut Fleischer, who, while affirming a humanist reading of Marx and wanting to unite the different strands of his approach to history, sees the writings of 1845-46 as being directed against Marx's earlier "anthropological definition of the meaning of history."[1] Although 1845-46 undoubtedly marked an important stage in the refinement of his previous perspective, Marx's materialist conception of history is still best viewed as complementary to his earlier description of the overcoming of alienation. Moreover, as we shall see later, already by 1844 Marx had gone some way in laying the preliminary foundations for his materialist conception.

Marx's theory of history retained the humanist and utopian impulse of his early writings, and it is possible to offer an interpretation of historical materialism which is not only consistent with, but actually demands, a utopian orientation. The basis for such an account lies in the crucial emphasis which Marx always gave to the role of *consciousness* in historical change. This chapter attempts to elucidate this, together with the humanist and nondeterminist character of Marx's materialism, from which its affinity with a utopian perspective is also evident.

The Genesis of Marx's Materialist Conception of History

In the Germany of Marx's youth Hegelian idealism dominated philosophical thinking and, like many others of his generation, Marx fell under its influence.[2] The spell of the Hegelian synthesis was not, however, to captivate Marx forever, and in his journalistic writings of 1842-43, where he began to concern himself with material and economic issues, the process which was to eventually lead to his detachment from Hegel was already underway.

That these writings represent a significant turning point is supported by Marx's autobiographical reflections in the 1859 Preface to his *Critique of Political Economy*, where he indicates the context in which he developed his materialist conception of history. Referring to his editorship of the *Rheinische Zeitung* in 1842-43, Marx writes that he "experienced for the first time the embarrassment of having to take part in discussions on so-called material interests." Mentioning his articles on the debates in the Rhenish Parliament on wood gathering, and the conditions of the Moselle wine growers, he says that these "provided the first occasions for occupying myself with economic questions." His denunciation in these articles of the undemocratic and unrepresentative character of the Prussian political system which furthered only partial interests, namely, those of the propertied at the expense of the poor, contrasted with the Hegelian conception of the reconciling role of political institutions in the state. However, at this stage Marx's thought was still in transition, and he did not as yet question Hegel's philosophy. He merely criticized the existing state in terms of the ideal state, on the grounds that because of its universal character the state should never place itself at the service of private interests. Nevertheless, when the opportunity came "to withdraw from the public stage into the study," further reflection seems to have persuaded him that it was in fact Hegel's view of the state that must be reconsidered.[3]

Hegel understood Reason (referred to as the Idea or Absolute Spirit) as a cosmic force, and saw the historical process as the unfolding of Reason in various social and cultural institutions. He reconciled the ideal with the real by conceiving reality as the unfolding of the Idea, and thereby rational. However, Marx in his 1843 *Critique of Hegel's Philosophy of Right* came to reject Hegel's system as too speculative, and emphasized instead the opposition between ideals and reality. Although Hegel's philosophy claimed to bridge the gap between the rational and the actual, Marx came to the conclusion that it did not stand up to the test when confronted with concrete political and historical reality.[4]

This fundamental shift in Marx's thinking, and the development of a systematic critique of Hegel, owed much to his reading of Feuerbach. Of particular importance was Feuerbach's *Preliminary Theses for a Reform of Philosophy* and his *Principles of the Philosophy of the Future*, published in 1843.[5] Feuerbach argued that Hegel had supposed thought to be the subject, and existence to be a mere predicate; thus, for Hegel, nature itself had become simply a predicate of thought. He considered that Hegel's idealism was bound to lead to mystification. In opposition to Hegel, he contended that "the true relationship of thought to being is this: being is the subject, thought the predicate. Thought arises from being, being does not arise from thought." Feuerbach proposed a reform of philosophy which would reverse the traditional role of subject and predicate. To arrive at the truth, Hegelian philosophy must undergo a materialist transformation: "We need only make the predicate into the subject and thus reverse speculative philosophy in order to arrive at the unconcealed, pure and naked truth."[6]

In his 1843 *Critique* Marx applied Feuerbach's transformative method to Hegel's theory of the state. Marx considered that with Hegel there was an inversion of the real social relations. Hegel began with the idea of the state, and then understood real empirical history as an expression of the idea of the state. In contrast, Marx insisted that the state is in fact an outgrowth of civil society: "Family and civil society are the presuppositions of the state, they are its properly active elements. But in speculation the relationship is inverted. When the Idea is made a subject, the real subjects, the civil society, the family, 'circumstances, caprice, etc.' become unreal objective phases of the idea and have a completely different significance."[7] In Hegel's political philosophy the clash of social forces in civil society was transcended by the universality of the state. For Marx, however, political institutions only masked the particularistic, egoistic interests of civil society. Thus Hegel's attempted reconciliation was unsuccessful, and did not correspond with the actual social situation, but rather was contradicted by the existence of alienation in modern society. In his 1859 *Preface*, Marx recalled the conclusions of his study of Hegel: "My investigation led to the result that legal relations as well as forms of state are to be grasped neither from themselves nor from the so-called general development of the human mind, but rather have their roots in the material conditions of life."[8]

It was not just his journalistic experience and work on Hegel's theory of the state, however, which led Marx to his recognition of the social and economic realm as being fundamental. During the early 1840s, Marx was in close personal contact with Moses Hess and had read his various writings, welcoming the primacy which Hess gave to social and economic factors.[9] By 1842 Marx had had his first meeting with Engels, whom he treated rather frostily, believing him to be a representative of the Berlin Young Hegelians. Nevertheless, when, at the end of 1843, Engels submitted his *Outlines of a Critique of Political Economy* for publication in the *Deutsch-Französische Jahrbücher*, it was greeted with particular enthusiasm by Marx. It was this work that helped launch Marx on his own study of political economy, which was to preoccupy him for the rest of his life.[10]

Marx's materialist standpoint formed the basis of his critique of religion in his 1844 *Critique of Hegel's Philosophy of Right: Introduction*, and it is in this text that he first ascribes a crucial role to the proletariat in social emancipation. Reviewing the progress in contemporary German politics and philosophy, he considers the possibility of genuine human emancipation in Germany. This, he concludes, can be achieved only by the practical realization of philosophy through a radical revolution that requires the existence of a universal class—the proletariat. He sees theory and practical action as forming a unity: "As philosophy finds in the proletariat its material weapons so the proletariat finds in philosophy its intellectual weapons and as soon as the lightning of thought has struck deep into the virgin soil of the people, the emancipation of Germans into men will be completed." The really interesting feature here is the weight still given to philosophy, and the implicit recognition that economic conditions alone will not give rise to revolution. Marx's rejection of speculative idealism did not imply any abandonment of the crucial role of consciousness and ideas in the process of social change: "Theory, too, will become material force as soon as it seizes the masses."[11]

Thus right at the outset of his discovery of the role of the proletariat, the infusion of revolutionary consciousness was, for Marx, the essential prerequisite of revolutionary transformation. Indeed, so strong was his emphasis on the role of consciousness at this time that he wrote to Ruge in the following terms: "The reform of consciousness consists only in the world becoming aware of its own consciousness, awakening it from vague dreams of itself and showing it what its true activity is....Then it will be seen that the world has long been dreaming of things that it only needs to become aware of in order to possess them in reality."[12] What distinguishes Marx's position from idealistic forms of utopianism is the stress upon, and analysis of, real material conditions already evident in his work of 1843.

In the *Paris Manuscripts* of 1844 it is the primacy of human labor which provided the focus for Marx's reflections. Amid the wide- ranging discussions in these documents, some of the main features of his materialist conception of history can be discerned, although only in embryonic form. "World history," Marx insists, "is nothing but the creation of man by human labour and the development of nature for man." In accord with his basic conception of the ontological priority of human labor, he argues that to understand the phenomenon of private property and the nature of society generally, it is necessary to begin with alienated labor in the process of material production: "This material, immediately sensuous, private property, is the material, sensuous expression of man's alienated life....Religion, family, state, law, morality, science and art are only particular forms of production and fall under its general law." Marx's mature account of historical materialism is also foreshadowed in the brief treatment he gives of the crucial significance of industrial development in human history.[13]

Marx used the *Paris Manuscripts* to outline his relation to Hegel's dialectic. Although he rejected Hegel's idealist vision, he considered Hegel, albeit in a mystified fashion, to have perceived the centrality within the historical process of the self-creation of human beings through their labor:

> The human character of nature and of historically produced nature, the product of man, appears as such in that they are products of abstract mind, and thus phases of the mind, conceptual beings. The *Phenomenology* is thus concealed criticism that is still obscure to itself and mystifying; but in so far as it grasps the alienation of man, even though man appears only in the form of mind, it contains all the elements of criticism concealed, often already prepared and elaborated in a way that far surpasses Hegel's own point of view.[14]

Marx's own dialectic was based upon an appropriation of the conception of historical movement, human labor, and the process of alienation within the Hegelian dialectic, but with the priority given to material reality—a process he describes as inversion. Throughout his life he acknowledged this indebtedness.[15]

In *The Holy Family*, published in February 1845, Marx begins by contrasting his materialism with speculative idealism. Rejecting the excesses of Bruno Bauer, who regarded the masses as a reactionary influence and thought society to be shaped only by "ideas," he insists: "In order to carry out ideas men are needed who can exert practical force."[16] Marx saw the emancipatory role of the masses as crucial, and in the section dealing with Proudhon's work on property, he outlines the historical movement toward communism through the emergence of private property and the proletariat. He sees the path to revolution as the outcome of both need and consciousness. The inhuman conditions and alienation experienced by the proletariat drive it toward conscious action to secure its emancipation. Thus he speaks of "misery conscious of its spiritual and physical misery," and "dehumanization conscious of its dehumanization and therefore self-abolishing."[17]

This stress upon the self-awareness of the proletariat shows that Marx did not envisage revolution as arising inevitably from historical forces independent of human beings. Historical necessity and conscious human action should not be placed in opposition, since class consciousness is both the product of historical development and the vehicle of revolutionary transition. Referring to England and France he comments that "a large part of the English and French proletariat is already conscious of its historic task and is constantly working to develop that consciousness into complete clarity."[18]

From this brief outline of Marx's revolutionary theory it is clear that he did not subscribe to a mechanistic form of materialism. Thus he distances himself from the metaphysical materialism of the seventeenth century derived from Descartes, and emphasizes the significance of the trend stemming from Locke, leading to the more humanist materialism of thinkers such as Helvétius and d'Holbach. This anti-metaphysical humanist strand he also associates with the French communists.

The humanist and social implications of this materialism captivated Marx and formed the basis of his own exposition of communism: "There is no need of any great penetration to see from the teaching of materialism on the natural goodness and equal intellectual endowment of men, the omnipotence of experience, habit, education, and the influence of the environment on man, the great significance of industry, the justification of enjoyment, etc., how necessarily materialism is connected with communism and socialism." However, the identification was limited, in that he assigned a much more active role to the human subject, and thereby rejected the mechanistic implications of the materialism of Helvétius and d'Holbach, who considered human beings in terms of the way they are passively moulded by external circumstances. Thus he continues: "If man draws all his knowledge, sensation, etc., from the world of senses and the experience gained in it, the empirical world must be so arranged so that in it man experiences and gets used to what is really human and that he becomes aware of himself as man....If man is shaped by his surroundings, his surroundings must be made human."[19] For Marx, conscious human activity always exercised a constitutive role in shaping the external world of nature, and he accordingly rejected mechanistic forms of materialism, whether of the metaphysical or anti-metaphysical variety. From *The Holy Family* it is thus evident how wide of the mark is the determinist metaphysics of the Second and Third Internationals.[20]

Understanding the evolution of Marx's materialist conception of history requires further examination of his relation to Feuerbach's materialism. For Feuerbach, philosophy ought not to begin with the Absolute Spirit or the Idea, but with humanity together with nature. In the *Paris Manuscripts*, this anthropology is closely reflected in Marx's picture of the "real man of flesh and blood, standing on the solid, round earth and breathing in and out all the powers of nature." Feuerbach, said Marx, "founded true materialism and real science by making the social relationship of 'man to man' the basic principle of his theory."[21]

Such indebtedness was, however, never uncritical. Feuerbach provided only a starting point for Marx, who turned Feuerbach's abstract anthropology into something much more specific through the consideration of human beings in relation to their social and economic situation. Marx had soon begun to sense Feuerbach's limitations, and as early as 1843 voiced some uneasiness in a letter to Ruge: "Feuerbach's aphorisms only seem to be amiss in one point in that he refers too much to nature and not enough to politics. Nevertheless that is the only link by which present philosophy can become a reality."[22] Even where Feuerbach's influence was at its strongest, in his *Critique* of 1843, Marx included a social and historical dimension which was lacking in Feuerbach. Again, in the *Paris Manuscripts*, despite his praise for Feuerbach, Marx's preoccupation with social and economic questions represents a radical shift from Feuerbach's abstract anthropological humanism.[23]

It was not, however, until his *Theses on Feuerbach* in 1845, that Marx consciously sought to elaborate his differences with Feuerbach, and to attach theoretical import to them. He now wished to define his position in opposition not just to Hegelian idealism, but also to Feuerbachian materialism. First priority was given to the "active side" in materialism, and in part at least his *Theses* were self-criticism. With this stress on the active subject shaping the external world of nature, the historical and human element within Marx's materialism was even stronger, and in this sense the *Theses* are something of a landmark.[24] Many years later Engels describes them as "the first document in which is deposited the brilliant germ of the new world outlook."[25]

Marx considered the prime defect in Feuerbach's philosophy to be that it was purely contemplative. He rejected the way in which, in Feuerbach's materialism, people are reduced to the status of observers of the world, and insisted that reality must always be understood in relation to human practice. His third thesis highlights the internal contradictions resulting from a view of human nature as simply the product of material conditions: "The materialist doctrine concerning the changing of circumstances and upbringing forgets that circumstances are changed by men and that it is essential to educate the educator himself....The coincidence of the changing of circumstances and of human activity or self-changing can be conceived and rationally understood only as revolutionary practice."[26] Thus, for Marx, the primary influence of material conditions must not be understood in such a way as to exclude the crucial role exercised by human consciousness itself.

Marx's *Theses* also indicated his differences with idealism. Although idealism develops the "active side," it does so only "abstractly," and "does not know real, sensuous activity as such." Marx saw the role of human activity in shaping the material world as providing the solution to the problems posed by speculative idealism. Hegel's attempted reconciliation of the ideal with the real was refuted by the continuing existence of alienation. For reality to be reconciled with ideality, and alienation to be overcome, reality itself must undergo a revolutionary transformation. Thus what was needed was not new interpretations of the world, but practical action. In his eleventh thesis Marx had in mind the whole of German philosophy since Hegel: "The philosophers have only interpreted the world, in various ways; the point is to change it."[27]

The Theory Outlined

It is in *The German Ideology*, written in cooperation with Engels, that we find the first really comprehensive presentation of Marx's materialist conception of history. Here Marx and Engels distanced their views from those of Feuerbach and the Young Hegelians, attempting, as Marx puts it in the

Preface of 1859, "to settle accounts with our erstwhile philosophical conscience."

If a date is to be given by which Marx had established his theory of history then it should be 1845-46, with *The German Ideology* in conjunction with the *Theses on Feuerbach*. Scholars who suggest an earlier date underestimate the clarification and more positive elaboration of his ideas achieved within these documents. Such an assessment also contradicts Marx's own testimony in his 1859 *Preface*, where he says that the investigation he began in Paris, he continued in Brussels, and only then goes on to speak of "the general result at which I arrived."[28]

The main charge made by Marx and Engels against the Young Hegelian ideologists was that they philosophize without any reference whatsoever to the real material world. "The premises from which we begin," they declare, "are not arbitrary ones, not dogmas, but real premises from which abstraction can only begin in the imagination. They are the real individuals, their activity and the material conditions under which they live, both those which they find already existing and those produced by their activity." Marx's differences with Feuerbach, and the emphasis on the interchange between human beings and nature, are reiterated at length:

> Feuerbach's "conception" of the sensuous world is confined on the one hand to mere contemplation of it, and on the other to mere feeling; he says "man" instead of "real historical man."... He does not see how the sensuous world around him is, not a thing given direct from all eternity, remaining ever the same, but the product of industry and the state of society; and, indeed, in the sense that it is an historical product....Even the objects of the simplest "sensuous certainty" are only given him through social development, industry and commercial intercourse. The cherry-tree, like almost all fruit-trees, was, as is well known, only a few centuries ago transplanted by *commerce* into our zone, and therefore only *by* this action of a definite society in a definite age it has become "sensuous certainty" for Feuerbach.[29]

It is this understanding of humanity's special relationship with nature that distinguishes Marx's materialism, and makes it, in fact, an *historical* materialism.

For Marx and Engels, it is productive activity which forms the fundamental basis of human existence. Thus they write: "As individuals express their life, so they are. What they are, therefore, coincides with their production." The relationship between the development of the productive forces and the division of labor is then considered: "How far the productive forces of a nation are developed is shown most manifestly by the degree to which the division of labour has been carried."[30] In turn, different stages in the division of labor result in different forms of ownership, such as tribal, ancient, and feudal forms. From these observations, Marx and Engels then draw the following conclusion:

> The fact is, therefore, that definite individuals who are productively active in a definite way enter into these definite social and political relations. Empirical observation must in each separate instance bring out empirically, and without any mystification and speculation, the connection of the social and political structure with production. The social structure and the State are continually evolving out of the life-process of definite individuals, but of individuals, not as they may appear in their own or other people's imagination, but as they *really* are; i.e., as they operate, produce materially, and hence as they work under definite material limits, presuppositions and conditions independent of their will.[31]

The state, in particular, is associated with the social conflict that results from the division of labor and private property: "Out of this very contradiction between the interest of the individual and that of the community the latter takes an independent form as the *State*, divorced from the real interests of individual and community, and at the same time as an illusory communal life, always based, however, on the real ties...."[32]

The analysis is extended to include the realm of ideology. Just as the forms of society and the state have their roots in material life, so do people's ideas, which are also generated under particular circumstances and conditions: "Men are the producers of their conceptions, ideas, etc.—real, active men, as they are conditioned by a definite development of the productive forces and of the intercourse corresponding to these." The formation of ideas must be explained from "material practice," that is, from human productive activity and its associated forms of cooperation: "Morality, religion, metaphysics, all the rest of ideology and their corresponding forms of consciousness, thus no longer retain the semblance of independence. They have no history, no development; but men, developing their material production and their material intercourse, alter, along with this their real existence, their thinking and the products of their thinking."[33]

Marx's materialist conception of history was by no means a straightforward materialist inversion of Hegelian idealism. If at times he appeared to be implying a crude mechanistic materialism, then the polemical context in which he and Engels were writing must be remembered. It was the attempt of speculative philosophy to make the world of ideas autonomous and independent of concrete material conditions which they were anxious to reject.

However, the fact that ideas have their origin in material conditions did not in any way lessen their crucial role in the social system and in the process of social transition. Indeed the section "Ruling Class and Ruling Ideas" opens by saying: "The ideas of the ruling class are in every epoch the ruling ideas, i.e., the class which is the ruling *material* force in society, is at the same time its ruling *intellectual* force."[34] Marx and Engels link the development of the productive forces with the growth of consciousness, writing that from the proletariat there "emanates the consciousness of the necessity of a fundamental revolution." It is this consciousness which—when heightened in the revolutionary process itself—makes revolution possible. Thus it is conscious human intervention, and not mechanistic processes, that leads the way to communist society.[35]

The central thesis of *The German Ideology*, concerning the primacy of material production, is rather crudely summarized in Marx's book *The Poverty of Philosophy*, published in 1847.

> In acquiring new productive forces men change their mode of production; and in changing their mode of production, in changing the way of earning their living, they change all their social relations. The hand mill gives you society with the feudal lord, the steam-mill, society with the industrial capitalist.[36]

Although this seems to suggest a very determinist approach, it is the polemical context that must again be taken into consideration. Through a confused application of Hegel's philosophy, Proudhon had treated economic categories and social relations as though they were eternal and not historical, namely, the result of particular conditions of production.[37] Not that this exonerates Marx, it merely helps explain the deficiency in his work. Many years later Engels conceded the shortcomings of his and Marx's earlier works, citing the circumstances under which they were writing: "Marx and I are ourselves partly to blame for the fact that younger writers sometimes lay more stress on the economic side than is due to it. We had to emphasize this main principle *vis-à-vis* our adversaries, who denied it, and we had not always the time, the place or the opportunity to give their due to the other elements involved in the interaction."[38] Marx, in particular, was inclined to the use of epigrammatic phrases, often at the expense of expressing his ideas with the precision they required—and this failure was not confined to his early life.

That Marx did not subscribe to a narrow determinism is evident from the way he continued to give a central place to the role of consciousness in historical change. In *The Poverty of Philosophy* he sees industrial development as eventually bringing about a situation where the struggle of the proletariat begins to assume a more pronounced form and becomes political in character. A point is reached where the proletariat "constitutes itself as a class for itself," and its antagonism to the bourgeoisie becomes a "political struggle."[39] This change is reflected in the work of theoreticians of the socialist and communist movement which, when capitalism is in its infancy is only utopian, but later becomes revolutionary:

> So long as they look for science and merely make systems, so long as they are at the beginning of the struggle, they see in poverty nothing but poverty, without seeing in it the revolutionary, subversive side, which will overthrow the old society. From the moment they see this side, science, which is produced by the historical movement and associating itself consciously with it, has ceased to be doctrinaire and has become revolutionary.[40]

Thus, for Marx, theory and practical action unite in a struggle which is conscious, organized and political, and historical transition is perceived first and foremost as the product of human activity.

"Base," "Superstructure," and the Priority of the Productive Forces in Marx's Materialism

The most widely discussed statement of Marx's materialist conception of history occurs in the 1859 *Preface* to his *Critique of Political Economy*, where his influential metaphor of "base" and "superstructure" is to be found in its most developed form. Describing his materialist method as the "guiding thread" of his studies, he outlined a concise summary, part of which is here quoted:

> In the social production of their life, men enter into definite relations that are indispensable and independent of their will, relations of production which correspond to a definite stage of development of their material productive forces. The sum total of these relations of production constitutes the economic structure of society, the real foundation, on which rises a legal and political superstructure and to which correspond definite forms of social consciousness. The mode of production of material life conditions the social, political, and intellectual life process in general. It is not the consciousness of men that determines their being, but, on the contrary, their social being that determines their consciousness.[41]

In the *Preface* account it is the relations of production, and not the productive forces, which form the "economic structure of society"—the "real foundation." However, the relations of production into which human beings enter "correspond to a definite stage of development of their material productive forces." Thus the economic structure of society is, in turn, dependent on the productive forces. When Marx speaks of the relations of production, he does not have in mind the work relations (i.e., forms of cooperation) appropriate to a given technology, which are included by him among the productive forces, but the property relations associated with particular forms of production.[42]

The nature of Marx's claim is essentially that the character of production determines, in general, the relations of production or property relations, which form the economic structure of society, and to which correspond the state, ideology, and so on. If this claim is abandoned, and the relations of production are regarded as independent of the productive forces, such a view can no longer in any meaningful sense be regarded as materialist.

Marx's position need not imply the adoption of an extreme form of technological determinism, since assigning a central role to the level of development of the productive forces is consistent with a whole host of variations within the general pattern of historical development. For example, there may be more than one set of possible productive relations for a given set of productive forces. The most obvious example here is the way Western democracies, fascist dictatorships, and bureaucratic collectivist states, despite their political diversity, all subsist under broadly similar industrial conditions. Recognition of this very considerable scope for diversity does not render historical materialism devoid of content since, for any given technology, specific types of society are excluded. Thus the above example could not be extended to also encompass ancient or feudal societies.[43]

The case for productive force primacy has recently been cogently articulated in Gerald Cohen's *Karl Marx's Theory of History: A Defence*. Arguing for a "technological" reading of historical materialism, Cohen maintains "that the productive forces strongly determine the character of the economic structure, while forming no part of it."[44] He goes on to formulate what he calls the primacy thesis: "The nature of the production relations of a society is explained by the level of development of its productive forces." In close association with the belief in the primacy of the productive forces, he introduces another thesis—the "development thesis"—which he summarizes as follows: "The productive forces tend to develop throughout history."[45]

Cohen sees evidence for both theses in Marx's *Preface*. The development thesis is presupposed throughout, and commitment to the primacy thesis is suggested by Marx's claim that "production relations *correspond* to productive forces." Moreover, this correspondence is one way, since when forces and relations come into conflict "the tension is resolved in favour of the forces, by transformation of the relations."[46] He also gives an impressive array of quotes from outside the *Preface* in support of the primacy thesis.[47]

Leaving aside Marx's view, Cohen goes on to provide his own arguments for the two theses. The development thesis has its basis in the character and attributes of human nature, namely, that human beings are rational creatures who in historical circumstances of scarcity have the intelligence and wherewithal to improve their situation through developing the productive forces. In support of the primacy thesis, Cohen writes that "a given level of productive power is compatible only with a certain type, or certain types, of economic structure." (He gives the example of slavery in a society with computer technology).[48] However, this mutual constraint is not sufficient on its own, and the development thesis must be added if the primacy of the forces is to be assured. Given the developing productive forces, it follows that either the relations change, or there is a contradiction between forces and relations which must be resolved in favor of the forces, otherwise development will be impeded.

For Cohen, the character of the productive forces "functionally" explains the corresponding relations: *"The production relations are of a kind R at time t because relations of the kind R are suitable to the use and development of the productive forces at t, given the level of development of the latter at t."*[49] Whether or not a given set of relations continue depends on whether they promote or frustrate the progressive development of the productive forces.

Cohen is at pains to stress that with his reading of the primacy thesis "the effect of the relations on the forces is emphasized," and he is also ready to concede that "the forces do not explain all the features of the relations."[50] The flexibility of his approach is evident in the generality of his periodization of different economic epochs. He lists only four: preclass society (no surplus); precapitalist class society (some surplus); capitalist society (moderately high surplus); and post-class society (massive surplus). No attempt is made to place the ancient and feudal modes in sequence, and he quotes Marx's comment in the *Grundrisse*: "'Between the full development of the foundation of industrial society and the patriarchal condition, many intermediate stages, endless nuances' occur."[51]

The question of whether Marx's treatment of the genesis of capitalism in *Capital* contradicts the primacy thesis is also discussed. He refers to Part VIII, Volume 1, where Marx gives an account of the expropriation of the peasantry and the creation of a proletarian class confronted by a capitalist class. John Plamenatz' objection to the primacy thesis is then quoted: "A considerable part of the first volume of *Capital* is taken up with explaining how the decay of feudal relations of production made possible the development of new productive methods. There is no question there of the methods of production peculiar to capitalism being born in the womb of feudal society and then gradually transforming it into a capitalist society as feudal relations of property, now become fetters on these methods, give way to other relations more in harmony with them...."[52] In opposition to Plamenatz, Cohen argues that fettering does not just apply to existing forces, but also occurs when "relations block the formation and/or entry into the productive sphere of new forces." He also points out that it was superior methods of tillage, that is, a growth in productive power, that led to the disfranchisement of the peasantry. Industrial production was similarly inhibited by the guild system, which had therefore to be abolished. Although these particular productive forces were not "peculiar to capitalism," he notes that "the primacy thesis does not say that forces *characteristic* of capitalism preceded its arrival."[53]

Cohen's book has done much to reinstate the case for productive force primacy. Its major defect is the hard and fast distinctions made regarding the productive forces, the production relations, and the superstructure. In particular, he tends to separate the human dimension from the productive forces, and removes altogether legal terms from the production relations which, as we shall argue later, cannot be justified. However, this does not thereby vitiate his overall argument, which can be taken as a defense of historical materialism that has the important virtue of not overstating the case.[54]

A common objection to assigning priority to the productive forces is that this leads to an impersonal determinism that denies the human element within history. Insofar as Cohen excludes the human dimension from the productive forces this is a fair criticism of his work, which does tend to fetishize the productive forces. It should be remembered that the productive forces always remain the product of women and men, and do not possess an autonomous status. Whatever influence they may exercise is owed entirely to humankind, whose history always remains a process of self-creation. As Helmut Fleischer puts it, "the *primum movens* of history is man," and not the "methods of production."[55]

Marx's basic insight concerning the priority of the productive forces can therefore be understood in terms that are fully consistent with his humanist standpoint and belief in the central role of human consciousness and action. The case for a determinist reading of Marx in fact becomes increasingly less viable as we examine the texts.

The *Preface* is frequently interpreted by both Marxists and non-Marxists alike in a narrowly materialist sense, as necessarily implying a form of economic determinism. However, a close consideration of Marx's language suggests that such a conclusion is not justified. For example, the word "conditions" need not imply an absolute determination. The reference to forms of social consciousness which "correspond" to the economic structure still leaves scope for other than economic causes. Marx's claim that social being "determines" consciousness could be seen as an inversion intended to counter the idealist perspective; in any case "determines" can be understood in a more relaxed sense to mean *influences, helps shape*, or *sets certain limits upon*. Although Marx certainly implies a close connection or correlation between base and superstructure, his overall choice of words—especially when taken in context—avoids a strictly causal framework. Thus, a little earlier in the *Preface*, he only speaks of legal relations and forms of the state as having their "roots" in material conditions, an expression open to fairly wide interpretation.[56]

Regrettably, the base/superstructure metaphor has tended to be regarded as a simple cause-effect model. Marx understood the relationship between "base" and "superstructure" in a much more complex manner. Thus, within the *Preface*, when commenting on the process of revolutionary change, he writes:

> In considering such transformations a distinction should always be made between the natural transformation of the economic conditions of production, which can be determined with the precision of natural science, and the legal, political, religious, aesthetic, or philosophical—in short, ideological forms in which men become conscious of this conflict and fight it out.[57]

Marx thus conceived superstructural elements as playing a central role in producing historical change, and consequently in altering production relations and the economic foundation. This emphasis on interaction is found throughout Marx's writings. In a passage in *The German Ideology* that closely parallels his later *Preface*, he refers to "the reciprocal action of these various sides on one another." Similarly, in his *Theories of Surplus Value* he comments: "If material production itself is not conceived in its *specific historical* form, it is impossible to understand what is specific in the spiritual production corresponding to it and the reciprocal influence of the one on the other."[58]

On closer examination the whole of the argument in the *Preface* in fact suggests a nonreductive interpretation. For Marx, the "relations of production" correspond to the material forces of production, and, as a consequence of the development of the productive forces, changes in the "relations of production" are produced. However, since it is always conscious human beings living in a specific social, political and ideological situation who actually develop the productive forces, there must inevitably be some circular interaction between "base" and "superstructure." As a consequence, if only implicitly, the mutual interaction between "base" and "superstructure" is confirmed.

A narrowly determinist interpretation of the *Preface* would conflict with Marx's earlier critique of Feuerbach's materialism. As has already been mentioned when discussing Feuerbach's third thesis, Marx ascribed a crucial role to human consciousness in initiating revolutionary transformation. When opposing idealism in *The German Ideology*, he says only that "circumstances make men just as much as men make circumstances," and still therefore considered human activity itself as fundamental.[59] A crude cause-effect determinism completely fails to understand Marx's own dialectical approach to material reality.

After Marx's death, Engels attempted to refute some of the economistic interpretations of their followers, and sought to highlight the interaction between the different levels. Writing to J. Bloch in 1890, he says:

> According to the materialist conception of history, the *ultimately* determining element in history is the production and reproduction of real life. More than this Marx nor I have ever asserted. Hence if somebody twists this into saying that the economic element is the *only* determining one, he transforms that proposition into a meaningless, abstract, senseless phrase. The economic situation is the basis, but the various elements of the superstructure...also exercise their influence upon the course of historical struggles and in many cases preponderate in determining their *form*. There is an interaction of all these elements in which...the economic movement finally asserts itself as necessary.[60]

Similarly, in a letter to H. Starkenburg in 1894, he writes:

> It is not that the economic position is the *cause* and *alone active*, while everything else only has a passive effect. There is, rather, interaction on the basis of economic necessity, which *ultimately* asserts itself.[61]

Despite their significant qualifications, these letters are still couched in fairly determinist terms, and indicate that Engels remained very much a prisoner of an economist perspective himself. Nevertheless, his stress on mutual interaction throws valuable light on how Marx's model should be regarded.

It is unfortunate that both supporters and critics alike often interpret Marx too rigidly. This tendency is particularly evident in attempts to universalize his theory of history as though it predicted a pattern of linear and uninterrupted historical development. Marx's overall schema was in fact much more flexible, and his typology of the different epochs should not be seen as strictly sequential. Hence his criticism of Mikhailovsky's review of *Capital*: "He feels he absolutely must metamorphose my historical sketch of the genesis of capitalism in Western Europe into a historico-philosophic theory of the general path every people is fated to tread, whatever the historical circumstances in which it finds itself."[62] Another problem that remains is the question of the relative autonomy from the economic sphere of certain cultural and spiritual elements. Here it is important to be clear about the precise nature of Marx's claim. His materialism does not commit him to the view that *all* superstructural phenomena are expressions of the base, but only that the superstructure as a whole is influenced and conditioned by the base in such a way that when historical development is considered in epochal terms the economic basis remains the dominant factor. Without this kind of interpretation, the "spiritual" and its influence on history is seriously underestimated—and this was not intended by Marx, as is shown by his reference to "free spiritual production" in his *Theories of Surplus Value*.

The degree of independence which he was frequently prepared to assign to law, literature, art, morality is noteworthy. For example, Marx recognized that the Roman legal system still influenced European law long after it had lost any economic foundation. (Engels conceded that law is also shaped by tradition and concepts of justice.) Marx welcomed the contribution of those novelists who in their work rose above their own economic background and class outlook, and so often powerfully portrayed the reality and injustice of class rule. He also recognized that art does not stand in direct relation to economic development. Despite his rejection of bourgeois morality as little more than the reflection of class interests, he was no relativist and moral concerns always remained fundamental for him.[63]

Although recognition of the process of interaction and the existence of autonomous cultural creations undoubtedly makes Marx's metaphor more credible and defensible, it is still perhaps questionable whether such a rigid and static image is at all helpful for understanding historical change. To attempt to equate society with a building is an exercise that is not surprisingly fraught with difficulties. Thus, not unreasonably, E. P. Thompson, deems "this metaphor from constructional engineering" to be "inadequate to describe the flux of conflict, the dialectic of a changing social process."[64]

Insofar as the notion "base" tends to suggest only a material content, it must be conceded that it does not do justice to the complexity of Marx's thought.[65] The economic foundation or "base" is not something purely material, consisting as it does of the activities and relations of humans in their material production. Nor should the forces of production themselves be considered solely in material terms, since Marx included the workers, and on one occasion "the revolutionary class itself," among the productive forces.[66] Fresh inventions and new social relations of production, like the appropriate superstructures that correspond to them, are all the product of human activity.

The most serious objection to Marx's metaphor is in fact its false polarization of "base" and "superstructure." It is this more than anything else that compounds the confusion and confirms the unsuitability of the metaphor. Thus, for example, the various relations within the economic foundation cannot be properly considered apart from the legal and ideological domain of the superstructure or vice versa. However, when scholars such as Acton and Plamenatz claim this objection refutes historical materialism they press the point too far, since it is only the limitations of this particular model that is highlighted.[67] Cohen's attempt to meet this criticism by excluding all legal terminology from Marx's account of production relations is somewhat contrived, and violates the fundamental unity of the various interacting elements in the historical process.[68] Similar considerations apply to his treatment of the productive forces, where the human dimension is sacrificed in the attempt to impose his own particular analytical framework. If any use is to be made of Marx's model, then the various levels of base and superstructure must be understood as interpenetrating each other dialectically and forming a unity.[69]

Toward a Humanist and Utopian Reading of Historical Materialism

It is as well, given its many inadequacies, that we are not solely dependent on Marx's base/superstructure metaphor for assessing his materialist conception of history. In his writings on history, and in his frequent adoption of a much more organic model of society, Marx provides us with alternative perspectives from which to view his theory of history.

In his historical writings Marx does not consider the drama of events solely in relation to economic and technological factors. Thus in *The Class Struggles in France* and *The Eighteenth Brumaire of Louis Bonaparte* he does not begin with a consideration of the productive forces, but rather with property relations and the divisions in the ruling class between industrial and financial interests. In this analysis it is the tensions between contending social classes and the ideological and political aspects of this struggle that are dominant, and the unfolding pattern of historical events is shaped by them as well as by a considerable amount of contingency.[70]

It is impossible to read the opening pages of Marx's *Eighteenth Brumaire* without appreciating the importance he attaches to the role of ideas within history. In periods of revolutionary crisis, he tells us, people "anxiously conjure up the spirits of the past to their service and borrow from them names, battle cries and costumes in order to present the new scene of world history in this time-honored disguise and this borrowed language." Cromwell and the English people, he continues, "borrowed speech, passions and illusions from the Old Testament for their bourgeois revolution."

Marx cites several examples from previous bourgeois revolutions—the limitations of which he was quick to point out. Thus, with the completion of the English bourgeois revolution, "Locke supplanted Habakkuk." The proletarian revolution, he insisted, would take on a very different form, and although it too would draw upon passions, images and poetry, Marx describes these in strikingly utopian language as deriving not from the past but the future:

> The social revolution of the nineteenth century cannot draw its poetry from the past, but only from the future. It cannot begin with itself before it has stripped off all superstition in regard to the past. Earlier revolutions required recollections of past world history in order to drug themselves concerning their own content. In order to arrive at its own content, the revolution of the nineteenth century must let the dead bury their dead. There the phrase went beyond the content; here the content goes beyond the phrase.[71]

It is difficult to envisage how images of the future can be wholly independent of the past, and Marx would seem to concede the point when he refers to the content going beyond the phrase. He clearly wished to stress that the new society instituted through socialism would be qualitatively different from anything in the past, but that he envisaged its inception as being crucially dependent on the existence of a subjective human consciousness imbued with socialist ideas and vision cannot be in doubt.

When we come to his mature economic writings, we find that Marx worked more with an understanding of society as an organic whole than the base/superstructure model. He inherited this organic view of society from Hegel. As early as 1843, despite his criticisms, he had described Hegel's account of the state as an organism as "a great advance." By the time he came to write up his economic studies in the late 1850s he was again—albeit critically—consciously making much use of Hegel.[72] Thus, in the *Grundrisse* he considers society in organic terms:

> While in the completed bourgeois system every economic relation presupposes every other in its bourgeois economic form, and everything posited is thus also a presupposition, this is the case with every organic system. This organic system itself, as a totality, has its presuppositions, and its development to its totality consists precisely in subordinating all elements of society to itself, or in creating out of the organs which it still lacks. This is historically how it becomes a totality.[73]

Similarly in *Capital*, Volume 1, he specifically describes society as an organism: "the present society is no solid crystal, but an organism capable of change, and it is constantly changing."[74]

Marx's model of organic totality does not, however, simply imply mutual interrelatedness, since within the various interacting elements it is production that predominates—hence the title of the first volume of *Capital*, "The Production Process of Capital." The positive side of the base/superstructure model is that this priority is assured, and the fact that the two models coexist in Marx's thought suggests each should be interpreted in the light of the other. The advantage of the organic model is, as Melvin Rader points out, that it "retains the strengths and avoids the weaknesses of the base/superstructure model."[75] In particular, it makes it possible to affirm the basis of society in the mode of production, but still give full weight to the importance of superstructural elements.

Given the abundant evidence for the flexibility and openness of Marx's materialist conception of history, it is perhaps surprising that it has so frequently been dismissed out of hand. However, the development of Marx's materialism by Engels into an all embracing philosophical theory along the lines of the natural sciences has undoubtedly decisively shaped the general perception of Marx's materialism as a form of determinism. Through adapting Hegel's methodology and dialectical theory, Engels sought to apply the materialist method to both nature and history. In his *Anti-Dühring* he writes: "In nature, amid the welter of innumerable changes, the same dialectical laws of motion force their way through as those which in history govern the apparent fortuitousness of events."[76] Engels claimed that he had read the whole of the text of *Anti-Dühring* to Marx, and, especially after Marx's death, tended to identify his own materialist philosophy with the views of Marx. However, the positive evidence that Marx specifically accepted Engels' materialist dialectics is simply not there, and an examination of Marx's writings shows that he considered his own project to be much more limited in scope and primarily concerned with developing a critique of political economy. For Marx, it was always *social* being that determined consciousness.[77]

Influenced by Engels' philosophical materialism, the dominant interpretation of Marx's materialism in the Second and Third Internationals was in metaphysical and economistic terms. Marx's materialist outlook was thus transmuted into what came to be commonly known as "dialectical materialism," and, as expounded by theoreticians such as Plekhanov, Kautsky, and Lenin, became a pseudo-scientific doctrine devoid of its original humanist character. Thus, Franz Jakubowski observes that with Kautsky the dialectic is turned "from a critical and revolutionary method into a mechanical scheme of development," while with Lenin, matter is considered to be independent of consciousness, which becomes mere "reflection."[78]

The importance of the above interpretation for twentieth-century Marxism can scarcely be exaggerated. However, the eventual emergence of alternative perspectives in the writings of thinkers such as Korsch, Lukács, and Gramsci—along with the publication of Marx's writings prior to *Capital*—has led to Marxism becoming a much more variegated phenomenon, no longer indistinguishable from the determinist perspective set in train by Engels' later work. Gramsci's work, in particular, which firmly reinstated the significance of "ideological," "spiritual," and "cultural" elements for historical change, represents a major corrective to economistic readings of Marx's doctrine, and has been especially influential within Western Marxism.

Despite his own occasional lapses into positivist language in *Capital*, Marx's perspective remained an essentially humanist one, and he always assigned a positive role to human consciousness and action.[79] This role assumes critical importance in periods of revolutionary transition, as Marx makes clear in his *Preface* of 1859. In such times of crisis the various elements of the superstructure that normally serve to validate the existing structure of society, now themselves become agents for change. In these circumstances, "ideology," as John McMurtry observes, instead of being simply a defense mechanism, "becomes a mobilizer." He goes on to write: "Ideology can and does truly, if exceptionally, spring men into economic action—its public formulations no longer merely the excuse, concealer, opiate of social rationalization, but penetrating to the secrets of the old economic system, as a sort of public self-recognition taking place in the final act of the historical dramas of the *ancien regime* and resolving its conflicts into a new, unwritten plot."[80]

This crisis comes about as a consequence of the development of the productive forces beyond a level that is compatible with the existing economic structure and its corresponding superstructural forms. Revolutionary action will be effectual only when the forces of production have developed sufficiently to make a socialist structure of society possible. Thus Marx's humanist imperative to create the new society of human freedom beyond capitalism is grounded in his analysis of historical development. His *utopia* of communist society is the product of history itself; it is not conjured out of nowhere, but matures within the "womb" of existing capitalist society. However, when deterministic interpreters of Marx speak of inevitability or necessity in the movement to communism, they neglect the centrality of human action. Communism is only a *possibility* that emerges at a particular stage of history; its attainment depends on conscious human intervention.

In order to fulfill this task there must exist a positive vision of the prospect of genuine human emancipation provided by socialism. How else is the struggle at the all-important ideological level to be properly informed and sustained? Once the crucial role of the superstructure in revolutionary change is acknowledged, it is but a short step to the recognition that Marxism needs its utopian dynamic if it is to effectively enlist, organize, and give vitality and direction to the maturing *subjective* productive forces that alone can achieve socialism. Utopia, as Leszek Kolakowski writes, "invades the consciousness of a mass movement and becomes one of its essential driving forces."[81]

Without any image of the future where is the basis for action in the present? Human beings are not automatons and require motivation and inspiration, but from where is this to come? As Marx has it in his *Eighteenth Brumaire*, images, passions, and poetry must not only be conjured up, but, to express the liberating content of socialism, must be drawn from the future. *Belief* in the socialist utopia must therefore once again be seen as essential for its realization. Without it history finds only impasse, and not the place where the realm of freedom really begins.

Chapter 3

Economics, Alienation, and Future Communist Society

It has usually been understood that whereas a utopian current is to be found in Marx's earlier writings, his later economic theory is wholly scientific in content. Little serious consideration has so far been given to the utopianism implicit in Marx's later work—a deficiency which stands in need of correction.

It was the onset of the economic crisis of 1857 which stimulated Marx to formulate the conception of political economy which had been maturing for the previous fifteen years. In a letter to Engels he writes: "I am working like mad all night and every night collating my economic studies so that I at least get the outlines clear before the *deluge*."[1] By the spring of 1858 he had produced a manuscript of some eight hundred pages, which is known as the *Grundrisse* (Outlines of a Critique of Political Economy). Unpublished in English until 1973, it is now widely recognized as being a crucial text for understanding Marx. Thus David McLellan calls the *Grundrisse* the "centerpiece of Marx's thought," claiming it contradicts any notion of a sharp break between the early and later Marx.[2] The work in fact was to serve as a rough draft for *Capital*, which was the first part of the ambitious plan of work Marx had projected in 1858.[3]

In the *Grundrisse* Marx's economic theory is interwoven with detailed treatment of the themes of alienation, species-being, and the new social individual, all of which are to be found in his writings of 1844. However, whereas in the *Paris Manuscripts*, philosophy and economics were treated in different sections, in the *Grundrisse* Marx had achieved a synthesis of his ideas. Accordingly, the first exposition of Marx's mature economics (the distinction between exchange-value and use-value, the labor theory of value, the discovery of surplus value, and the tendency of the rate of profit to fall), appears in the context of an exploration of the humanist concerns that were an abiding feature of his thought.[4]

The degree of affinity with the *Manuscripts* should not obscure the advance that had taken place in Marx's understanding of economics. The most significant change was in his attitude to the labor theory of value. In 1844, along with Engels, he had rejected the labor theory of value, arguing that value and costs of production were not related to one another. Although he was won over by the time he wrote *The German Ideology*, it is clear from *The Poverty of Philosophy*, written in 1847, that at this stage he simply equated value with price. It is not until the *Grundrisse* that we find the fully developed value theory, which became the cornerstone of Marx's economics.[5]

The Labor Theory of Value

Marx's labor theory of value is hotly disputed, not only by bourgeois economists, but also among Marxists. What follows is not a comprehensive exposition and evaluation—which would be beyond the scope of the present work—but an attempt to outline Marx's value theory and indicate its relation to his conception of alienation. In *accepting* Marx's theory of value, its centrality to the whole theoretical project of Marx's mature economics is acknowledged, along with its superiority over the crude empiricism of the marginal-utility school and its validity despite the various criticisms that have been advanced.[6]

Marx's analysis of value in the *Grundrisse* introduces the distinction between use-value and exchange-value. For commodities to exchange, independently of their subjective use-value, there must exist a common substance or exchange-value, which Marx defined as the labor time necessary for their production: "Every commodity (product or instrument of production) is = the objectification of a given amount of labour time." No longer equating value with price, Marx insisted that embodied human labor time was only the essence of value: "Because labour time as the measure of value exists only as the ideal, it cannot serve as the matter of price comparisons." Prices are determined by fluctuations in the market.[7]

For the process of circulation to take place money is required as a medium of exchange: "The exchange-value of a commodity, as a separate form of existence accompanying the commodity itself, is *money*; the form in which all commodities equate, compare, measure themselves."[8] Marx uses the shorthand C-M-M-C to denote the process of circulation which replaces primitive barter.[9] When his analysis of commodity circulation is completed he goes on to consider money as capital. This, he says, initially arises from the process of "buying in order to sell, which makes up the formal aspect of commerce, of capital as merchant capital." For this, he adopts the shorthand M-C-C-M, and describes merchant capital as the first form of capital.[10] However, capital proper does not appear until later, and is associated with production rather than circulation.

The *Grundrisse* sketches out an historical account of the formation of the capital-labor relation, which Marx was to develop later in *Capital*. The creation of the propertyless worker required the dissolution of those relations which tied the peasant to the land, and the separation of the craftsman from his instruments of production. This emergence of the modern laborer was accompanied by the growth of mercantile wealth and the gradual extension of its control over materials and implements of production. Thus the relation between capital and wage labor arises historically as the end product of a complex series of legal and political changes: "The same process which placed the mass face to face with the *objective conditions of labour* as free workers also placed these conditions, as *capital*, face to face with the free workers."[11]

In his detailed examination of the capital-labor relation Marx introduced the all-important distinction between "labor" and "labor power," or "living labor" and "objectified labor," from which he proceeded to his discovery of surplus value. He reasoned that in the exchange transaction, what the capitalist obtained from the worker was the use-value of labor for a definite exchange-value corresponding to the worker's "labor power," which functioned as a commodity. The value of this commodity is fixed, being simply the labor required to reproduce the worker himself, which in this case amounts to the means of subsistence.[12] However, in acquiring the use-value of labor, the capitalist is in the enviable position of having obtained "labour itself, as value-positing activity, as productive labour, i.e., he obtains the productive force which maintains and multiplies capital."[13] This is because labor power differs from other commodities in that when deployed in the production process it produces fresh wealth, through putting labor to work, creating a value over and above its exchange-value.[14]

Identifying the three components of the production as raw material, instruments of production, and "the labour time objectified in the price of labour," Marx claimed that the first two remained unchanged as values even if they change their form, and that only with the third component "does capital exchange one thing for something qualitatively different; a given amount of objectified labour for an amount of living labour."[15] He went on to argue that if in production only a portion of the total labor time (which a little later he calls necessary labor) is required to cover the worker's means of subsistence, then the remainder is surplus labor, to which there corresponds a surplus value. Thus arises the creation of surplus labor and value, which he considered to be "the great historic quality of capital."[16] Although this surplus originates in production and not in circulation or exchange, it is intimately related to exchange in that it follows from the way the worker "exchanges value-positing activity for a predetermined value, regardless of the result of his activity."[17]

Capital is necessarily exploitative since it can only grow by the expropriation of surplus labor in production. The capitalist will only employ labor so long as he is able to strike a surplus, and the wage bargain where the worker is seemingly paid in full for his labor simply masks this exploitation.[18] Although the capital-labor relation has the appearance of an ordinary exchange relation, what the capitalist buys is labor-power, the value of which is always less than the value it produces, since the capitalist ensures the laborer works longer than is required to reproduce the value of his labor power. Marx demystifies the exploitative nature of this transaction when he writes that it "posits the exchange of objectified labour for labour capacity, and therefore the appropriation of living labour without exchange."[19]

The freedom and equality of the marketplace is only apparent, since economic necessity forces workers to place their labor at the disposal of capital. The nonownership of the means of production gives workers no practical alternative but to sell their labor to the capitalist who owns the means of production. Thus Marx writes that the exchange of labor "*rests on the foundation of the worker's propertylessness,*" and "implies compulsion over the individual."[20] Although the worker may be free in a formal sense, this is "a mere *semblance,* and a *deceptive semblance.*"[21] The freedom of the worker in bourgeois society has as its basis the rule of capital, and only results in subjection and enslavement: "This kind of individual freedom is therefore at the same time the most complete suspension of all individual freedom, and the most complete subjection of individuality under social conditions which assume the form of objective powers."[22]

The above account can be usefully supplemented from the more lengthy treatment of value to be found in *Capital.* Here Marx defined the ratio of surplus labor to necessary labor as the rate of surplus value. The significance of this particular parameter for the further development of his economics should not distract attention from its function as an indicator of the worker's exploitation—Marx in fact describes it as an exact expression of the degree of exploitation of the worker.[23] The wage-form is simply an illusion that serves an ideological function, since it "extinguishes every trace of the division of the working day into necessary labour and surplus labour, into paid and unpaid labour."[24]

Concerning the juridical and political freedoms the worker enjoyed in bourgeois society, Marx wholeheartedly welcomed these, and wished only to draw attention to the fact that capitalist society stood in the way of their fulfillment. Hence his caustic comments in *Capital* concerning the rights of the worker:

> The sphere of circulation or commodity exchange, within whose boundaries the sale and purchase of labour-power goes on, is in fact a very Eden of the innate rights of man. It is the exclusive realm of Freedom, Equality, Property and Bentham. Freedom, because both buyer and seller of a commodity, let us say of labour-power, are determined only by their own free will. They contract as free persons, who are equal before the law. Their contract is the final result in which their joint will finds a common legal expression. Equality because each enters into relation with the other, as with a simple owner of commodities, and they exchange equivalent for equivalent. Property, because each disposes only what is his own. And Bentham, because each looks only to his own advantage.[25]

Marx's point was that all these freedoms are of no avail, since this formal legal equality serves only to conceal the class domination to which the worker is subject. In reality, capitalist and propertyless worker confront one another on terms which favor capital, and human labor is both forced and exploitative. It is only through considering the creation of surplus value in the production process itself that the fundamentally exploitative character of the capital-labor relation can be properly understood. The apparent exchange of equivalents at the level of circulation throws a veil over the true state of affairs:

> The relation of exchange between capitalist and worker becomes a mere semblance belonging only to the process of circulation, it becomes a mere form, which is alien to the content of the transaction itself, and merely mystifies it. The constant sale and purchase of labour-power is the form; the content is the constant appropriation by the capitalist, without equivalent, of a portion of the labour of others....[26]

Value Theory and the Concept of Alienation

From the above outline of Marx's value theory, its relation to his understanding of alienation is immediately evident.

Value, for Marx, is "objectified labour in its general social form."[27] This designation of abstract human labor as the substance of value assumes a society where the products of labor take the form of commodities. In modern bourgeois society the commodity form is dominant, and objects are not produced for their utility or use-value, but for their exchange-value. Labor is no longer carried out under the worker's control, but in subjection both to the wishes of the capitalist and the impersonal dictates of the market. In exchange the worker's human labor is reduced to the status of a mere commodity (labor power), to be bought and sold like any other, having a value only equal to the labor required to reproduce it. Commenting on this situation Georg Lukács writes: "This transformation of a human function into a commodity reveals in all its starkness the dehumanized and dehumanizing function of the commodity relation."[28] Thus, in equating value with labor, Marx had in mind alienated labor in particular. For him, value is *alienated labor*.[29]

Given the way in which the generation of surplus value is based on the worker's subjection and exploitation, this economic category too has its origin in alienated human labor. Marx also recognized that capital, profit, rent, interest, money, and so on are in fact mystified expressions of alienated labor. Whatever their role as important categories for the development of economic science, they have their origin in the worker's alienated productive activity. The existence of the value form and the creation of surplus value, from which all these categories derive, would not be possible unless the worker was subject to the power of capital and exploited by it. Thus Marx's economics unfolded from his alienation theory, and far from being abandoned, the initial philosophical and essentially humanist impulse that inspired the younger Marx is made the starting point for his mature economics.

John Elliott helpfully sums up this basic interrelation between economics and social theory in Marx when he writes:

> ...just as many of Marx's mature ideas on economics are suggested or implied, at least in embryonic form, in his early writings on alienation, so too may the concept of alienation be derived or implied from his mature economic analysis. Labor power, value, exchange, production, and capital, for example, are all explicitly formulated constituent elements in Marx's analysis of capitalist

economic relations. Simultaneously, for Marx, they are all manifestations of the underlying phenomenon of alienated man in alienated society.[30]

Ernest Mandel is wrong to criticize scholars who insist on the interrelation between alienation theory and Marx's economics, and when he attempts to impose an arbitrary and artificial separation. The conceptual link between the two cannot be reduced simply to the status of a happy coincidence. Thus when he claims that Marx's economics "has an independent value of its own," and "results from a strictly scientific study," he is making a concession to positivism that would have been quite foreign to Marx. The fact-value distinction had no place in the thought of Marx, for whom humanism and science always went hand in hand.[31]

Jerrold Seigel is also incorrect when he argues that Marx elaborated his economics in the *Grundrisse* independently of alienation theory. He points to Marx's insistence that the concept of capital is derived from value, not labor. However, although Marx first developed his concept of capital through a consideration of value and surplus value, given that value itself is alienated labor this can hardly be said to imply that capital does not have its roots in alienated human labor. Indeed, in *Capital*, Volume 3, Marx explicitly describes capital as "an alienated social power."[32] The origin of the various economic categories in the worker's condition of alienation is supported in the unpublished sixth chapter of *Capital*, Volume 1, where Marx refers to "the social forms of labour which present themselves as forms of the development of capital."[33]

The continuing centrality of Marx's concept of alienation is illustrated by the way in which the fourfold aspects of the worker's alienation, first outlined in the *Paris Manuscripts*, reappear in the *Grundrisse* in the context of the development of his economics.[34]

In the exchange which takes place between the capitalist and the worker, the worker becomes alienated from the product of labor, since by selling this labor to the capitalist, the worker "obtains a right only to the *price of labour*, not to the *product of this labour*."[35] In such a situation, "the product of labour appears as *alien property*, as a mode of existence confronting living labour as independent."[36]

The activity of labor itself also involves alienation for the worker, since living labor is active within the production process, "in such a way that, as it realizes itself in the objective conditions, it simultaneously repulses this realization from itself as an alien reality." In language very similar to his account in the *Manuscripts* of the activity of labor as self-alienation, Marx goes on to conclude: "This realization process is at the same time the de-realization process of labour."[37]

Although Marx does not specifically refer to workers being alienated from their "species-being," he continues to use the term and clearly retained the conception of species-being, which he had outlined in 1844. This can be seen in his criticism of Adam Smith's views on labor, where Marx insists that the human individual "needs a normal portion of work, and of the suspension of tranquillity," and speaks of human labor—at least potentially—as "a liberating activity," a means of "self-realization," and "an activity regulating all the forces of nature."[38]

The notion of species-being is explicitly referred to at the very outset of the chapter on "Capital," without any suggestion whatsoever that Marx had abandoned his former understanding of the term.[39] Virtually the whole of the *Grundrisse* could in fact be described as an implicit commentary on the way capitalism alienates workers from their fundamental humanity—their species-being. Instead of free human labor being able to realize itself through constructing and controlling its environment, the worker is confronted by "the objective world of wealth as a power alien to labour." There is no escape from this situation: "The greater the extent to which labour objectifies itself, the greater becomes the objective world of values, which stands opposite to it as alien—alien property."[40] The exchange transaction has the consequence that the worker "alienates his life-expression," and "impoverishes himself... because the creative power of his labour establishes itself as the power of capital, as an *alien power* confronting him."[41] Discussing the role of money Marx sums up the predicament facing the individual in bourgeois society: "Individuals are subsumed under social production; social production exists outside them as their fate; but social production is not subsumed under individuals, manageable by them as their common wealth."[42]

The alienation of workers from each other follows from the particular obligation imposed on them, which Marx describes as "the duty of respecting the products of one's own labour, and one's own labour itself, as values belonging to others."[43] When workers divest themselves of their labor, it is the capitalist who appropriates it. Marx sees capital as the antithesis of the worker, and the "others" he refers to represents the capitalist class - the relationship between capital and labor being produced and reproduced through the process of exchange on which production is based.[44]

The way in which the *Grundrisse* links the younger and the mature Marx must refute those interpretations which argue for a break between the two.[45] The social theory of the *Manuscripts* forms the basis for the elaboration of

Marx's economics. Moreover, this remains true for *Capital*, where it is quite incorrect to say that the term "alienation" is no longer present. Not only does the term occasionally appear in *Capital*, but the manner in which it is used is fully consistent with Marx's previous writings. Thus describing the consequence of the exchange process for the worker, in Volume 1, Marx writes:

> Before he enters the process, his own labour has already been alienated [*entfremdet*] from him, appropriated by the capitalist, and incorporated with capital, it now, in the course of the process, constantly objectifies itself so that it becomes a product alien to him [*fremder Produkt*]... the worker himself constantly produces objective wealth, in the form of capital, an alien power that dominates and exploits him....[46]

Attention must also be drawn to the sixth chapter of *Capital*, Volume 1, which for unknown reasons Marx did not include in the published version. This missing section gives a fairly extended discussion of alienation in language which closely parallels that of the *Manuscripts*. Marx specifically refers to the "process of alienation," and speaks of "the domination of the capitalist over the worker." The means of production, he asserts, "are not subject to the worker, but it is he who is subject to them." In this situation of subjection to the rule of capital, "the world of wealth swells before the worker like a world which is alien to him and which dominates him."[47] Specific references to alienation are also to be found in the other volumes of *Capital*. For example, in Volume 3 capital and land are described as "alienated from labour and confronting it independently."[48]

It is not just a matter of terminology, however, and Ronald Meek is surely right when he describes *Capital* as a book about alienation.[49] Marx's project in *Capital* was concerned with the way in which production in capitalist society is not carried out under social control, but is subjected to the inhuman power of capital. That this involves alienation for the worker is self-evident, and the whole of *Capital* can therefore be seen as a commentary on this alienation. It is in this context that the lengthy and graphic descriptions which Marx gives us of the plight of the worker should be located. The strong emphasis throughout *Capital* which Marx places on the worker's exploitation also illustrates the point. The laborer could not be exploited without also being alienated, since, as we have seen, exploitation involves coercion, unequal exchange, and the worker's loss of control over the product. The degree of exploitation in fact provides a measure of the laborer's alienation. Thus the frequent use of the term "exploitation" complements rather than replaces the concept of alienation. Or as John Elliott puts it: "Exploitation, though clearly the more explicitly and heavily discussed topic, supplements rather than supplants alienation."[50]

Ernest Mandel, while fully accepting that alienation retained a central place in Marx's thinking, maintains that he had progressed from an anthropological to an historical conception of alienation. However, contrary to what Mandel suggests, at no point in the *Manuscripts* did Marx contend that alienation arises in "*human nature* itself," or "*nature in general*."[51] He thought of nature and humanity together, describing nature as "the inorganic body of man," and on this basis merely asserted that alienation occurs within the world of nature.[52] Marx (as Mandel acknowledges), specifically rejected the identification of alienation with objectification.[53] Moreover, the fact that he considered it possible for alienation to be overcome, is also difficult to square with the interpretation offered by Mandel, who is forced to charge Marx with inconsistency, and argue that his thought was still in the process of "transition."

Mandel claims that Marx escaped from his contradictory position by abandoning the unhistorical notion of species-being. However, in his idea of species-being Marx was simply outlining his view of human beings' self-consciousness and universality, and consequent relation to the external world of nature. Far from being unhistorical, this view actually became the starting point for his materialist interpretation of history! Although he borrowed the term "species-being" from Feuerbach, when he used it in the *Manuscripts* he invested it with his own meaning and did not take it to refer to some abstract generic human essence. Despite his enormous debt to Feuerbach, Marx had attained a critical relation to his thought well before he wrote his famous eleven theses.[54] As has already been shown, Marx retained his conception of species-being, and although he came to prefer terms like "social individual," it remained implicit in his later work. Thus, the discussion of human labor in *Capital* as "a process between man and nature," particularly closely parallels the 1844 account of species-being.[55]

The Utopian Prospect of the Overcoming of Alienation

Along with the *Paris Manuscripts*, the *Grundrisse* also holds out the prospect of the future "unalienated" or "free" individual. Marx understood the worker's alienation as corresponding to a particular stage of social development—the bourgeois mode of production—rather than an absolute necessity of production itself. Historical development would create the conditions for a changed foundation of production, and alienation would give way to the free and full development of the truly social individual. Thus he speaks of a third stage of history: "Free individuality, which is founded on the universal development of individuals, and the dominion of their communal and social productivity, which has become their social power, is the third stage."[56]

In future communist society workers will no longer be ruled by capital as an external power, but will themselves control and regulate the production process. Thus, referring to the alienation in bourgeois society, Marx writes: "With the positing of the activity of individuals as immediate general or *social* activity, the objective moments of production are stripped of this form of alienation; they are thereby posited as property, as the organic social body within which the individuals reproduce themselves as individuals, but as social individuals."[57]

Marx sees capitalism's continuous revolutionizing of the productive forces as eventually creating "the material elements for the development of the rich individuality which is as all-sided in its production as in its consumption, and whose labour also therefore appears no longer as labour, but as the full development of activity itself."[58] At the heart of his argument concerning this new emancipated individual is his account of the way in which modern machinery reduces labor time to a minimum, and thereby undermines the bourgeois mode of production resting on value expansion, as well as creating the preconditions for socialism. The massive growth of the means of production is "instrumental in creating the means of social disposable time," and thus freeing "everyone's time for their own development." Again he writes: "The saving of labour time is equal to an increase of free time, i.e., time for the full development of the individual."[59]

In a particularly futuristic manner, given the time in which he was writing, Marx anticipated the implications of the technological transformation of the productive forces which capitalism would accomplish. The essence of his vision is that in its relentless pursuit of surplus value, capital, through the application of science, revolutionizes the productive forces, thus reducing necessary labor time to a minimum and creating material conditions incompatible with the continuance of capitalism, while making the full all-round development of the individual possible.

Marx envisaged a situation arising where automation would make the worker the regulator and supervisor of the production process, and the creation of wealth would come to depend not so much on labor time but "on the power of the agencies set in motion during labour time, whose 'powerful effectiveness' is in turn out of all proportion to the direct labor time spent in their production, but depends rather on the general state of science and on the progress of technology." Once such progress has been achieved, productive activity is no longer subject to previous constraints and becomes a matter of the worker's "appropriation of his own general productive power, his understanding of nature and his mastery over it by virtue of his presence as a social body." Thus Marx speaks of the "social individual" appearing as "the great foundation-stone of production and of wealth." With industrial production taking this new form, the general reduction of necessary labor time for society makes possible "the artistic and scientific development of the individuals in the time set free."[60] Furthermore, human labor in the sphere of material production, which now assumes a "social" and "scientific" character, is no longer alienating.[61]

Marx's historical conception of alienation, and his utopian expectation of its supersession with the emergence of the fully developed individual in future communist society, is in complete continuity with his earlier writings. To be sure, in the *Grundrisse* the language is even richer, and Marx's schema is supported by the considerable intellectual achievement of his mature economic theory, but the vision still remains the same as that first adumbrated, albeit in a more sketchy and impressionistic form, some fifteen years earlier.

In *Capital* Marx also outlines the prospect of the overcoming of alienation. Thus, in Volume 1, he strikingly contrasts the crippled individual worker of capitalist society with the fully developed individual:

> Modern industry, indeed, compels society, under the penalty of death, to replace the detail-worker of today, crippled by life-long repetition of one and the same trivial operation, and thus reduced to the mere fragment of a man, by the fully developed individual, fit for a variety of labours, ready to face any change of production, and to whom the different social functions he performs, are but so many modes of giving free scope to his own natural and acquired powers.[62]

In Volume 3 Marx contrasts the "realm of natural necessity" with the "realm of freedom," and in something of a departure from his previous treatment of these questions, now maintains that real freedom lies beyond the sphere of material production. Concerning the realm of natural necessity, he writes:

> Freedom, in this sphere, can consist only in this, that socialized man, the associated producers, govern the human metabolism with nature in a rational way, bringing it under their collective control instead of being dominated by

it as a blind power; accomplishing it with the least expenditure of energy and in conditions most worthy and appropriate for their human nature. But this always remains the realm of necessity. The true realm of freedom, the development of human powers as an end in itself, begins beyond it, though it can only flourish with this realm of necessity as its basis. The reduction of the working day is the basic prerequisite.[63]

Marx is right that the reduction of necessary labor is of the utmost importance, since without it, even if production was subject to social control, the sheer physical obligations it imposed would in themselves have a stunting effect on the full development of human individuality. However, when mastery over nature through scientific control of the means of production has reached a high level, the element of drudgery will be reduced to negligible proportions, and work concerned with material production will involve the creative use of the individual's powers through the application of technical and scientific talents, with plenty of time left for cultural and artistic development. Marx's suggestion that material production can never become a sphere of unalienated human activity is in fact inconsistent with the rest of his work. It is, as we have seen, specifically denied in the *Grundrisse*, and cannot easily be reconciled with his *Critique of the Gotha Programme* of 1875, where labor in the higher phase of communist society is described as "life's prime want."[64]

The point is that a stage is surely reached where the quantitative reduction of necessary social labor leads to a *qualitative* change in its overall significance. In the automated communist society of the future, where necessary labor has been vastly reduced, and more arduous and unpleasant tasks have been eliminated by machines, the more positive features of the experience of work will be ascendant. A fifteen-hour week, with twelve weeks holiday and optional early retirement, helps provide a structure and rhythm to life that is conducive to physical and emotional well-being; the social contacts which work furnishes and the sense of self-esteem that derives from contributing to the good of society are also positive and upbuilding; and shorter hours liberates the free time needed for personal development.

Another feature of such a society will be that more highly skilled professions, such as medicine, scientific work, and teaching—which will also involve shorter working hours—will be open to much wider participation. Factory workers will have the option of undergoing professional training. Similarly, professional workers could take a break if they chose, and try their hand at truck driving, button pushing, administration, or whatever they chose. It is this general interchangeability of roles and lack of restrictions which lies at the heart of Marx's vision of the "all-round" individual of communist society. In such a culture the previous subordination of all relations to the demands of the market is replaced by a new harmony between the individual and society, with the activity of labor no longer being alienating, but enriching social existence and human community.[65]

Marx's distinction between the realms of freedom and necessity, despite the way in which he identifies alienation with material production as such, was nonetheless suggestive, and introduces the question of the phases of communist society which he later dealt with along the following lines in his *Critique of the Gotha Programme*. It is only when material scarcity has been overcome, and labor has been reduced to the extent that it no longer is a burden on overall human development, that the higher phase of communism as the true realm of human freedom will arrive. The total overcoming of alienation will thus not be instantaneously achieved, but will involve a progressive process of disalienation, humanity firstly exerting social control over the means of production, and then increasingly experiencing autonomy and freedom in relation to the sphere of production as the application of science further transforms it.

It is therefore evident that whatever its shortcomings, the brief account Marx gives us in *Capital* of the "fully developed" individual and the future "realm of freedom" fits into the general framework of his thought, his language in particular indicating its utopian content.

Commodity Fetishism and the Demystification of Capitalism

Closely associated with Marx's preoccupation with the worker's alienation and how it will be overcome in future communist society is his account of the fetishism of commodities in *Capital*.[66]

An object becomes a fetish when it is invested with powers it does not possess in itself. Marx maintained that commodities in bourgeois society exhibit a fetish character, in that they appear to have an exchange-value which belongs to them inherently, whereas in fact it is derived from human labor. This "mysterious" and "enigmatic" quality of commodities consists, Marx writes, "in the fact that the commodity reflects the social characteristics of man's own labour as objective characteristics of the products of labour themselves, as the socio-natural properties of these things." This fetishization has dire implications for human social relations: "It is nothing but the definite social relations between men themselves, which assumes here, for them, the fantastic form of a relation between things."[67]

This mystification is accompanied by the external domination to which workers are subject: "Their own movement within society has for them the form of a movement made by things, and these things, far from being under their control, in fact control them."[68] Instead of dealing with other people directly, workers now relate to them only via the market, with the consequence that they no longer exercise their human freedom, but become the plaything of economic forces. As Paul Sweezy puts it: "The world of commodities has, so to speak, achieved its independence and subjected the producers to its sway."[69]

The commodity-form is only one instance of fetishism in capitalist society. Money, with its all-pervasive mediating function in the exchange economy, is invested with a fetish character, its powers being ascribed to it as though they were natural attributes. In this role, Marx writes, it is "changed into a true god, for *the intermediary reigns in real power over the thing it mediates for me*. Its cult becomes an end in itself."[70]

Capital also displays a fetish character, since its ability to increase its value appears to be an inherent property, rather than resulting from the creation of surplus value through the exploitation of human labor in the production process: "In interest-bearing capital, therefore, this automatic fetish is elaborated into its pure form, self-valorizing value, money breeding money, and in this form it no longer bears any marks of its origin. The social relation is consummated in the relationship of a thing, money, to itself....Thus it becomes as completely the property of money to create value, to yield interest, as it is the property of a pear tree to bear pears."[71] In his treatment of the "The Trinity Formula" (capital-profit, land-rent, labor-wages), further instances of fetishism are cited.[72]

In his theory of fetishism Marx owed much to Feuerbach, whose ideas on religion, modified in accord with his own materialist premises, he now applied to the field of economics. This would seem to be suggested by his reference to finding an analogy with fetishism in the "misty realm" of religion: "There the products of the human brain appear as autonomous figures endowed with a life of their own, which enter into relations both with each other and with the human race. So it is in the world of commodities with the products of men's hands."[73]

Marx's discussion of fetishism both parallels and develops his treatment of alienation, species-being, and the role of money in the early writings and the *Grundrisse*. Iring Fetscher goes as far as to write: "What Marx calls in this context *fetishism*, he described in his early writings as *alienation*."[74] However, while the examples Marx gives us of fetishism are indeed particular instances of alienation, the concept of alienation is a more generalized one which he did not wish to abandon, and his discussion of fetishism should be seen as complementing his account of alienation, and not replacing it. Interestingly, Marx's unpublished sixth chapter of *Capital*, Volume 1, in fact includes a sentence which refers to both alienation and fetishism: "The objective conditions essential to the realization of labour are *alienated* from the worker and become manifest as *fetishes* endowed with a will and soul of their own."[75]

It is important that the various forms of fetishism which Marx identifies should not be regarded as simply an illusion. In capitalist society social relations do find expression as relations between things; money does dominate human social relations; although not as a natural property, capital does expand its value; and so on.[76] Accordingly, consciousness of fetishism, however necessary, must not be equated with its abolition. Fetishism itself can only be overcome through a social revolution in which production becomes subject to social control by free individuals. Thus, directly alongside his account of fetishism, Marx alludes to the utopian prospect of a new society where social relations assume a transparent and rational form: "The veil is not removed from the countenance of the social life-process, i.e., the process of material production, until it becomes production by freely associated men, and stands under their conscious and planned control."[77]

Marx goes on to refer to the "material foundation" required for the overcoming of fetishism, and the chapter on fetishism should be seen in the wider context of Marx's economic analysis of capitalism's revolutionizing of the productive forces, which occupies the rest of *Capital*. It is only as the end product of capitalist development that the conditions of production are raised into "general, communal, social conditions."[78] Unfortunately Marx's discussion of future communist society in his treatment of commodity fetishism is tantalizingly brief and vague. He gives little account of what production by "freely associated men" might mean, and the distinction between socialism and the higher stage of communism, so important in his *Critique of the Gotha Programme*, is not even mentioned.

The most important contribution of the theory of fetishism in *Capital* is undoubtedly the way in which it demonstrates how the mystification of social relations makes awareness of the worker's real situation much more problematic. Capitalism disguises its more fundamental reality, so that the basic underlying relations of alienation become suppressed, and the surface level of appearance dominates. Even the laws of political economy are seen as fixed and unalterable, taking on the appearance of natural law.[79] The worker's general alienation as a result is compounded and the true condition remains hidden from view. In his theory of fetishism Marx sought to expose capitalism's limited historical character, its contradictions, and its roots in the exploitation and alienation of the worker. This unraveling of the basic reality of bourgeois society was crucial if the proletariat was to attain a revolutionary consciousness and fulfill its historic role. Colletti highlights this revolutionary intent, when he observes that the "anti-fetishistic discourse of *Capital* comes to coincide with the *self-consciousness of the working class*."[80]

The way in which Marx's work on fetishism enabled him to demystify the workings of bourgeois society was very much in line with the declared intention behind his critique of political economy. Marx's basic concern was to penetrate beneath the surface appearance of capitalist society, and to discover the hidden underlying reality, in order to equip the workers in their struggle for emancipation. His economics was to be more than a contribution to theoretical study, and was to serve the practical purpose of enabling the proletariat to attain a revolutionary consciousness.[81] Thus when describing the fetish character of interest-bearing capital, the revolutionary motive underlying his critique is evident: "For vulgar economics, which seeks to present capital as an independent source of wealth, of value creation, this form is of course a godsend, a form in which the source of profit is no longer recognizable."[82]

Marx recognized the way in which bourgeois society does not present itself as exploitative and dehumanizing, but tries to hide this reality behind an exterior of equal exchange, the legal rights of the citizen, harmonious laws, and so forth. If the workers were to fully realize their true subjugation and alienation this would help put an end to their acquiescence and make them much more of a threat to the existing social order. The revolutionary consciousness Marx endeavored to promote was inspired by the utopian vision of a society where human relations no longer assumed a fetishized form, but brought genuine human freedom. Not that consciousness alone would be enough. Marx more than anyone realized that the capitalist mode of production had to develop through the outworking of its internal dynamic before its contradictions would make it ripe for its final overthrow. In this respect, he remained a Hegelian: necessity and freedom must be combined.

Chapter 4

Profit Law, Proletariat, and Utopian Consciousness

The whole purpose of Marx's analysis of the capitalist mode of production had been to uncover capitalism's internal "laws of motion," and in the profit law he considered he had grasped one of the most fundamental features of capitalist development.[1] It was this law above all else which provided the foundation for his conviction concerning bourgeois society's eventual transformation. The law must, however, be seen within the overall context of Marx's vision of future communism. Too often the debate about its validity has been restricted to comment on empirical evidence or the detail of Marx's argument. The intention in this chapter is to supplement an examination of the profit law with an emphasis on subjective factors and insistence upon the implicit utopianism within Marx's thought.

The Law Itself

To understand the profit law we need to begin with a consideration of the basic categories of Marx's economic theory. In the *Grundrisse*, building upon his labor theory of value and surplus value, Marx argues that the rate of profit must be defined as the ratio of surplus value to the total capital expended in production. From this he inferred that the greater the fixed or constant capital (machines and raw materials), the lower the rate of profit, if the surplus value remains the same. Whether the gross profit rises or falls depends on whether the change in the rate of profit is offset by the rise in total capital. Marx uses c, v, and s to denote constant capital, variable capital (the expenditure on labor), and surplus value, respectively. Given that the rate of profit = s/c+v, from this simple algebraic expression it can be seen that the rate of profit will decline as constant capital increases in relation to variable. This change in relation between constant and variable capital follows from the development of the productive powers of labor brought about by industrial advance, which Marx associates with "the decline of the part of capital which exchanges for living labour relative to the parts of it which participate in the production process as objectified labour." Thus with remarkable simplicity he arrived at what he calls the law of the *"tendency of the profit rate to decline."*[2]

Marx's views on the profit law must be considered in conjunction with earlier sections of the *Grundrisse*. (He in fact includes a footnote to pages 333ff.) In this earlier treatment of the relation between "surplus value and productive force," the conclusions reached are particularly germane to later discussions. Using arithmetical illustrations, he argues that increases in productivity do not give corresponding increases in surplus value. Thus, if half a day's labor was surplus, and the productive power of labor were doubled, then surplus value would only increase by a further one-quarter, that is, from one-half to three-quarters. Pursuing this line of reasoning he arrived at the conclusion: "The more developed capital already is, the more surplus labour it has already created, the more terribly must it develop the productive force in order to realize itself in only smaller proportion, i.e., to add surplus value."[3]

This inherent difficulty in expanding the realization of surplus value has important implications for the theory of the falling rate of profit, insofar as it demonstrates the impossibility of off-setting rises in constant capital through improved surplus value realization. There exists a definite upper limit to surplus labor, since it can never be greater than the amount of living labor employed. Thus, although in the specific section on the profit law Marx assumes the rate of surplus value to be constant, his deliberations elsewhere indicate that he took full account of variations in its rate.

Marx in fact alludes to the consequences of the limitations to surplus value realization when dealing with the question of the general rate of profit, and speaks of a decline "if the proportion of surplus to necessary labour falls *relatively*." This, he says, takes place "if the part of capital which exchanges for living labour is very small compared to that which exchanges for machinery and raw material."[4] The point Marx appears to be making, both here and elsewhere, is that if the amount of living labor in a commodity falls sufficiently in relation to the elements of constant capital, then even if it is virtually all unpaid labor, the profit rate will still decline.

Marx regarded the decline in the rate of profit as an expression of the enormous increase in the productive power of industry, the diminishing amount of labor required, and the extension of capitalism on a world scale. It was on the basis of this law that he deduced that "beyond a certain point, the development of the powers of production becomes a barrier for capital; hence the capital relation a barrier for the development of the productive powers of labour." At this stage contradictions and crises emerge, and the system of wage labor must cease. Marx concludes laconically: "The violent destruction of capital not by relations external to it, but rather as a condition of its self-preservation, is the most striking form in which advice is given it to be gone and to give room to a higher state of social production."[5]

The operation of the profit law is linked with the workings of the industrial cycle and its pattern of periodic devaluations of capital and fluctuations in wages. Marx maintained that given the pressure from the falling rate of profit, capital would attempt to check the process by increasing the ratio of surplus to necessary labor. Hence the paradox that the highest development of productive power coincides with the "degradation of the laborer, and a most straitened exhaustion of his vital powers." As contradictions develop they are resolved through the mediation of crises, "in which by momentaneous suspension of labour and annihilation of a great portion of capital the latter is violently reduced to the point where it can go on." However, the respite for capital is not permanent and a point is reached where "regularly recurring catastrophes lead to their repetition on a higher scale, and finally to its violent overthrow."[6]

The whole of Part Three of the third volume of *Capital* discusses Marx's theory of the falling rate of profit, under the heading "The Law of the Tendential Fall in the Rate of Profit." In his discussion Marx draws upon his treatment in Volume 1 of constant and variable capital, and the organic composition of capital (an expression used to quantify the relation between constant and variable capital—usually defined as c/c+v).[7]

He begins by arguing that with the same rate of surplus (s/v), the profit rate will fall as the constant capital rises. He assumed that the value of constant capital would rise with its material volume, and that this change in the composition of capital applies to all the decisive spheres of production, and therefore the fall in the rate of profit is generalized. A second formulation of the law no longer stipulates an unchanged rate of surplus value. "With the progressive decline in the variable capital in relation to the constant capital, this tendency leads to a rising organic composition of capital, and the direct result of this is that the rate of surplus-value, with the level of exploitation remaining the same or even rising, is expressed in a steadily falling general rate of profit."[8] Marx considered this trend to be a product of capitalism's progressive development of the productivity of labor.

All this does not prevent the absolute mass of labor employed and the surplus value from growing, since the fall in the profit rate corresponds to a relative, not an absolute, decline in variable capital and mass of profit. Indeed, given that capitalist production is essentially a process of accumulation, despite fluctuations, the mass of surplus labor and surplus value must grow. For this to happen total capital must increase at a faster rate than the profit rate falls. However, as capitalism develops, ever greater capital is needed to employ the same labor power, and there arises a "disproportion between the progressive growth of capital and the relative decline in its need for a growing population."[9] The mass of profits is dependent on both the rate of surplus value and the number of workers, and for accumulation either must increase.[10]

Falling individual commodity prices are consistent with a greater mass of profits on a larger number of commodities. This is only true, however, within certain limits, and Marx again refers to the barrier to surplus value creation. He writes: "With the enormous decrease, in the course of the advance of productivity, of the absolute amount of living labour newly added to the individual commodity, the unpaid labour it contains also undergoes an absolute decline, no matter how much it may have grown in relation to the paid portion."[11]

Marx acknowledges that there are in fact counteracting influences at work which give the law of the falling rate of profit only the character of a tendency. He begins by considering increases in the level of exploitation. These can be achieved by prolonging the working day and making labor more intense through measures such as raising the speed of machinery. The application of new technology before its use becomes generalized is another factor. Other counteracting influences include: the reduction of wages below their value; the cheapening of the elements of constant capital, which because of increases in productivity in turn become cheaper to produce; the creation of relative surplus population, which makes cheap labor available for new labor intensive branches of production which yield high profits and therefore raise the general rate profit; benefits from foreign trade, which cheapen both the elements of constant capital and the means of subsistence, as well as yielding higher profits from overseas trade.[12]

Commenting on these various counteracting factors, Marx writes that

> the same causes that bring about a fall in the general rate of profit provoke counter-effects that inhibit this fall, delay it and in part even paralyze it. These do not annul the law, but they weaken its effect. If this were not the case, it would not be the fall in the general rate of profit that would be incomprehensible, but rather the relative slowness of this fall. The law operates therefore simply as a tendency, whose effect is decisive only under certain particular circumstances and over long periods.[13]

Mindful of other possible explanations for declining profit rates, Marx points out that although the quantity of living labor in commodities falls, the unpaid portion still grows relative to the paid. Thus the tendential fall in the rate of profit is linked with an increased level of exploitation, and should not be explained by high wages, other than in exceptional cases: "The profit rate does not fall because labour becomes less productive but rather because it becomes more productive."[14]

As well as considering the various counteracting influences, Marx also discusses the role of crises and their relation to the operation of the profit law. It is when an expanded amount of capital only produces the same surplus as before, or even less, that capitalism's most serious difficulties emerge. In this situation competition intensifies; each capitalist seeks to avoid losses, but loss for the class as a whole is inevitable. A period of stagnation and crisis begins, where wages are lowered and workers dismissed. The mass of constant capital grows but its value falls, and the stagnation in production prepares the way for later expansion. This takes place within the limits imposed by capitalism, and a new cycle repeats the previous one, again leading to crisis.[15]

Drawing attention to what he describes as the "overproduction of capital," Marx describes how unemployment rises because excess capital is not used on account of the low level of profit. Hence the scandal of surplus capital and surplus labor side by side. Capitalist production is determined by profit expectations and not social needs, with the consequence that "production comes to a standstill not at the point where needs are satisfied, but rather where the production and realization of profit impose this."[16]

Marx stresses that as the capital required to employ a given amount of labor increased, the surplus created had certain limits regardless of the rate of surplus value. Total surplus value is determined by the rate of surplus value and by the number of workers set in motion. For a given capital, the first rises while the second falls, which means, therefore, that the compensation for the reduced number of workers by an increased level of exploitation has definite limits. Given these inherent obstacles in raising surplus value, he concludes, accumulation will come under threat no matter how efficient capital becomes.[17]

Since the rate of profit is the driving force of capitalism, its decline must eventually bring to an end the capitalist mode of production. Marx comments that capitalism is not an absolute, but only an "historic mode of production, corresponding to a specific and limited epoch in the development of the material conditions of production."[18]

The Law and Its Critics

Marx's theory of the tendency of the rate of profit to fall has received much attention in recent years. Given the importance Marx himself attached to it, and the seriousness of its refutation for Marxism, criticisms of the law must be carefully examined. Although there have been various studies of the empirical evidence for the law, it would be beyond the scope of this work to evaluate these, and the discussion below will be confined to considerations of Marx's basic argument.[19]

In his book *The Theory of Capitalist Development*, Paul Sweezy rejects Marx's formulation of the law of the tendency of the rate of profit to fall. Criticizing Marx for assuming that the rate of surplus value remains constant while the organic composition of capital rises, Sweezy maintains that in fact the rate of surplus value also increases and that this compensates for any rise in the organic composition. He also argues that although in physical terms the amount of machinery and materials has tended to increase, because of rising productivity this is not the same as a growth in the organic composition of capital, which is "a *value* expression." Sweezy rejects the possibility that the organic composition might be the dominant variable, insisting that "the direction in which the rate of profit will change becomes indeterminate."[20] In a later essay Sweezy modifies his position and acknowledges that Marx did in fact take account of the increases in the rate of surplus value which accompany a rising organic composition of capital. However, he continues to argue that there is no reason why the organic composition should increase relatively more rapidly.[21]

In response to Sweezy it should be noted that for Marx the organic composition was the dominant factor because of the definite limits to possible increases in surplus value that do not exist in the case of the organic composition. Marx accepted that the organic composition of capital would not rise as fast as the technical composition (its material volume), but still considered it would dramatically increase as capitalism progressed despite all the counteracting influences. In contrast, as we have seen, Marx was emphatic that increased surplus value realization confronted certain inherent barriers. Although Sweezy alludes to this line of argument, he too readily dismisses it as belonging to the realm of "science-fiction."[22]

Geoff Hodgson maintains that the validity of the theory of the falling rate of profit is dependent on whether or not the organic composition of capital does actually rise.[23] Hodgson regards technical innovation as an important factor in checking the rise in the organic composition of capital. Furthermore, technical change "often takes the form of replacing one machine by another *different* one. In which case we cannot talk about an increase or decrease in the *mass* of machinery."[24] Hodgson draws upon the work of Mark Blaug, who emphasizes the importance of technological changes in reducing the cost of fixed capital. Blaug's main criticism of Marx is that he failed to take proper account of the way in which market pressures result in technical developments that lead to savings in the costs of constant capital. The consequence of this is to reduce any imbalance between the respective expenditures on capital and labor. Blaug even goes so far as to claim that "Marx erred in not envisaging the possibility that labour might become the relative scarcer factor."[25]

In highlighting the role of technical development in reducing the organic composition of capital, Hodgson and Blaug are drawing attention to a factor which Marx did not sufficiently emphasize, even though he considered it as a counteracting influence. It is interesting to note that Engels seems to have taken a more ambivalent view of the profit law. Marx had left one chapter of *Capital*, Volume 3, unwritten ("The Effect of Turnover on the Rate of Profit"), and Engels inserted a short chapter of his own in which he discussed the consequences of the shortening of the turnover periods for capital investment due to improved means of transport and communication. He also stressed the importance for the profit rate of advances in labor productivity which reduce the turnover period and do not increase capital outlay—citing new methods in metallurgy and the chemical industry.[26]

Epoch-making inventions and technical improvements that significantly reduce costs are undoubtedly a crucial factor in determining the long-term trend in the rate of profit. However, although technical change need not always increase the value of constant capital, and can indeed reduce it, insofar as technological advance revolutionizes the production process and ultimately reduces labor time to a minimum as a proportion of total capital, the eventual outcome must be that capital costs become the more significant factor of production. Thus Marx's profit law is perhaps better described as an *ultimate trend* rather than a "tendency." It is an expression of the fact that capitalist development will reach a stage where the inherited productive wealth of humankind, represented in the means of production, will require only the most modest amount of active labor time for the successful operation of the production process.

This claim would be readily accepted by many people besides Marx. Such persons would also no doubt dismiss as banal Blaug's suggestion that labor might become relatively the scarcer factor. Marx's achievement, however, was to correctly draw the inference from all this for the trajectory of capitalist evolution, namely, that in such a situation profits will fall, and production based on profit will become impossible.

The Question of Agency

Attributing such importance to the profit law might seem to suggest a more determinist than utopian reading of Marx. It is certainly the case that forms of Marxism which stress historical necessity to the neglect of the active role of women and men are often espoused by those hostile to utopianism. Scientific determinism may postulate future communist society, but leaves little room for the constructive role of utopian imagination. It follows that the profit law could be consistent with a utopian interpretation of Marxism only if conscious human agency still remained a *sine qua non* for the transition to socialism. Here, however, the major difficulty is that the crucial text for understanding Marx's economics, the *Grundrisse*, intriguingly contains little reference to the role of the proletariat in achieving socialism. Indeed the impression is sometimes left that Marx may have abandoned his previous perspective on discovering a more satisfactory basis for his understanding of the emergence of future communist society. Several scholars have in fact argued precisely this point.

In an article on this question of the role of the proletariat, entitled "Proletariat and Middle Class in Marx: Hegelian Choreography and Capitalist Dialectic," Martin Nicolaus suggests that Marx came to reject the outlook of his earlier writing—most notably the *Communist Manifesto* of 1848.[27] Marx's former belief, says Nicolaus, was that "capitalist society must inevitably become polarized into two directly antagonistic classes, and that, in this polarization, the industrial proletariat must play the role of successful negation."[28]

This emphasis on class opposition and the role of the proletariat Nicolaus attributes largely to the influence of Hegel, at a time when Marx had only a limited knowledge of political economy. This earlier assessment, with its crude schema of class polarization and the absolute impoverishment of the working class, was at variance with the implications of Marx's mature economics, and led Marx to adopt a new perspective. Nicolaus sums up his argument:

> My thesis is that Marx's major contributions to the understanding of capitalism—the labor theory of value, the theory of surplus value, the law of the tendential decline of the profit rate—constitute a body of theory from which the failure of capitalist society to polarize, the rise of a new middle class, and the declining militancy of the industrial proletariat—in other words, the essential features of advanced industrial society—can be accurately predicted and explained, and indeed that Marx himself did so.[29]

Focusing in particular on Marx's theory of surplus value, Nicolaus highlights the crucial significance of the swelling mass of surplus value, as capitalism develops, for the relationship between the capitalist and working classes. This increased surplus, he says, "enables the capitalist class to face workers' demands for higher wages with an unprecedented degree of flexibility." In such circumstances, wage increases become less significant for capital and more a matter of policy:

> What happens then, Marx foresaw, is that the workers' submission to the capitalist class is clothed [He continues quoting *Capital* Vol. 1]...in bearable, or as Eden says, "comfortable and liberal" forms....From the workers' own swelling surplus product, a part of which is constantly being converted into additional capital, a greater portion flows back to them in cash, so that they can broaden the sphere of their consumption, equip themselves better with clothing and furniture, etc., and develop a small reserve of savings.[30]

The consequence of all this is that social polarization is attenuated and the perspectives of the Manifesto no longer hold.

The rising mass of surplus value also explains the emergence of the new middle class: "It [the surplus] *enables* the capitalist class to create a class of people who are not productive workers, but who perform services either for the individual capitalists or, more important, for the capitalist class as a whole." Nicolaus supports this contention with references to the middle class in Marx. Thus he quotes *Theories of Surplus Value*, where discussing the mass of surplus, Marx chastises Ricardo for forgetting to emphasize "*the constant increase of the middle classes, who stand in the middle between the workers on one side and the capitalists and landed proprietors on the other side, who are for the most part supported directly by revenue, who rest as a burden on the labouring foundation, and who increase the social security and the power of the upper ten thousand.*"[31]

A rising standard of living for the working class and the growth of the middle class is indeed a far cry from what many would consider the usual path to revolution. But in another essay Nicolaus positively welcomes this:

> It would be a paltry theory indeed which predicted the breakdown of the capitalist order only when that consisted of child labour, sweatshops, famine, chronic malnutrition, pestilence, and all other scourges of its primitive stages. No genius and little science are required to reveal the contradictions of such a condition. Marx, however, proceeds by imagining the strongest possible case in favour of the capitalist system, by granting the system the full development of all the powers inherent in it—and then exposing the contradictions which must lead to its collapse.[32]

The assessment offered by Nicolaus is open to question for a number of reasons. To attribute Marx's early views on class polarization and the role of the proletariat solely to his dependence on Hegel is a gross oversimplification. It neglects the importance of Marx's study of economics which began as far back as 1843-44, his indebtedness to the work of bourgeois historians for his understanding of classes, and the decisive influence of his contact with utopian socialists and with artisan political organizations while in Paris.[33]

The belief that improved living standards in advanced capitalism will make the proletariat no longer a revolutionary force is also problematic. The assumption that the rising living standards associated with a particular phase of accumulation can be indefinitely sustained is unwarranted, and discounts the possibility (and effects) of serious economic crises. It also gives insufficient weight to the particular difficulties that arise when constant capital has increased enormously in relation to variable capital and the falling profit rate threatens the accumulation process. When this occurs the search for new capital must be intensified, since this will be desperately needed to sustain the expansion on which future profits depend. All this increases the precariousness of bourgeois society and brings with it the prospect of bankruptcy and unemployment. The very success of those units of capital which do survive by further automating the productive process also creates unemployment. Higher unemployment in turn requires increased government expenditure, which further reduces the state's resources to manage the crisis. The consequence of all this for industrial workers is that they will find their pay subject to pressure from employers seeking to maintain profits and from the state requiring its revenues. Combined with the specter of mass unemployment, this is hardly a scenario conducive to political stability.

On the question of the new middle class, Nicolaus correctly stresses its significance as a feature of developed bourgeois society, which Marx anticipated on the basis of his theory of surplus value. However, as the long-term decline in profits eventually causes the mass of surplus value to fall, or at least to prove insufficient for the investment required for further accumulation, the same pressures that bear down on the working class and unemployed also threaten the middle class. Thus, while in certain historical periods this class may contribute to social cohesion and thereby reduce class polarization, it cannot permanently escape the consequences of capitalism's contradictions, and will therefore also be drawn into its deepening crisis.

Nicolaus later retracted his position, with only minimal explanation.[34] However, the importance of the issues at stake merit the detailed response given above. It should also at this point be noted that several other scholars have suggested that Marx substantially revised his political theory. David McLellan says that virtually nothing is said in the *Grundrisse* of the transition from capitalism to communism, and goes on to claim that "the revolutionary activity of the proletariat—is never alluded to." Commenting on this situation he identifies "a tension between the long-term view of the *Grundrisse* and the prospects of fairly imminent revolution implicit in some of Marx's later writings."[35]

Paul Walton, in his discussion of the *Grundrisse*, speaks of "the demise of the proletarian revolution," and says of the labor theory of value "that there is no empirical prediction of proletarian revolution which can be drawn from the theory."[36]

It is certainly the case that however graphic the description of both capitalism and communism in the *Grundrisse*, the question of the transition from one to the other is neglected. When the "barrier" to capitalist development is mentioned it is usually presented as a problem affecting the internal logic of capital, with no consideration given to the role of the proletariat. Albrecht Wellmer refers to "an unnoticed blurring of the distinctions between a revolutionary transformation and an organic metamorphosis of the capitalist system."[37] This failure to adequately demonstrate the link between capitalism's deepening contradictions and the question of agency is acknowledged by scholars who nevertheless insist that Marx retained his belief in the revolutionary role of the proletariat in the

Grundrisse. Thus, Allen Oakley describes Marx's arguments as "scattered and sketchy."[38]

Part of the confusion over whether Marx abandoned his belief in the revolutionary role of the proletariat is perhaps attributable to an important change in perspective that did occur. In 1848, Marx expected the worker's lot to become progressively worse in an absolute sense. The "modern labourer," he writes, "instead of rising with the progress of industry, sinks deeper and deeper below the conditions of existence of his own class. He becomes a pauper, and pauperism develops more swiftly than population and wealth."[39] This belief in the absolute impoverishment of the working class was, however, to undergo substantial revision.[40] Thus, in the *Grundrisse*, when discussing wage fluctuations in the upward stage of the economic cycle, Marx refers to the possibility of "the worker's participation in the higher, even cultural satisfactions, the agitation for his own interests, newspaper subscriptions, attending lectures, educating his children, developing his taste etc...."[41]

In *Capital*, Volume 1, Marx states that as capitalism advances the level of needs develop beyond mere physical subsistence, and that "the determination of the value of labour-power contains a historical and moral element."[42] However, although he readily conceded that at certain stages of capitalist development the living standards of workers would rise, he insisted they remained exploited nonetheless.[43] His theory of surplus value implied only the *relative* impoverishment of the working class, since an increased rate of exploitation is perfectly consistent with a rising standard of living for the workers.[44] Unlike Ricardo, he did not see wages and profits as being inversely related.[45]

That Marx came to subscribe to a theory of only relative impoverishment can be more or less directly confirmed from a number of quotations. Thus, in *Capital*, Volume 1, he qualifies what he has to say concerning the plight of the laborer: "The situation of the worker, be his payment high or low, must grow worse."[46] In *Theories of Surplus Value*, when discussing the extent to which the worker shares in the benefits of productivity increases, he says that the workers will not permit wages "to be reduced to an absolute minimum; on the contrary, they achieve a certain quantitative participation in the general growth of wealth."[47]

Marx's theory of wages became much more flexible, with physical subsistence serving as only an absolute minimum above which wages fluctuate, the upper limit being determined by "the respective power of the combatants," that is, the class struggle.[48] However, although the impoverishment was relative, it still remained significant as an indicator of the worker's oppression and alienation. When Nicolaus quotes Marx's reference to the worker's submission taking "comfortable and liberal forms," he takes it completely out of context, since Marx was only discussing a particular phase of accumulation when the ratio of constant to variable capital remains unchanged, and even then he insisted the worker remained exploited.[49] At other times downward pressure on wages would emerge in crises to threaten previously accepted living standards. It is in this sense that we should understand those passages which refer to the worker's immiserization and impoverishment in the later writings, rather than seeing them as simply an unqualified restatement of views held in the *Manifesto*.

The assessment of the conditions of life of the proletariat under capitalism is not the only area where the *Manifesto* and Marx's mature economics differ. Marx increasingly came to recognize the need for a much longer period of capitalist development before bourgeois society would be ready for revolutionary transformation. The excitement of the upheavals of 1848 having died down, Marx obtained during 1850 a reading ticket for the British Museum, where he threw himself into an intensive period of study of economics, and already by late 1850 he had began to distance himself from his earlier perspective of permanent revolution. Many years later Engels acknowledged that history had proved Marx and himself to be wrong in the 1840s, and to have mistaken the birth pangs of capitalism for its death throes.[50] In the *Grundrisse* the necessity for capitalism to first run its full course is stressed throughout, replacing the imminent expectation of revolution.[51]

In recognizing that Marx abandoned some of his former analysis we are, however, far from proposing that he no longer regarded the proletariat as the bearer of socialism. *Capital* and Marx's later political writings give abundant testimony to the contrary. Furthermore, whatever its theoretical weaknesses, the *Grundrisse* cannot be said to justify such a conclusion. David McLellan overstates his case when he suggests that the revolutionary role of the proletariat is never alluded to, and a number of passages can be cited in this respect. For example, when considering the possible effects on capitalism of technological improvements, Marx concludes:

> If it [capital] succeeds too well at the first, then it suffers from surplus production, and then necessary labour is interrupted, because *no surplus labor can be realized by capital*. The more this contradiction develops, the more does it become evident that the growth of the forces of production can no longer be bound up with the appropriation of alien labour, but that the mass of workers must themselves appropriate their own surplus labour.[52]

Another pertinent passage, from which we have already quoted, is to be found amid Marx's reflections concerning the falling rate of profit:

...the highest development of productive power together with the greatest expansion of existing wealth will coincide with depreciation of capital, degradation of the labourer, and a most straitened exhaustion of his vital powers. These contradictions lead to explosions, cataclysms, crises, in which by momentaneous suspension of labour and annihilation of a great portion of capital the latter is violently reduced to the point where it can go on.... Yet, these regularly recurring catastrophes lead to their repetition on a higher scale, and finally to its violent overthrow.[53]

For Marx, the unfolding of capitalism's internal contradictions and the creation of the conditions for its own supersession, were not viewed in isolation from the advancing self- consciousness and social significance of the proletariat. Thus, when discussing the question of transition he interjects: "At a certain point, a development of the forces of material production is at the same time a development of the forces of the working class—*suspends capital itself* [sic]."[54]

However, significant as these references may be in calling into question any alleged *volte-face* in Marx's position, when David McLellan writes that it can "plausibly be claimed that the lack of anything 'political' seriously detracts from the view of the *Grundrisse* as the most complete of Marx's work," he is undoubtedly identifying a major theoretical shortcoming of this otherwise outstanding text.[55]

The *Grundrisse*, in its description of future communist society, presents a vision of what capitalism could make possible through its revolutionizing of the productive forces. Whether this possibility will be actually realized is dependent on subjective factors. Capitalism only creates the *conditions* for future emancipation. The benefits of capitalism's high level of development appear only in a contradictory and distorted form, namely, in the context of widespread unemployment, regional and global inequalities, and recurring crises. To suggest, as some scholars have done, that Marx envisaged a greatly increased standard of living combined with massively reduced labor time for the whole of society *within* capitalism, misinterprets what Marx is saying in the *Grundrisse*, and ignores those passages—and the many more in *Capital*—that emphasize the powerful forces to which workers remain subject throughout capitalist development.[56]

To be sure, Marx's economic theory implied only relative and not absolute impoverishment, and was consistent with rising real wages in particular historical conjunctures. Nevertheless, there remains the pressure to overcome crises and contradictions at the expense of the working class and to the detriment of historically established material expectations.

It is the consequence of capitalism's unfolding contradictions that heightens the likelihood that workers will embrace more revolutionary aspirations.[57] This would seem to be the thrust of Marx's remarks about "crises," where he envisages the "degradation of the labourer" leading to capitalism's "overthrow."[58] Marx recognized that the deepening crises of capitalism would expose the irrationality of the capitalist mode of production. His vision of future communist society indicated the repressed potential within capitalism, and given that the capitalist class cannot be expected to relinquish power voluntarily, this vision is not only compatible with, but *requires* the intervention of the proletariat. Although Marx did not always make this very clear, it is surely the more accurate reading of the *Grundrisse*.

Marx's account of the transition to socialism is of continuing importance, and although modern bourgeois society is composed of many different strata, the implications of his theory of surplus value are still consistent with affirming the revolutionary transformation of that society. Within the international economy the growing ranks of lower paid and unemployed workers clearly have little to gain from capitalism. Even highly paid industrial workers still experience alienation, along with the constant threat of unemployment due to further technological advance, and the possibility of falling real wages whether directly via their employer or through taxation. Nor, as we have seen, can the middle classes assume that their privileged position is invulnerable. Thus, despite the existence of a much more variegated proletariat or class of "nonowners," there remains a considerable common interest in the creation of socialism.

In the earlier post-war period skepticism about the possibility of socialist transition was perhaps more justified. The trade cycle was less in evidence, and crises, when they came, were much less severe. In such a situation of rising living standards, Marx seemed much less relevant. However, the slow-down of economic growth, the reemergence of recession, and widespread unemployment in the economically advanced countries—all in the context of more efficient technology and powerful productive capacity—makes his predictions much more pertinent. It is significant in this respect that despite the economic upturn following the recession of the early 1980s, structural unemployment still persists. Fortuitously such concerns have been somewhat overtaken by recent events in Eastern Europe, and in the short term at least a period of further capitalist expansion is in prospect. It cannot, however, be assumed that capitalism will continually be able to manage crises by regulative measures, or contain workers' demands by granting higher wages combined with social reforms, and yet these are historically precisely the means by which it has maintained social stability.

The Need for Utopian Vision

Marx's theory of the falling rate of profit should in fact never be seen in isolation, either from the question of agency in the transition to socialism or from his vision of the future communist society, to which we must now give further attention.

The profit law pointed not only to capitalism's demise, but also toward the future emancipated society of free individuals, where capitalist productive forces and relations are discarded and replaced by a new mode of production, making possible genuinely human social relations.[59] In the *Grundrisse*, Marx considers the falling rate of profit to be "identical in meaning" with the enormous development of the productive forces, and the reduction of labor time to a minimum.[60] Yet it was precisely this growth of production by automatic machines and the concomitant reduction of labor time—both being the culmination of capitalism's revolutionizing of industry—which provided the basis for the new communist society. Thus the very factors which undermined the basis of capitalist production through the operation of the profit law create the conditions for overall human development. The profit law and Marx's vision of future communist society each in different ways reflects the implications of the massive growth in productivity in advanced bourgeois society.

The decline in the rate of profit strikes at the very heart of the central dynamic of capitalism—the accumulation process. In doing so it prepares the way for the emergence of socialism. Marx envisaged both the profit rate and the total mass of profit as coming under threat. Eventually a point is reached where the self-realization of capital is suspended, and capitalist social relations are negated:

> ...the development of the productive forces brought about by the historical development of capital itself, when it reaches a certain point, suspends the self-realization of capital, instead of positing it. Beyond a certain point, the development of the powers of production becomes a barrier for capital; hence the capital relation a barrier for the development of the productive powers of labour. When it has reached this point, capital, i.e., wage labour, enters into the same relation toward the development of social wealth and of the forces of production as the guild system, serfdom, slavery, and is necessarily stripped off as a fetter. The last form of servitude

assumed by human activity, that of wage labour on the one side, capital on the other, is thereby cast off like a skin....[61]

While it is the convulsions caused by the crisis in profit realization which signal the demise of capitalist social relations, the decline in the rate of profit is only an expression of a deeper underlying development, namely, that production has come to depend less on labor time and more on the level of science and automation. In such circumstances capitalism loses its *raison d'être*, since the capital-labor relation on which it is based becomes less and less relevant. "Capital thus works toward its own dissolution as the form dominating production."[62] Throughout the *Grundrisse* Marx returns to his conviction that capitalism is not the final form of the development of the productive forces, and that there is an inherent barrier to production based on capital.[63]Through its revolutionizing of the productive forces, capitalism reduces labor time to a minimum, but in doing so it thereby creates the material conditions for its own downfall. The conflict between the forces of production and the social relations to which Marx briefly alludes in the famous Preface to his *Critique of Political Economy* of 1859, is elaborated in the *Grundrisse* as the heart of the argument:

> On the one side, then, it [capital] calls to life all the powers of science and of nature, as of social combination and social intercourse, in order to make the creation of wealth independent (relatively) of the labour time employed on it. On the other side, it wants to use labour time as the measuring rod for the giant social forces thereby created, and to confine them within the limits required to maintain the already created value as value. Forces of production and social relations—two sides of the development of the social individual—appear to capital as mere means, and are merely means for it to produce on its limited foundation. In fact, however, they are the material conditions to blow the foundation sky-high.[64]

Marx sees reduced labor time as also providing the foundation for the future communist society:

> As soon as labour in the direct form has ceased to be the great well-spring of wealth, labour time ceases and must cease to be its measure, and hence exchange-value [must cease to be the measure] of use-value. The *surplus labour of the masses* has ceased to be the condition for the development of general wealth....With that, production based on exchange-value breaks down, and the direct, material production process is stripped of the form of penury and antithesis. The free development of individualities, and hence not the reduction of necessary labour time so as to posit surplus labour, but rather the general reduction of the necessary labour of society to a minimum, which then corresponds to the artistic, scientific etc. development of the individuals in the time set free, and with the means created, for all of them.[65]

Commenting on the eventual consequence of the shortening of labor time through the application of science to the production process, Marx writes: "This will redound to the benefit of emancipated labour, and is the condition of its emancipation."[66] As well as vastly reduced labor time for society as a whole, with all its implications for the free development of individuals, work in future communist society also loses its alienating character and becomes a means of self-realization.[67]

The fundamental irrationality of capitalism under advanced technical conditions makes its continuance more and more of an anachronism, and Marx points us toward the rich potential that would stem from the socialization of industry and the harnessing of productive power to serve human ends. In *Capital* the link between the profit law and the future communist society, though less strong, is still present. Thus, discussing the unfolding of the law in Volume 3, Marx writes:

> The contradiction between the general social power into which capital has developed and the private power of the individual capitalists over these social conditions of production develops ever more blatantly, while this development also contains the solution to this situation, in that it simultaneously raises the conditions of production into general, communal, social conditions.[68]

The outline of future communist society which Marx gives us in his mature economics firmly demonstrates that utopian anticipation remained at the heart of his socialism. His utopian vision of the future was no idealist dreaming, but was informed by the glaring contrast between existing social conditions and what had become objectively possible once capitalism had reached its maturity. Marx's profit law, the historic role of the proletariat, and the vision of future communist society are all best seen as interdependent elements, which although insufficiently integrated, nevertheless form a theoretical whole. This can be seen from a consideration of the question of the transition to socialism. The intervention of the proletariat and social strata acting in alliance is necessary as it would be naive to assume that those with power will voluntarily relinquish it without contest. But the existence of such class forces is not by itself enough, since capitalism too must be ripe for transition. Finally, those opposed to existing conditions must possess a revolutionary consciousness in order to fulfill their historic role, and it is here that the need for utopian vision is paramount.

It would of course be wrong to deny that the attempt to understand Marx as a utopian thinker is without problems. Discussion of future communist society is much more limited in *Capital*. Marx's dismissive attitude to utopian speculation in the postface to the second edition, where he speaks of "recipes...for the cook-shops of the future," is also often mentioned.[69] Such criticisms can nevertheless be countered by a consideration of Marx's objectives in writing *Capital*. In the preface, he describes the ultimate aim of his work as being to "reveal the economic law of motion of modern society."[70] Thus his reference to "recipes" for the future should be taken as applying to speculation divorced from concrete analysis.

In his *Critique of the Gotha Programme*, written several years later, Marx in fact speaks freely and in detail of post-capitalist society.[71] Writing on the Paris Commune in 1871 he praises the Commune for its decentralization and direct democracy, and regards it as an anticipation of the forms of political organization appropriate to communist society.[72] The evidence is thus overwhelming that discussion and predictions concerning future communist society did have a place in his work. If he had been able to complete his studies it is clearly a matter of conjecture as to how he would have proceeded. Bertell Ollman draws attention to the draft plan for *Capital* Marx was working on in 1851, which indicates that in the final volume he "intended to present his views on communism in a more systematic manner." Citing a letter to Marx, Ollman refers to Engels' later comment that "'the famous positive,' what you 'really want' was never written."[73] All things considered, it can therefore reasonably be argued that the task of reinvigorating Marxism through the renewal of its utopian dimension can claim a starting point in Marx himself. Indeed, the unfinished and unresolved nature of his work both suggests and legitimizes such an endeavor.

For Marx, the worker's recognition of alienation and the need to overcome it was of enormous significance. In the *Grundrisse* he writes:

> The recognition [*Erkennung*] of the products as its own, and the judgement that its separation from the conditions of its realization is improper—forcibly imposed—is an enormous [advance in] awareness [*Bewusstsein*], itself the product of the mode of production resting on capital, and as much the knell to its doom as, with the slave's awareness that he *cannot be the property of another*, with the consciousness of himself as a person, the existence of slavery becomes a merely artificial, vegetative existence, and ceases to prevail as the basis of production.[74]

This passage not only indicates that Marx was by no means oblivious to the significance of utopian aspirations, but also helps explain the importance he attached to the problem of fetishism later in *Capital*. The possibility of workers gaining knowledge of their true situation is always in danger of being thwarted by the veil of appearance which hides the underlying reality, yet such awareness is a prerequisite if workers are to act in their own interests, and begin openly challenging capital.[75] The conflict between revolutionary aspirations which arise from the worker's experience of alienation and the fetishization which hinders these is not satisfactorily examined by Marx, who gives insufficient attention to the implications of capitalism's mystification of social relations. The process of defetishizing bourgeois social relations, and the forms of struggle that assist this, require much more consideration.[76]

As Gramsci and others have pointed out, Marx did not have sufficient to say concerning the growth of working-class consciousness.[77] Indeed, it was the paucity of his work on this matter that made it possible for Lenin to claim that workers by themselves could attain trade union consciousness only and that socialist ideas needed to be introduced into the proletariat by intellectuals—hence the leading role of the party. Marx far too readily talked of the "mere fragment of a man" becoming the "fully developed individual," without attempting to bridge the chasm between the two.[78] He did not place enough emphasis on the need for the working class to change itself through engaging in struggle at every level against the dominance of bourgeois society and its ideology. Jack Lindsay's comments in his discussion of Gramsci are particularly apposite: "The transition to socialism needed the construction of a new common sense (good sense), a new culture in all spheres, a new philosophy, a *new consciousness* [my italics]....Marxist parties with a purely political programme, which leave cultural and moral hegemony unchallenged in the control of the ruling class and its exponents, have no hope of success."[79]

As the nurturing of consciousness is of the utmost significance, the relevance of the utopian orientation found in Marx is immediately apparent. The vision of future communist society provides the means of awakening and sustaining *confidence* concerning the prospect of real social transformation.

The dissemination of such a perspective has important strategic and programmatic implications. It suggests a much more positive acceptance of the inheritance of the religious and cultural traditions associated with utopianism; the need for socialist education to be given a higher priority; the importance of a greater reliance on mass participation and action, broad alliances, and so on, rather than the Leninist subordination of the masses to the party; the urgency of combating the negative visions of communist society presented by existing distorted forms of socialism; the necessity of intermediate objectives which provide a measure of realization of socialist aspirations and an incentive to further action. This list is not intended to be exhaustive, but only to *indicate* the kind of redirection of socialist thinking that is envisaged.

Above all, the vision of socialism that is articulated must be *comprehensive*. The degree of stratification of modern bourgeois society requires the formation of alliances between various social groups. The insights of feminist, ecological, and peace movements should be accepted as a valuable critique of the socialist tradition and a much-needed challenge to it to broaden its scope—Marx himself gave little attention to women's oppression or ecological issues, and could hardly have anticipated the importance of peace and disarmament in a nuclear age.[80] Socialism too must increasingly be seen in global terms, with the struggle for emancipation in the West being linked with the hopes for greater democracy and individual rights in the existing communist world, and the moral imperative to work to reverse the mounting deprivation and poverty in the poorer countries. Recognition of our global interdependence, the fragility of our natural environment, and the alarming depletion of the earth's resources will mean that no expansion—even socialist—can go unchecked. Marx far too casually talked of production in abundance. Socialism is not consumerism, and the pursuit of the socialist ideal will require the clarification of what constitute genuine human needs and a much greater emphasis on *qualitative* rather than quantitative economic growth.

A utopian renewal of socialism would have important consequences in any consideration of the relation between reform and revolution. A reformism which does not even envisage the ending of capitalist social relations would be rejected, since it cannot be said to correspond to a radically new social order and is therefore devoid of utopian content. However, given that the transition to socialism will not occur automatically (either through the collapse of capitalism or as a Pavlovian reaction to ever-increasing misery), but only through conscious human action, all this implies the need for a process of growing strength, assertiveness, and confidence among working people within existing capitalist society. Defense of previous gains and a desire for further concessions and reforms is fully consistent with the longer term aim of the conquest of political power as a precondition for the construction of future communist society. Once people are convinced that they have more to gain from the dismantling of capitalism than from its continuance they will support more radical economic measures, such as increased public ownership and greater democratic control over the economy, and the way will then be open to embracing more avowedly socialist objectives.

It must, however, always be stressed that consciousness alone will not be sufficient without the objective economic preconditions for socialism. Marx saw evidence of capitalism's readiness for transition not only in declining profits and economic crises, but also in certain important changes that were already beginning to take place. In *Capital* he regards forms of social ownership such as factory cooperatives, and the emergence of joint-stock companies, as changes in capitalist society which prefigured its impending transformation. Thus he refers to cooperatives as the first examples of the emergence of the new form of society within the old: "These factories show how, at a certain stage of development of the material forces of production, and of the social forms of production corresponding to them, a new mode of production develops and is formed naturally out of the old." He speaks in similarly positive terms of the change from ownership by individual entrepreneurs to joint-stock companies, describing corporate capitalist ownership as a transitional form between ownership by the single capitalist and ownership by the associated producers: "Capitalist joint-stock companies as much as cooperative factories should be viewed as transition forms from the capitalist mode of production to the associated one."[81]

Widespread state intervention, public and private monopolies, and the dramatic growth of transnational companies indicate the potential for the socialization of the means of production within present capitalist society. In its laissez-faire stage capitalism consisted of numerous competitive units, and the possibilities for exerting social control were very different. However, many of the developments that were only just beginning to emerge in Marx's time have now considerably altered capitalism and make its rational, planned, and democratic control ever more urgent. All this calls for a consciousness inspired by a vision of the society of human freedom beyond capitalism. Utopia must be embraced as both means and end.

Chapter 5

Ernst Bloch's Messianic Marxism

> Once man has comprehended himself and has established his
> own domain in real democracy, without depersonalization and
> alienation, something arises in the world which all men have
> glimpsed in childhood: a place and a state in which no one has
> yet been. And the name of this something is home or homeland.
> —*Ernst Bloch*

No thinker has done more to reinstate the utopian elements in Marxism than
the German Marxist philosopher, Ernst Bloch. Esoteric and often organized
in an eclectic and frustrating manner, his utopian philosophy has been
dismissed, by Christians and Marxists alike, as a confused and idiosyncratic
amalgam of heresies. Yet within his writings, which span half a century (born
in 1885, he died at ninety two), there can be shown to be a remarkable unity
of thought.[1] Furthermore, themes and perspectives can be discerned which
continue even today to be of relevance to both Christianity and Marxism and
to the dialogue between them, and which make Bloch a philosopher of more
than just historical interest.

The central thesis of his work was that Marxism had become distorted and
impoverished through the exclusion of utopian elements. He considered that
within the Marxist tradition there had been too great a progress from utopia
to science, and he sought to revitalize Marxism through a creative incorporation of utopianism. (Initially he spoke in terms of adding a utopian dimension
to Marx, but later came to recognize the utopianism implicit in Marx.[2]) His
magnum opus, *Das Prinzip Hoffnung* (*The Principle of Hope*), set forth his
fully developed system of theoretical messianism. Using a wide variety of
sources, he showed the potency of the human yearning for a better world.

Overwhelmingly, though, he took the Judeo-Christian tradition as his model and inspiration, and attempted to claim the heritage of religious messianism for a renewed Marxism. In so doing he helped reassert the eschatological content of Christianity, and stimulated important developments in modern theology, most notably Jürgen Moltmann's "theology of hope" and much of liberation theology.

Marxism as a Humanist Utopianism

Bloch's Marxism is essentially humanist in its orientation: "True Marxism, in its dynamics of the class struggle, and in its substantive goal, is, and must be, humanism and humanitarianism enhanced." For Bloch the revolutionary project was concerned above all with the struggle for the full liberation of human potential from the dehumanization of capitalist society. He was insistent that a humanist interpretation of Marxism is the only one faithful to Marx:

> For Marx, the humane, even as a remote goal of the tendency of society, is completely dominant. Marxism properly pursued, effectively unburdening itself, and emancipating itself from evil neighbors, has been since its inception "humanity in action," the human countenance coming to fulfillment.[3]

Thus Bloch emphasized the continuity in Marx's thought, and saw no contradiction between the early and later Marx.[4]

With himself and other middle-class intellectuals in mind, Bloch rhetorically asked: "What has brought to the red flag those who did not, in a sense, need it?" For his answer he looked no further than Marx himself, who "offers a secure paradigm for the red path of the intellect: the model of a humanism that concerns itself in action."[5] Although he was highly critical of sentimental forms of socialism, Bloch placed a very strong emphasis on the ethical dimension of socialism: "Love for mankind, insofar as it clearly understands itself as directed toward the exploited, and progresses toward true knowledge, is unquestionably an indispensable factor in socialism."[6]

This recognition of the humanist foundations of Marxism does not in any way detract from the need for a detailed analysis of society, but only confirms it. "The humanitarianism of Marx, as directed to the least of his brethren, proves itself in his endeavor to understand from their roots the degradation and induced nullity of most of his brethren, in order to attack their very roots."[7] For Bloch, Marx's fourth thesis on Feuerbach—that the secular basis of human alienation must be "understood in its contradiction and revolutionized in practice"—provides a positive mandate for both scientific analysis and revolutionary activity. It is quite mistaken to suppose that there is any conflict between the two:

> The new proletarian standpoint does not in any way eliminate the value concept of humanism. On the contrary, it allows that concept to be realized for the first time. The more scientific socialism is, the *more concrete is the concern for man at its center*, and the more certain is the real elimination *of his self-alienation as its goal.*[8]

Thus, Bloch is insistent that scientific analysis should not obscure Marxism's utopian intention to transform the world. "Marxism never renounces its heritage, and least of all the primal intention: the Golden Age. In all its *analyses* Marxism plays the part of a sober detective, yet takes the legend seriously, and reacts pragmatically to the *dream of the Golden Age.*"[9]

For Bloch, the realm of human freedom, which he calls the "regnum humanum," to which all previous utopias point, constitutes Marxism's "concrete utopia." He also (as in the quotation with which this chapter opened) uses the term "homeland" to describe the future unalienated socialist society. Bloch draws inspiration for this "concrete utopia" from the *Paris Manuscripts* and Marx's radically utopian theme of the "humanization of nature" and the "naturalization of man." In his revolutionary humanism Bloch sees the emergence of full human individuality in a transformed world as occurring through the historical process itself:

> Marx indicates that his ultimate intention is "the development of the wealth of human nature." This *human* wealth, like that of *nature* as a whole, lies exclusively in the trend latency in which the world finds itself....It follows that man everywhere is still living in prehistory, and that all things are still in the stage prior to the just and true creation of the world. *The true genesis is not at the beginning, but at the end.*

Central to Bloch's use of concrete utopia is his view that the future exists already in the present, in the form of latency. In a somewhat surprising departure for a professed Marxist, he uses the Aristotelian concept of "entelechy," claiming that matter itself is in a process of development, and thus provides an ontology to support his utopian perspective.[10]

Bloch's concept of utopia must be distinguished from that of the utopian socialists, who lacked any notion of class struggle. His "concrete utopia" presupposes the class struggle, and is directed toward revolutionary activity in line with the real tendencies of the historical situation. For him, utopian thought does not contradict, but rather enriches, historical materialism. Thus he speaks of the unity of "sobriety" and "enthusiasm," and maintains that Marxism has both a "warm stream" and a "cold stream." The "warm stream" which he identifies within Marxism refers to the revolutionary passion to change the world, along with man's capacity for hope and for "dreaming ahead," while the "cold stream" refers to Marxism's rigorous scientific analysis of society.[11]

Since revolutionary practice, while based on sober analysis, must be informed by an awareness of the final goal, Bloch is highly critical of economistic interpretations of Marxism which exclude both ideals and utopian ends. "Ideal images," he writes, "hasten ahead of and precede an objective historical tendency." "Concrete utopia," he contends, "is bound up with historical materialism and prevents it from defaulting—prevents it from discarding its visions of a goal ahead and gives it the *novum* of a dialectical-*utopian* materialism."[12]

To describe the content of the authentic hope which is consistent with the Marxist vision of the future, Bloch uses the term "*docta spes*," "hope conceived in materialist terms."[13] For the Marxist, hope, and its rational basis, must be held together in a dialectical unity: "Reason cannot blossom without hope, and hope cannot speak without reason: both must operate in a Marxist unity."[14]

In his discussion of historical materialism, Bloch stresses the importance of superstructural elements and assigns a relative autonomy to the superstructure, which he maintains contains a genuinely utopian surplus. The emphasis on the "warm stream," on "hope," "dreaming ahead," and utopian imagination concerning the future socialist society, are all necessary to stimulate the creation of revolutionary consciousness. Bloch had a better insight into human nature than most of his Marxist contemporaries. Dry determinism and cold mechanistic dogma, however "scientific," do not do justice to the complex interplay of emotional, psychological, spiritual, as well as rational, faculties that constitute the human subject. Bloch's utopianism, however, is consistent with such a holistic anthropology.

What Bloch offers us are suggestive insights for restructuring historical materialism on the basis of a reassertion of the importance of consciousness, and a constructive use of the cultural legacies of the past. However, the sheer variety and complexity of the sources he uses, some of which seem very strange bedfellows with Marxism, raises the question of whether Bloch is too syncretistic a thinker. Many aspects of his thought are clearly far too mystical and fanciful to be considered compatible with Marxism. For example, social utopias are one thing, but Bloch's speculative materialism ("entelechy"), is quite another. Such an ontological basis for a Marxist utopianism does more to undermine than commend it.

Religion and Utopia

Bloch's utopianism always remained deeply rooted in his interpretation of religion. In contrast to other scholars, who so often begin their discussion of utopianism with Thomas More's *Utopia*, Bloch regarded utopian thinking as a basic human propensity, and in his work on religion he traces its development from the early biblical period through Jewish and Christian history.

For Bloch, Scripture first becomes historical with the Exodus, which gives the Bible "a basic tone it has not lost."[15] The Exodus story tells of how a Bedouin tribe led by Moses is delivered from oppression and slavery, by its God, Yahweh, who is henceforth understood as a God of liberation. After settling in the promised land of Canaan and adopting an agricultural way of life, these people still retain a deep memory of the nomadic institutions and primitive semi-communism that characterized their previous social organization. However, in the agrarian society inherited from the Canaanites, there quickly emerges a sharp polarization between rich and poor, and intense exploitation. It is in this context that Bloch locates the prophets: "Amidst this exploitation the *prophets* appeared, thundering against it, projecting the judgment and along with it the *very first plans for a social utopia*."[16] The prophets acted in league with the semi-nomadic opposition, the Nazarites and Rechabites, who kept alive the tradition of Yahweh as a God of the poor, to whom private property was completely alien.

Bloch points out that the prophets' denunciation of apostasy takes on its special significance from the way it represents the struggle between Yahweh the God of the poor and Baal the God of the expropriators. Yahweh is invoked as the enemy of the oppressors and the judge of those who accumulate wealth at the expense of the poor. As prophetism develops, from the old image of a tribal God there eventually emerges an image which associates Yahweh with a definite socio-moral message. "From Amos to Isaiah, and even further, the moral message was conceived of as Yahweh's primordial will: 'Learn to do good; seek justice, correct oppression; defend the fatherless, plead for the widow' (Isaiah 1:7)."[17] For the prophets, Yahweh becomes the embodiment of moral reason, and the God of liberation "a true God of morality, an ideal God whose qualities could now really be a model for men."[18] Along with this there comes the idea of free moral choice, which subjects fate to the power of human decision. Finally, at the height of the prophetic tradition there appears the messianic hopes of the future liberation that Yahweh, the Exodus God, will bring, not only for Israel but for all the nations of the earth. Thus the writings of Isaiah and Micah are filled with utopian visions, which form the basis of later Christian social utopias.

The fierce prophetic condemnation of injustice, and a taking up of the cause of the poor and exploited, is again, Bloch notes, evident with the Nazarite John the Baptist and Jesus himself. He sees Jesus as an eschatological prophet, whose Gospel of the Kingdom was essentially a proclamation of a new social order of love-communism. Only with the disaster of the cross was the Kingdom interpreted as lying beyond and above history, and Jesus' love-communism relaxed and spiritualized. Bloch is highly critical of Pauline Christianity, and observes how the call for a radically new social order was gradually replaced by a concentration on inwardness and belief in a beyond: "Instead of a radical renewal of this world, an institute of the beyond appeared—the Church—and interpreted the Christian social utopia as referring to itself."[19]

Bloch criticizes Augustine for his accommodation with Rome and his lack of interest in the state, both of which follow from his exclusive preoccupation with God and the soul, and the Manichaean influences he did not entirely free himself from. He also objects to Augustine's interpretation of history, and in particular his tendency to equate the Church with the millennium: "In Augustine's book, *civitas Dei* is hailed as virtually present in the Jewish Levi State and in the Church of Christ. So vast a dream as the millennium is sacrificed to the Church."[20] However, Bloch recognizes that elsewhere Augustine makes it clear that the City of God will not fully appear until the end of present history: "It is not in the existing world, nor beyond it, but after this world that the City of God appears in full."[21] Bloch thus acknowledges that *civitas Dei* constitutes a political utopia. He also notes how *civitas Dei* itself challenged the Church's millennial claims, and that throughout the Middle Ages and the early modern age, chiliasm kept erupting.

It was with the revolutionary movements and heretical sects that chiliasm again came into its own. Bloch considers Joachim di Fiore to be especially important. Joachim taught that there were three stages of history—the stages of the Father, Son, and Holy Spirit. These corresponded to the Old Testament "stage of fear and of known law"; the New Testament "stage of love and of a Church divided into clerks and laymen"; and the third stage of the Holy

x millenarianism

Spirit with "the illumination of all men in a mystical democracy, without masters and without a Church."[22] Joachim believed his own time to be that of the final kingdom, and he condemned passionately feudal and ecclesiastical rule. His message was essentially a return to the eschatological preaching of Christ. Bloch refers enthusiastically to Joachim's "complete transfer of the kingdom of light *from the beyond, from the consolation of hoping for the beyond, into history*."[23] Bloch identifies a whole tradition, stemming from Joachim, which included the Hussites, the Anabaptists, Münzer, the Diggers, and concludes: "Joachim was cogently the spirit of *revolutionary Christian social utopianism.*"[24]

Bloch's identification of an heretical strain in Christianity in line with the revolutionary and eschatological preaching of Jesus is undoubtedly instructive. Although he imposes too neat a classification upon these very diverse dissenting groups, the eschatological hopes suppressed by the Church did tend to migrate into these sects. Not surprisingly, and as Bloch himself notes, theologians and Church historians tend to give heretical groups a bad press, or else to simply neglect them.[25] The present century, however, has seen a recovery of interest in chiliasm. Since Weiss and Schweitzer, New Testament theology has been forced to reconcile itself to the fact that Jesus was an apocalyptic and eschatological figure, with conceptions of the world that were quite foreign to modern thinking—at any rate, modern bourgeois thinking. The existence of a sharp break between Jesus and Paul has also come to be widely accepted, although insufficient attention has been paid to the implications of this break. In addition, it has come to be widely recognized that the question of whether, in becoming a state religion by the fourth century, Christianity baptized Rome or vice versa, is a very real one.

Bloch was well informed on developments in modern theology, and in his own right has made some important contributions to theological debate. He observes that Weiss and Schweitzer, despite their brilliantly perceptive insights, eventually retreated to the safe haven of nineteenth- century cultural Christianity.[26] He also gives an excellent critique of both Bultmann and Barth, who in their different ways were responding to the breakdown of Liberal Protestantism and the rediscovery of eschatology.[27] He castigates Bultmann's use of Heideggerian existentialism in his treatment of myth, claiming that Bultmann replaces the eschatological, social, and cosmic dimensions of reality with a preoccupation with mere individualism. Although commending Barth as a stalwart anti-fascist, he rejects his conception of God as "Utterly-other," and argues that while Barth recognized the importance of eschatology, he confused it with "other-worldliness," and consequently concluded that eschatology no longer has any real relationship with the world.

From a socialist viewpoint, the various revolutionary heretical movements which Bloch identifies were bound to fail, given the primitive social conditions in which they arose. However, although their hopes and aspirations were unrealizable at the time, they constitute a cultural legacy which assumes critical importance when the objective conditions for their fulfillment arise, and Bloch's appeal for socialism to enter into a creative inheritance of the traditions of the past, in order to inform its vision for actively transforming the future, is vital if socialist politics is more than a belief in determinism. To be sure, the utopian hopes of revolutionary chiliasm, as Bloch points out, need to be rectified (set "on their feet"), but this happens through their incorporation into the "concrete utopia" of the future socialist society. We have already referred to the importance of a "holistic" anthropology. A particularly valuable contribution that chiliasm can make is to draw attention to the need for socialism to mobilize the deeper lying vital and elemental levels of the human psyche, which Marxism has tended to neglect.[28]

Religious Inheritance

Bloch's identification of the utopian dimension of religion led him to a thorough reevaluation of the Marxist critique of religion. He recognized an ambiguity inherent in religion, and saw in Marx's "opium" quote support for the claim that, while acting as an ideology which confirms human beings in their situation of alienation, religion is also a *protest* against human estrangement.[29] Bloch understood this ambiguity to be rooted in the situation which gives rise to religion, and he developed his analysis through a reconsideration of Feuerbach's work on religion.

Bloch had a very high estimation of Feuerbach, whom he considered to have advanced beyond much of the atheism of the enlightenment by addressing the problem of religious inheritance. Feuerbach's religious criticism had reduced theology to anthropology, making of religion a series of positive affirmations about human beings. Thus from religion there emerges a definite heritage, and Bloch commends Feuerbach for his insights in this respect: "No one has made a more concerted effort than he did to turn the flow of human ideals away from the Beyond and back to man whom these ideals reflect."[30]

However, Feuerbach's unhistorical anthropology inhibited him from seeing the need for a utopian concept of the human essence, rather than one which is statically settled. Accordingly, Bloch imaginatively reworks Feuerbach's anthropological critique of religion, replacing Feuerbach's reduction of the divine hypostasis to abstract "species man," with the utopian ideal of the *humanum*, so that the *deus absconditus* becomes a *homo absconditus* which awaits realization. For Bloch, only atheism is consistent with messianism, since it makes possible the appearance of the very things theism devalued, and opens the way for real human freedom.

Bloch insisted that the utopian impulse implicit in religion still continues to exist when the illusion of an hypostasized deity has been shattered, since what was conceived of as God is but a "draft on the human content that has not yet appeared."[31] He maintains that there is a wish-content and a depth of hope in religion which should be retained, and argues that Marxism needs to actively inherit the *topos* into which religion projects the God-postulate, replacing it with the utopia of the kingdom of freedom. The consequence of this is a creative union of historical materialism with religious utopianism, a union which is rooted in Bloch's process ontology, which completes his system of theoretical messianism. Thus he writes:

> When dialectical materialism hears and grasps the import of the mighty voice of tendency in the world which it has made its own, and when it calls on men to work for the goal revealed by that voice, it shows decisively that it has taken hold of the living soul of a dead religion, the *transcendere* without transcendence, the subject-object of a well-founded hope. That is what lives on when the opium, the fools paradise of the Other-world, has been burnt away to ashes. That remains as a call, signalling the way to the fulfilled This-world of a new earth.[32]

It is only when religion becomes a "binding back" to a static, mythological God of the beginning that Marxism must break with it. Within the Bible itself, there is a critique of this sort of religion, in favor of a religion which is radically utopian, and subversive of the present order. Thus Bloch sees a convergence between Marxism and a Christianity which substitutes for the future Kingdom of God a future kingdom of human freedom: "Implicit in Marxism—as the leap from the Kingdom of Necessity to that of Freedom—there lies the whole so subversive and un-static heritage of the Bible: a heritage which, in the exodus from the static order, showed itself far more as pure protest, as the archetype of the Kingdom of Freedom itself."[33] He uses the term "meta-religion" to describe the Marxist inheritance of religion. As far back as Moses, "instead of the visible nature god, there appears an invisible one of justice, of a kingdom of justice."[34] He argues that within Judeo-Christian history there is a progressive development away from theism, toward the human subject's increasing self-injection into religious mystery.

Bloch raises the question of what exactly is left after the God-hypothesis is abandoned. Although he speaks confidently of the open *topos* which lies ahead, he concedes that "nothingness and its futility is doubtless just as latent in the vacuum of atheism as the "all" of fulfillment by the *regnum humanum* or Kingdom."[35] This belief in the indeterminate outcome of history shows his position to be one which accords a special emphasis to subjective human agency. In the present nuclear age, where few would deny the precarious nature of human history, Bloch's positing of the possibility of nothingness and futility has a special poignancy.

As well as opening up possibilities for revitalizing Marxism, Bloch's analysis of religion is instructive in its own right. Most critiques of religion are concerned with explaining it away, and presuppose an acceptance of positivism (Freud and Durkheim) or nihilism (Nietzsche). In contrast, Bloch takes the religious question more seriously and seeks a positive inheritance of religion. He was right to point out the significance of Feuerbach in this respect, and his application of an historicized anthropology to Feuerbach's critique of religion can claim to be a legitimate development of Marxist religious criticism. Marx discerned the social roots of religious alienation, and was also aware that religion could function as protest. However, it took Bloch to fully discover the rich potential inheritance that lay within religion, which Marx, no doubt with eyes fixed more on Victorian Christianity than Thomas Münzer, only barely glimpsed.

Whether messianism and utopianism require atheism, as Bloch contends, is questionable. He speaks as though God and human beings were of one and the same essence, and therefore the existence of God is necessarily a threat to human freedom. However, in the Christian tradition, the Godhead is understood as possessing a totally different order of being, and from this particular ontological perspective, the sovereign and all-embracing purpose of God neither denies human freedom nor is ultimately frustrated by it.[36] Further, through giving an objective point of reference for human history, one which affirms the ultimate triumph of love, Christian theism provides a basis for utopian aspirations, and helps provide the hope and confidence for the courageous exercise of human freedom. Thus the social utopia of a classless society and human liberation can be understood in terms of a Christian philosophy of history and eschatology.

Admittedly, Christian theology has tended to be extremely conservative socially from St. Paul onward, and the Church as an institution in society has been anything but revolutionary. However, the emergence of recent political theology has heightened awareness of the subversive and socially radical current in Christianity and highlighted its revolutionary potential. Bloch himself was very much aware of the possibilities for cooperation and dialogue between a renewed Christianity and Marxism:

> When Christians are really concerned with the emancipation of those who labor and are heavy laden, and when Marxists retain the depths of the Kingdom of Freedom as the real content of revolutionary consciousness on the road to becoming the substance, the alliance between revolution and Christianity founded in the Peasant Wars may live again—this time with success.[37]

Reflections

As was said at the beginning of this chapter, although Bloch at first sought to add a utopian dimension to Marx's work, he later came to an awareness of the utopianism already present in Marx. As such a viewpoint has expounded throughout the previous chapters there is little to add here, save perhaps as Maynard Solomon has usefully pointed out, that utopian imagination was in fact central to Marx's anthropology and understanding of human labor. For Marx, the essential difference between human beings and animals is that human beings possess an image in their minds of the objects they produce in reality. Thus Marx (like Bloch) regarded a form of utopian anticipation as an integral element of the human condition.[38]

A utopian awareness of the final goal, and a conviction about the moral desirability of that goal, are clearly subversive of the present order, and are crucial factors in motivating people in the direction of revolutionary consciousness and action. For revolution to succeed enough people must *believe* in it, and utopianism is essential to sustaining such a belief. When such a utopian consciousness becomes widespread, it becomes a material force in human history. Thus Bertell Ollman is surely right in saying that Marx's vision of the future is of vital importance for raising class consciousness, and that the inability to conceive of a humanly superior way of life has impeded the growth of such consciousness. Hence his insistence: "Giving workers and indeed all oppressed classes a better notion of what their lives would be like under communism (something not to be gleaned from accounts of present-day Russia or China) is essential to the success of the socialist project."[39]

The lack of a positive image of the socialist alternative has undoubtedly greatly inhibited socialist advance. The standard objection to socialism, that present socialist states are unattractive and oppressive, is a very forceful one indeed. However, when existing models of genuine socialism are not ready to hand, the value of utopian ideas and imagination is even more evident.

Once the connection is made between utopianism and the infusing of revolutionary consciousness, a vast area of human inspiration, drives, and energies is opened up, and the tyranny of the present becomes subject to revolutionary hope. To be sure, any socialist renewal of interest in the future must not depart from Marx's basic method, since revolutionary hope which is not based on proper analysis will lead only to disillusionment. As a disciple of Hegel, Marx recognized that there was no place for abstract ideals divorced from the real movement of history. However, it is precisely here that the value of Bloch's contribution becomes clear, since he so very firmly situates his ideas within the context of historical materialism. The consequence of this is that the dangers which have hitherto accompanied utopian socialism are avoided, while the possibilities of utopianism for renewing Marxism are open to realization. Thus, although some of Bloch's more esoteric speculations, and particularly his notion that matter is in a process of development, must be rejected, a more modest renewal of utopianism within the framework of historical materialism is an enterprise that needs to be seriously considered.

Bloch's tendency to equate utopianism with chiliasm, however, has definite weaknesses. The future of which socialism speaks does not simply appear from nowhere, but at the climax of a long historical process, and as the end product of a period of intense revolutionary struggle. In the socialist vision of the future there is thus both continuity and discontinuity. Chiliasm, in contrast, places all the emphasis on radical discontinuity, and its more eruptive and ecstatic character raises the question of whether there is not a fundamental antipathy between chiliasm and historical materialism. Mannheim sees chiliasm as having more of an affinity with radical anarchism.[40] Although Bloch does maintain that the utopian hopes of revolutionary chiliasm need to be "rectified," he unfortunately pays too little attention to these basic differences.

But this is not all there is to say about Bloch's contribution. During the present century, as technological development has continued apace, the composition of the working class has altered dramatically. The proletariat is no longer a single homogeneous group but has become far more stratified, with, notably, a large and growing number of white-collar workers and technicians. In advanced industrial societies there is also a far higher general level of educational attainment. In such conditions, if there is to be a choice other than the outmoded insurrectionary politics of the vanguard and the modest achievements of welfare capitalism, then there must be a rebirth of a Marxism that can effectively wage the socialist struggle in the ideological and cultural domain. Second only perhaps to the work of Gramsci, Bloch's innovative development of the Marxist tradition, with its rediscovery of the historical power of utopia, indicates the way forward to such a Marxism.

Finally, recognition of the significance of utopian aspirations for socialist transformation, along with the insistence on the utopian content of religion, indicates possibilities for dialogue between Marxist socialism and Christian utopianism. At the practical level, the partial fusing of these two utopian projects could be extremely important, in terms of the alliance of social forces created.

Furthermore, such an alliance need not be a fudge, but could lead to a renewal of the potential of both socialism and Christianity. The problem, of course, with Bloch's meta-religion from the Christian point of view is that Christianity is completely superseded and absorbed by a revitalized Marxism. For the Christian theologian this would be unacceptable since there are elements of Christianity that cannot be thus surrendered. The most obvious of these is the doctrine of God, but also there is Christianity's perspective on certain basic questions, such as the meaning of life, the problem of suffering, and the finality of death. Accordingly, however strong an alliance is forged, Christianity would always need to remain distinct from Marxism. Thus, in a future socialist culture of human freedom religion would continue an independent existence, providing answers to questions that Marxism in itself cannot answer. The only alternative would be for socialism itself to undergo a complete transformation, and incorporate these elements of Christianity within itself, but this would involve a religious inheritance beyond that envisaged by Ernst Bloch.

Chapter 6

Paul Tillich's Religious Socialism: An Attempt at Synthesis

In Germany during the latter half of the nineteenth century, Socialism and Christianity remained sharply opposed—witness the 1848 counter-revolutionary Protestant reply to the *Communist Manifesto* made by J. H. Wichern. This statement considered "inner mission" and a program of charity to be the effective response to the "social question." From 1848 onward, the Church continued to ally itself with Prussian conservatism, and the split grew even wider. Socialism, for its part, either completely rejected religion or restricted it to the private sphere.[1]

Paul Tillich, the son of a Lutheran pastor in a small town in east-Elbian Prussia, was born in 1886, and was strongly influenced by the pervading political conservatism and antisocialist attitudes. In his essay "Autobiographical Reflections" (written in 1952) he tells us: "The existence of a parliament, democratic forces, socialist movements, and a strong criticism of the emperor and the army did not affect the conservative Lutheran groups of the East among whom I lived. All these democratic elements were rejected, distortedly represented and characterized as revolutionary, which meant criminal."[2]

Before World War I, Tillich adhered to the political conservatism of his background and upbringing. In typically patriotic spirit, loyal to both Throne and Altar, he volunteered for service at the outbreak of the war, and was appointed as a chaplain to the Western front, where he served for four years.[3] The war was to be for Tillich the great turning point of his life. At its beginning he was enthusiastic and politically naive, but as events progressed, and any hope of a quick victory was shattered, things began to take on a new complexion. The indescribable anguish of witnessing some of the terrible conflicts of the war had a profound effect upon him. He later referred to his experience in the war as "a personal kairos." James Luther Adams and John Stumme mention in particular the battle of Champagne in 1915. However, according to Wilhelm and Marion Pauck, although Tillich reckoned the transformation took place one night in 1915, it was actually a cumulative metamorphosis.[4] Be that as it may, the horrors of death in the trenches marked for Tillich the end of the era of bourgeois idealism. In his book *On the Boundary*, he refers to the disastrous effect of the war on idealist thought: "The experience of those four years of war revealed to me and to my entire generation an abyss in human existence that could not be ignored."[5]

In November 1918 the war came to an end, and Germany experienced revolution and civil war. Tillich, unlike most Lutherans, responded positively to the revolution and was keenly interested in the political situation. The war had given him personal contact with the proletariat, and he had become acutely aware of the bitterness of the troops, their situation of exploitation and alienation, and sense of complete betrayal by capitalist forces.[6] With the dethronement of the Kaiser, and the socialists in power—despite defeat in the war—November 1918 marked an exciting new beginning for Germany. Like many others, Tillich was gripped by the dynamism of the socialist movement. Later in his book *The Religious Situation*, he speaks of the transcendent element, and passionate eschatological tension in the original socialist movement.[7] When the call came to join the religious socialist movement, abandoning his previous political indifference, he responded positively, and having entered the movement became one of its leading theoreticians.[8]

To understand the background to Tillich's affirmation of religious socialism, it is necessary to consider in more detail his activity after the war. Following his return to Berlin, and the completion of his work as an army chaplain, Tillich spent a brief period in Church administration.[9] James Fisher has attempted to show that this was also a formative episode in his politicization.[10] Shortly after the 1918 revolution the new government proposed the separation of church and state. The conservative wing of the Church predictably opposed this, while many liberals supported the idea.

Various groups emerged at this time, concerned with the pressing question of separation. Karl Aner, in late November 1918, founded the *Bund Neue Kirche* (BNK). In a document published in December by this group, the creation of a new Church was suggested, "a Church which can cultivate and exhibit a dynamic religious life and can effect a genuinely religious culture."[11] In contrast to the political conservatism of the former Church, the new Church would stand firmly with the new Republic. This document was signed by members of a Berlin "steering committee" which included Paul Tillich! Fisher's research has given us some indication of Tillich's thinking as early as December 1918. Separation policy had provided a further catalyst to a consideration of the question of the relation of the Church toward socialism.

John Stumme writes that Tillich's entry into the religious socialist movement was through Siegmund Schultze's *Soziale Arbeitsgemeinschaft* (SAG). This group included Günther Dehn, Karl Mennicke, Friedrich Rittelmeyer, and others. Eventually Tillich and Mennicke separated from SAG, and a new circle emerged around them. By the first issue of *Blätter für Religiösen Sozialismus* in Easter 1920, the ethos of the group was decisively stamped by Tillich and Mennicke.[12]

Tillich's various activities in connection with religious socialism did not go unnoticed by the Church authorities, and in May 1919, following a lecture given by him and Carl Wegener to the Independent Social Democratic Party on "Christianity and Socialism," the Evangelical Consistory of Brandenburg inquired into his activity. For his reply he sent the substance of his lecture, which was later reworked and published in a pamphlet entitled "Socialism as a Question for the Church." Tillich's reply gives us his first full statement on Christianity and Socialism.[13] He argues that every attempt to identify Christianity with a particular social order must be rejected. However, Christianity has within it the power and the will to shape human life, and the Christian ethic is compatible with the socialist ideal. Reform policies and attempts to win the workers were rejected by Tillich—Fisher comments that this was an attack on the approach of groups like SAG. This helps explain his rift with SAG by 1920, and may also caution against overemphasizing its role in Tillich's politicization.[14]

By 1920, the circle around Tillich and Mennicke was referred to as "the Berlin Circle" or "the Kairos Circle."[15] The stimulus given by this group was particularly important as Tillich developed his ideas until 1924, when he left for Marburg. The Greek word "kairos" from the New Testament means "the right time," or "fullness of time," "the moment rich in content and significance."[16] The war and revolution was seen as a decisive turning point for Germany and Europe, and it was this common "kairos" awareness, rather than a uniformity of viewpoint, which gave the circle its impetus and identity.[17]

As well as Dehn and Mennicke, who were both pastors, other important members of the group were Eduard Heimann, Adolf Löwe, Alexander

Rüstow, and Arnold Wolfers. The Jewish intellectuals Heimann and Löwe brought their considerable expertise in the field of economics. Rüstow, a sociologist, was a free-thinking atheist and Tillich's opponent and rival in the group's discussions. Wolfers, an attorney from Switzerland, provided financial help for the group.[18]

The group discussed Barth's theology and various issues in relation to Marxism and socialism.[19] Barth, who had been a religious socialist, later distanced himself from such movements, and in a lecture he gave at Tambach in September 1919 he argued strongly for a radical distinction between the Kingdom of God and human political movements.[20] The Kairos Circle recognized that Barth had raised some important problems, but rejected his position. James Luther Adams writes that they "looked upon Barth as an escapist in the name of an extravagantly transcendent God," and that Tillich, in particular, thought that Barth "had lost the sense of the paradoxical immanence of the transcendent."[21] The intellectual and nonecclesiastical character of the circle distinguished it from the practical-political groups of religious socialists more concerned with Church policy. Tillich considered that these groups did not probe fundamental problems deeply enough, and were therefore "unable to bring about a transformation of either religion or socialism from the deepest level."[22]

Although largely dominated by theoretical interests, Tillich's religious socialism did not exclude practical engagement. In *On the Boundary*, he tells us that, albeit with mixed feelings, he did join the Social Democratic Party for practical political reasons.[23] He also had considerable sympathy and involvement with the young socialists, in their efforts to renew socialism.[24]

Tillich's teaching career was another important stimulus. Back in 1919, his first course of lectures had been entitled "Christianity and the Social Problems of the Present." After lecturing successively at Berlin, Marburg, Dresden, and Leipzig, in 1929 he came to Frankfurt and entered into a dialogue with members of what came to be known as the "Frankfurt School." Some of the thinkers he now had contact with were Max Horkheimer, Theodor Adorno, Erich Fromm, and Herbert Marcuse. Tillich shared the concern of the Frankfurt School for a thoroughgoing critical reexamination of Marxist theory, and acknowledges his indebtedness to the school, mentioning in particular their sociological analysis.[25] His subsequent writing is certainly consistent with influence from his Frankfurt colleagues (e.g., *The Socialist Decision* published in 1933).[26]

d vital mode of existence...points to the threat to, and the reality of the loss
, meaningful existence."[32] In an essay written a year earlier, however,
lich argued that through the class struggle and Marxist dialectic, the
oletariat finds meaning and an awareness of being supported by the
conditional.[33] His analysis thus demonstrated the religious character of
cialism—a view which he believed to be supported by historical evidence,
ich shows socialism to have Christian humanistic elements.[34] In a lecture
ven in 1946 on "Religion and Secular Culture," Tillich again highlighted
e religious nature of socialism by claiming that revolutionary movements
epresent an ultimate concern, a religious principle, hidden but effective in
em."[35]

For Tillich, the religious and political spheres could not be separated
ithout doing violence to both. The need for a theological interpretation of
olitical realities follows from the universal claim of Christianity itself, and
was in this sense that Tillich understood the proletarian situation as
onstituting a fundamental challenge to the unconditional claim to which
otestantism gives voice. In his 1931 essay "The Protestant Principle and
e Proletarian Situation," he makes a perceptive analysis of the relationship
etween Protestantism and the proletariat in modern society. The irrelevance
of an individualistic Protestantism for the proletarian masses reduces the
otestant message to "a religious possibility for only certain groups of
en."[36] Consequently, the universal character of the Protestant message
ecomes threatened, and can only be maintained if Protestantism adapts itself
o that the proletarian situation no longer remains inaccessible. This pos-
bility remains open for Protestantism since it "has a principle that stands
eyond all its realizations." This principle "contains the divine and human
otest against any absolute claim made for a relative reality, even if this
aim is made by the Protestant church." It is "the theological expression of
e true relation between the unconditioned and the conditioned or, religious-
' speaking, between God and man."[37]

Tillich maintains that the incongruity with the proletarian situation does
ot belong to the essence of Protestantism, but is a product of the contradic-
on between Protestantism and its own principle. This principle comes to
owerful expression in the proletarian situation. For example, the judgment
f the Protestant principle, concerning distortion in the human situation,
ecomes apparent in the proletarian situation where "the perversion of man's
ature shows its reality in the social realm."[38] To confine the application of
e Protestant principle to the individual dimension would be to impose an
bitrary and unjustified limitation. The Protestant principle applies to the

Some Basic Features of Tillich's Religious Socialism

Following on from the Swiss Blumhardt brothers, whom h
the fathers of continental religious socialism, Tillich maintair
attitude to secular culture. "The Blumhardts", he tells us, "re
God may speak for a time more powerfully through a nonreligic
anti-Christian, movement, such as early social democracy, tha
Christian churches."[27] It was this stance in relation to secular c
allowed him to embrace socialism, even though the roots of soci
go back to atheistic thinkers.

It was not, therefore, surprising that when invited to speak
Society in Berlin in 1919, Tillich should choose as his title "Or
a Theology of Culture." In this lecture he was concerned to dev
interpretation of the mutual immanence of religion and cu
religious principle," he said, "is actualized in all spheres of
cultural life."[28] The reason for this becomes clear when we c
understanding of the philosophy of religion. In his 1922 essay "Th
of the Concept of Religion in the Philosophy of Religion," he
"there is a function of the spirit which neither stands alongside
functions nor is their unity, but rather comes to expression in ar
them, namely the function of unconditonality. It is the root fun
function in which the spirit breaks through all its forms and penet
ground."[29] Later in the same essay he writes of "the breakthrou
unconditionally real as the ground or reality of the whole of cultur
functions."[30] This understanding of the philosophy of religion expla
for Tillich, there can be no distinction between the sacred and the s
any separation of religion from culture.

If religion can be manifest in secular reality, then there is no reas
in principle, socialism cannot be religious. In his 1919 essay Tillich
"Religion is directedness toward the unconditional." It is "a re
meaning...the ultimate and deepest meaning—reality which shakes tl
dation of all things and builds up anew."[31] The problem of the mea
life was central for Tillich, and it was this existential orientation that in
his understanding of religion. The question we must ask is whether, acc
to his understanding of religion, socialism is in fact religious in chara
his essay "Religious Socialism" (1930), he maintains that in the anthrop
of religious socialism the human essence is a "unity of the vital a
spiritual, of being and meaning." Describing the proletarian situation
where "man is radically threatened," he writes: "The loss of a mean

whole person, as a unity of body and spirit. Tillich also touches upon several other respects in which the Protestant principle finds vindication in the proletarian situation—for example, the demonic, ideology, and anticipation.

Tillich was highly critical of the absence of an adequate social ethics within the Lutheran tradition, and considered this to be a major factor in the failure of the German churches to respond to the issues raised by socialism.[39] Lutheranism had failed to develop an understanding of the Kingdom of God which embraced social and political realities, and Tillich in contrast refers to "the inestimable value of the Calvinistic idea of the Kingdom of God in the solution of social problems."[40] The tragedy of Lutheran dualism is that it excludes public life from the demands of the Kingdom. An understanding of religion as directedness to the unconditioned, operative in all spheres, precludes any such separation of the political from the spiritual.

Tillich was not alone in sensing the need for reconstruction in Protestant social ethics—Bonhoeffer is another example.[41] Tillich's approach was to attempt to find a way to meet the justifiable demands of the Protestant tradition, as powerfully voiced by Barth, without sacrificing a socio-political ethic. Thus although he rejected what he saw as socialism's utopianism, he insisted that an attempt be made "to unite the radical nature and the transcendence of the religious perspective with the concreteness of an immanent will to shape the world."[42] He made use of the term "*belief-ful realism*" to describe this particular attitude—a term he also used to refer to a style of art.[43] Tillich regarded the prophetic stance as the "inner attitude" essential to religious socialism.[44] It was through the concreteness of his prophetic eschatology that he was able to decisively break through the impasse in Protestant social ethics.

In overcoming the traditional opposition between religion and socialism, Tillich makes possible a constructive evaluation of socialist thought while his rejection of any naive identification of the two allows him to be critical in his assessment.[45] However, if *all* secular reality is potentially religious, then a variety of philosophies could be described as religious. For example, in the case of fascism it would be possible to speak of a religious fascism, and indeed Tillich does refer to fascism as demonic, and in that sense essentially religious. The question is whether there are any reasons why *socialism* should be considered inherently better than the alternatives. There are insufficient criteria in Tillich's work to support the contention that socialism should be accorded a unique significance—a shortcoming which will be discussed again in the following section (pp.119f).

The problem of the considerable diversity of influences upon Tillich's religious socialism, and therefore the very complex indebtedness, must also be mentioned. This raises the question as to whether his position can be considered a coherent one. To answer this satisfactorily an in-depth study of Tillich's appropriation of these various sources would be required, which is beyond the scope of the present work.

Another important issue has been addressed by Eduard Heimann, who is prepared to concede that Marxism is religious in the subjective sense, but adds: "Concretely, is not Marxism, however profoundly religious, an antireligion?"[46] He goes on to refer to the problem of the conflicting truth claims of various religions. Charles West makes a similar criticism when he describes Marx as the apostle of another faith.[47]

This leads to the question of whether religious socialism is not a contradiction in terms. For Tillich, the atheistic content of socialism was unnecessary—indeed, in order to renew itself socialism required the religious dimension. Moreover, Christianity had a responsibility to help shape the social order, which Tillich considered was best fulfilled through entering into a relationship (albeit critical) with socialism, thus making the term "religious socialism" meaningful. The terminology, however, remains problematic. One does not begin a dialogue by telling socialists that their views are really religious. Interestingly, in the Foreword to *The Socialist Decision* (1933), Tillich refers to the confusion arising from the name "religious socialism," "which has been challenged (with good reason) from the religious as well as socialist side"—though this does not seem to have dissuaded him from making regular use of it![48]

Leaving these observations aside, we must now turn to Tillich's attempt to construct a philosophy of history, through which he was to forge the major concepts of his religious socialism.

Eschatology and the Interpretation of History

It was the situation following the war which impressed upon Tillich the need for a Christian interpretation of history, and he refers to "the gap between the transcendent message of traditional Christianity and the immanent hopes of the revolutionary movements."[49] Thus Tillich's concern was with the problem of defining the relation of the transcendent to history, the eschatological to the historical. His interpretation of history has justly been described by J. L. Adams as "the most elaborate and substantial one that has been worked out in the history of Protestant philosophical theology." It included three main categories: "theonomy," "kairos," and "the demonic."[50]

The term "theonomy" had its origin in Tillich's theology of culture and philosophy of religion, and was used to describe a society in which all cultural forms were directed toward the unconditional or divine. The expectation of a new theonomy was created by the momentous events after the end of the war. The breakdown of bourgeois civilization brought with it the possibility of a reunion of religion and secular culture. In his 1922 essay "Kairos," theonomy is considered in close association with both heteronomy and autonomy. Heteronomy describes the attempt of religious or political authority to dominate cultural life through imposing an "alien law." Autonomy occurs when cultural forms are created in accord with reason but without any relation to the unconditional. Theonomy, in contrast, is a situation where "the consciousness of the presence of the unconditional permeates and guides all cultural functions and forms."[51]

The connection of theonomy with Tillich's philosophy of religion is evident in his lecture of 1919 on the theology of culture, where he proposes the hypothesis "that the autonomy of cultural functions is grounded in their form, in the laws governing their application, whereas theonomy is grounded in their substance or import."[52] In the "Kairos" essay Tillich describes autonomy as "the dynamic principle of history," whereas theonomy "is the substance and meaning of history." The dialectical relations of theonomy, autonomy, and heteronomy are central to an understanding of the historical process: "History comes from and moves toward periods of theonomy."[53]

Kairos was undoubtedly the most important concept in Tillich's eschatology and interpretation of history. For Tillich and indeed for many of his generation, the upheavals following the November revolution were experienced as both crisis and opportunity. Amid a disintegrating bourgeois world, Germany, precisely because of its military defeat, was uniquely placed to bring to the world religious socialism. This is the background of what Eduard Heimann calls "the exuberance of the call to the kairos."[54]

In his doctrine of kairos it was Tillich's intention to find a way between the exaggerated utopian hopes of socialism and the otherworldliness of Lutheran transcendentalism. Thus although he rejected the idea that the Kingdom of God can be fulfilled in history, he sought to positively relate Christian eschatology to the struggle for a new social order.[55] It was in his essay "Kairos" that Tillich first attempted to outline a philosophy of history in accord with his conception of kairos. The revolutionary situation in Germany was immediately placed in a theological context:

Kairos in its *unique* and universal sense is, for Christian faith, the appearing of Jesus as the Christ. Kairos in its *general* and special sense for the philosopher of history is every turning-point in history in which the eternal judges and transforms the temporal. Kairos in its *special* sense, as decisive for the present situation, is the coming of a new theonomy on the soil of a secularized and emptied autonomous culture.[56]

Tillich outlined his doctrine of kairos with reference to alternative philosophies of history. He begins with the absolute type of philosophy of history, where it is the final period of history that is most important. This has two forms. The first, the revolutionary-absolute type, negates the past and affirms the future, whether in history or beyond. The second form, the conservative transformation of the revolutionary form, represented by Augustine, understands the decisive event as lying in the past, the church representing the new reality that has been established. Both of these interpretations set up one historical reality as absolute, "whether it be an existing church or the expected rational society." However, in making a finite reality unconditional they fall into idolatry: "The unconditional cannot be identified with any given reality, whether past or future; there is no absolute church, there is no absolute kingdom of reason and justice in history." This Tillich sees as essentially the message of Barth's "theology of crisis." However, in contrast to Barth's emphasis on permanent crisis, Tillich does not view the kairos as always given in every moment of history, and therefore "indifferent to the special heights and depths of the historical process."[57]

In what Tillich identifies as the relative form of the philosophy of history, absolute judgments are replaced by a relativizing attitude toward historical events. Three types of the relative form are dealt with: the classical, the progressive, and the dialectical. In the classical type, represented by Leibniz, Goethe, and Ranke, "every epoch is immediately under God." The progressive-relative type emerges from the disappointed hopes of the revolutionary-absolute type, radical change being replaced by slow transformation. The dialectical type has three forms, the theological (e.g., Joachim of Floris), the logical (e.g., Hegel), and the sociological (e.g., Marx). The three forms of the dialectical interpretation of history give a positive evaluation of all periods; the past is not negated unconditionally. For example, with Joachim of Floris the period of the Spirit is prepared for by the periods of the Father and the Son. Also, the future is not affirmed unconditionally. Tillich argues that when Hegel, Marx, and others stop the dialectical process arbitrarily, they introduce an idea from the revolutionary-absolute interpretation and contradict the dialectical principle. Herein lies the limits of the dialectical type; either it stops the dialectical process arbitrarily, or adopts a doctrine of infinite repetition.[58]

Tillich used the above considerations to show the demands necessitated by an interpretation of history in accord with the meaning of kairos: "The tension characteristic of the absolute interpretation of history must be united with the universalism of the relative interpretations....What happens in the kairos should be absolute and yet not absolute, but under the judgment of the absolute." This happens "when the conditioned surrenders itself to become a vehicle for the unconditional." In his conception of kairos Tillich was concerned to establish the relationship between the conditional and the unconditional: "Everything can be a vessel of the unconditional, but nothing can be unconditioned itself."[59]

Although the doctrine of the kairos has close similarities with the dialectical interpretations of history, Tillich addressed three important differences. There is no final stage where the dialectic comes to a halt. Along with the horizontal dialectic there is also "the vertical dialectic operating between the unconditional and the conditioned." Finally, the historical process is not a matter of necessity, but a "unity of freedom and fate."[60]

Despite his regard for socialism as "the movement most strongly conscious of the kairos," Tillich was critical of socialism for failing to grasp the full significance of the unconditional both positively and negatively—it saw the kairos, but missed its depth. Religious socialism sought to make its criticism more radical and revolutionary by placing socialism itself under this criticism, and thereby making it all the more effective. He refers to religious socialism as "our attempt at interpreting and shaping socialism from the viewpoint of theonomy, from the vision of the kairos."[61]

The demonic formed the third central category of Tillich's interpretation of history. Commenting on his idea of the demonic, in his introduction to *The Protestant Era*, Tillich refers to it as one of the forgotten concepts of the New Testament, which despite its great importance for Jesus and the apostles, "has become obsolete in modern theology." He attributes this neglect to the reaction of the philosophers of the enlightenment against the misuse of the concept in the Middle Ages and in orthodox Protestantism.[62]

In his 1926 essay "The Demonic," Tillich's understanding of the demonic was distinguished from "a mythological or metaphysical affirmation of a world of spirits," and developed in close association with his philosophy of religion.[63] In his writing on the theology of culture he had worked with some rather problematic distinctions between form, content, and import, and the demonic is related to the notion of the importance of maintaining form under the impact of religious import or substance. Thus he writes that the demonic can never be without form, it is "the unity of form-creating and form-destroying strengths."[64] In the demonic, "the divine, the unity of bottom and abyss, of form and consumption of form, is still contained." But there is also in the demonic "the relatively independent eruption of the 'abyss.'" It is this formless eruption of the abyss which produces demonic distortion: "Demonry is the form-destroying eruption of the creative basis of things."[65] Nationalism and capitalism are singled out by Tillich as the two major current manifestations of the demonic—in their combination of creative and destructive power they both exhibit a demonic character. Capitalism, for example, has released enormously powerful productive capacity, but has at the same time involved destruction and degradation for the masses.[66]

Tillich's attempt at a theological interpretation of history was an ambitious project, and the endeavor gave expression to his deeply speculative mind. He was right to recognize that there is much more to a religious analysis of socialism than simply ethical questions, and that the philosophy of history implicit in socialism must be confronted.

Tillich understood that the problem with bourgeois society was not only its injustice, but also its lack of ultimacy and the way in which it destroyed all human bonds. His preoccupation with theonomy arose partly from the romantic critique of capitalism, to which the memories of the semi-feudal conditions of his childhood background had made him receptive.[67] However, it was also much more than a longing for the past, and constituted a real attempt to articulate some of the positive features of socialism. His vision of a future theonomous socialism offered the hope of a new social order where the empty autonomy of bourgeois culture, with all its destructiveness for human relations, was overcome in genuine and fulfilled human community. This belief in the emergence of a new theonomous society through the transforming power of the kairos has a definite utopian ring to it, and when Tillich speaks of being "grasped" by the kairos, something of its power to motivate action is evident. Although he refrained from using the word *utopian* to describe his hopes for a new theonomous society, because of the implications of perfection, he *did* possess this vision of a qualitatively new society.

The doctrine of kairos was undoubtedly a powerful means of relating social and political realities to the transcendent. The immediacy of the kairos expectation provides a definite thrust and impetus for political action. Traditionally in Christian theology, either the parousia is deferred indefinitely and thereby becomes irrelevant for the present, or a realized eschatology is adopted, leaving nothing for the future. Through relating transcendence to special moments in history, Tillich creates the interim hope of a particular kairos—the coming of a new theonomous age—and thus relates Christian hope to socialist expectation.

In his category of the demonic, Tillich made creative use of a concept which is too often neglected, and his awareness of the potential for structural evil and destructiveness adds considerable realism to his political thinking. Through contributing to an understanding of the ways in which nationalism and capitalism combine creative and destructive features a more effective basis is provided for the necessary attack upon them. To counter his claim that capitalism is demonic, with the assertion that socialism has also demonic manifestations (e.g., the Soviet Union), does not alter the validity of his description of capitalism. Tillich fully recognized that socialism too can become subject to demonic distortion.[68]

All this speaks positively. However, there were some major difficulties. The description of history as moving from and toward periods of theonomy, contrary to Tillich's best intentions, detracts from the notion of direction in history. Here the historical process is reduced to endless repetition, a view which is at variance with both socialism and prophetic interpretations of history. To avoid this Tillich would have had to show that all the various states of theonomy possess something qualitatively new. However, his description of theonomy, which draws so heavily on the categories of his philosophy of religion, makes it difficult to discern any difference between the states of theonomy. This has serious practical implications, since a sustained hope for the future, which can give the necessary confidence for political action, is completely undermined by the reduction of history to mere repetition.

Also problematic is Tillich's view of theonomy, as "the meaning and the goal of history," expressed in his essay "Church and Culture," written in 1924.[69] Does not the possibility of several theonomies mean therefore that there is more than one goal of history? Even if these goals are reduced to one goal, namely, the state of theonomy as such, the goal of history is still located within history itself—something Tillich elsewhere unequivocally excludes. Changing the goal of history from the transcendent Kingdom of God into a temporal reality only introduces inconsistency and confusion into his writings. In the same passage, Tillich refers to theonomy as an "indication" of the Kingdom of God. Yet the absence of any adequate discussion of the relationship of the various theonomies to one another, and to the transcendent fulfillment of the Kingdom of God, leaves the term with only limited eschatological significance. If he had more concretely related the idea of theonomy to the Kingdom of God, the uniqueness of each "theonomy" might have been more evident—each "theonomy" could then be understood to represent a unique manifestation of the Kingdom of God for that time.

Similar problems arise with Tillich's category of the demonic. This may help explain how the dialectical movement between heteronomy, autonomy, and theonomy is in fact maintained, but it too suffers from the absence of an eschatological dimension. To be sure, evil will always remain a feature of human existence, but the hideous structural forms of the demonic, manifest in socialist prehistory, must be consigned to the past if the new society of justice and equality ushered in by socialism is to be established.

Although Tillich rightly criticized the Barthian conception of history as ever-present crisis, indifferent to the heights and depths of the historical process, it must also be asked whether his understanding of kairos lacks an eschatological perspective. How are the separate kairoi related to each other? Like Barth, Tillich is also very dependent on Greek metaphysics, and the ontology which determines the structure of his doctrine of kairos does not easily fit into an eschatological framework. This serious deficiency goes some way to explain why his religious socialism lacked momentum and effectiveness.

The concept of kairos also lacks internal coherence. Tillich writes: "The appearance of the new is the concrete crisis of the old, the historical judgment against it. The new creation may be worse than the old one which is brought into crisis by it; and whether better or worse, it is subjected to judgment itself. But in the special historical moment it is *en kairo* (at the right time) while the old creation is not."[70] But if this is the case, it is difficult to see how this particular kairos is derived from the unique kairos, the appearance of the Christ.

This could have been avoided if Tillich had more systematically related his understanding of kairos to his category of the demonic. The secondary kairos, since it is derived from the unique kairos, cannot create a situation worse than the old one, but it is possible that the situation resulting from a creative derivative kairos subsequently becomes subject to demonic distortion. If the intention of Tillich's doctrine of kairos is to construct a generalized philosophy of history, accounting for all movement and change in history, then it must be related to an understanding of the demonic.

There remains the obvious problem of successfully identifying beforehand the coming kairos. Tillich's own record on this leaves him in a similar position to enthusiasts among the millenarian sects whose hopes were shattered. To account for the absence of the expected new theonomous age, after World War II he introduced the idea of a "sacred void," a term symbolic of the lack of ultimacy in present civilization. However, this makes for a peculiar consistency, since the earlier affirmation of an imminent kairos is now contradicted by his own revised theory, and the nonappearance of the socialist kairos![71]

There was, of course, a sense in which Tillich did judge historical events correctly. The period 1917-24 was extremely volatile, and the prospects for a European-wide socialist revolution were greater than they had ever been. For Lenin and Trotsky the idea of socialism in one country—especially in the conditions of backwardness of the Soviet Union—was nonsense. Their hopes for the October revolution were entirely dependent on the fall of tsarism precipitating the collapse of capitalism in its metropolitan heartland. It was only after the death of Lenin and the ascendency of Stalin that this prevailing orthodoxy was abandoned. In the meantime, through a series of finely balanced struggles bourgeois reaction and fascism had finally proved victorious in Germany. The Soviet Union was isolated, and all that lay ahead was the totalitarian degeneration of the Soviet experiment in socialism, which nearly seventy years later is threatened with collapse. Capitalism, for its part, proved a good deal more resilient than many anticipated, and following World War II entered into a period of expansion and comparative stability. Arguably, however, all this is consistent with the longer range perspective of Marx, for whom the precondition for socialism was *fully* developed capitalism. The possibility of a future kairos introducing a democratic and humane socialism in place of the endemic injustice and alienation of capitalist society still remains.

The question of the shortage of specific criteria to support Tillich's advocacy of religious socialism has already been mentioned. The doctrine of kairos only partially resolves this problem. In his 1926 essay "Kairos and Logos," where Tillich expounds the epistemological implications of kairos in dialogue with the various strands in the Western philosophical tradition, he argues that although thinking in terms of the kairos sets limits for the realization of the logos, it does not exclude the criterion of the logos. Tillich recognized that the problem with fascism is that it does not submit itself in any way to this criterion, which includes rationality, justice, and truth, but instead is arbitrary and irrational. Moreover, since the secondary kairos or dependent kairos is derived from the one unique kairos, and is therefore controlled by the logos character of the appearance of Christ in history, the special kairos bringing in the socialist society is under the control of the logos, and it is this which distinguishes religious socialism from a religious fascism.[72]

The difficulty, however, with Tillich's logos criterion and notion of kairos generally, is that it remains rather abstract. The danger existed that Tillich's concepts could be adopted and subverted to another use, and this indeed did happen in the work of Emanuel Hirsch, who used Tillich's work in constructing his own apologia for a Lutheranism that had become wedded to German nationalism.[73] In many ways Tillich's very achievement proved to be his downfall. His religious socialism was integral to his ambitious program of developing a philosophy of religion, a philosophy of history, and a theology of culture (which he saw as a necessary response to the crisis in traditional moral theology).[74] Not surprisingly, such an enormous undertaking involved weaknesses associated with the necessary level of abstraction. In his book *The Socialist Decision* (1933), where an emphasis upon "the demand of justice" is central to his whole analysis, Tillich went some way to providing a stronger ethical foundation for his position. In his later work, most notably his *Love, Power, and Justice* and *The Courage to Be*, the ethical dimension of his thinking was to receive fuller and more powerful expression.[75]

The critique of dialectical interpretations of history offered by Tillich in his idea of kairos does betray some serious misunderstandings. In the case of Hegel's idealism, Tillich was right that the dialectical process does eventually come to a halt—Hegel saw this as occurring when Spirit finally overcomes the alienation involved in its successive objectifications. But with Marx, for whom alienation is not equated with objectification as such, the overcoming of the workers' alienation in classless society only brings to a close prehistory and not history itself. Marx's discussion of the lower and higher phases of communist society indicates that he did not envisage that the ending of capitalist social relations would bring historical movement to a close.

As for Tillich's other criticism of dialectical philosophies of history, namely, that they exclude the "vertical" dimension of divine action characteristic of eschatological thinking, this again indicates the Platonic terms in which he understood transcendence. There are in fact good reasons to suggest that the difference is not as striking as it first appears. Firstly, the activity of God can and should be understood as *immanent* in the dialectical process itself. Secondly, transcendence need not necessarily involve using the metaphor "vertical," as Tillich does, but can also be expressed in terms of the *future*. If this is done, then the historical dialectic which points toward structural change and a new future also includes within itself the dimension of transcendence. This is what Roger Garaudy has in mind when he writes:

"Transcendence is translated into Hegelian or Marxist language as *moving beyond the present situation dialectically*."[76] If Tillich had developed his ideas along these lines, the similarity between Christian eschatology and the historical dialectic would have been even closer. However, he is right to recognize a difference between the two. The transcendence of eschatology is not just a product of structural change, but also has its roots in God himself. It is also even more radical, in that it embraces the full scope of the negative.[77]

Before concluding, we must briefly allude to Tillich's *Religiöese Verwirklichung (Religious Realization)*, published in 1929, which later appeared in *The Interpretation of History* (1936), where some of the issues associated with the interpretation of history were again dealt with.[78]

Pointing out the logical problems in talking about an "end" of time, Tillich argues that to think of "end" as a moment in time is contradictory, since the idea of a discontinuance of time is itself a time determined thought.[79] Attempting to redefine "beginning" and "end" from a Christological perspective, he writes: "Beginning is the event in which the genesis of that development is seen, for which the center has constituted itself a center. End is the goal of that development which is constituted by the center as a meaningful historical process."[80] In terms of his eschatology he concludes: "The end of historical time is its relation to the ultimate. Thus the ultimate stands equally close to and equally distant from each moment in history."[81] Here Tillich is not concerned with the last things in a temporal sense. Hence he translates "Ta eschata" as "the ultimate."[82]

Sadly, Tillich's understanding of the "end of historical time" as its relation to the ultimate is a destructive restructuring of the eschatological problem. By making all modes of time equally related to the ultimate, the eschaton is completely defuturized. Eschatology is reduced to the familiar problem of the manifestation of the eternal in the temporal, or, as Tillich so frequently puts it, the unconditional in the conditional. His view is not far removed from the mystical contemplation of the eternal beyond the temporal, which in his essay "Kairos" he describes as "unconscious" of history.[83]

In 1929, Tillich's interpretation of history was beset by the same difficulties, arising from the ontology he employed, which marred his categories of theonomy, kairos, and the demonic. The ontological framework of his eschatology remained Platonic in character and quite foreign to Hebrew thought, which he rightly points out is the real birthplace of historical consciousness. Both John Stumme and Carl Braaten have pointed to the antagonism in Tillich's theology between ontology and eschatology.[84] In Tillich's model the only way the future can have significance and priority is if the various manifestations of divine transcendence taken together form an eschatological schema. In fact, he understands belief in salvation as bringing the conviction that history is more than simply progression and regression. Also he conceives of the ultimate as giving a definite direction to time.[85] However, these insights cannot be adequately substantiated on the basis of his ontology, where the future is given no priority whatsoever. This is surely why "the end" is so important for biblical eschatology: it is a way of placing the emphasis decisively on the *future*.

Tillich's failure to develop an eschatology orientated to the future has serious implications for his religious socialism. Hope for a more meaningful society requires the dynamism of a forward-looking eschatological vision. However, this does not mean that Tillich's interpretation of history must be altogether abandoned, since the question still remains whether productive use can be made of his concepts of theonomy, kairos, and the demonic through integrating them into an ontology which accords priority to the future. If this is done, the possibility of their taking on a more *utopian* character emerges, and as symbols they are given added power and effectiveness. To be sure, Tillich's reservations about utopianism would have inhibited him from doing this. Whether this was justified will be considered in the course of the next chapter, where his attitude toward utopianism will be considered at greater length.

Chapter 7

Rethinking Socialism:
Tillich's Assessment of the Prospects for Socialism in Weimar Germany

The Weimar Republic, from its inception at the dethronement of the Kaiser to its collapse under the onslaught of conservative reaction and fascism, had been marked by continual instability and crises. With class forces too finely balanced, a working class split between social democracy and communism, and a vacillating executive implementing an inadequate socialist strategy, an historic opportunity for socialism had been lost. By 1933 the fatal consequences of this failure were emerging in the specter of the barbarism of Nazism.[1]

Tillich's most important political work, *The Socialist Decision*, published early in 1933, was the product of fourteen years' participation in the German religious socialist movement, and owed much to the "joint labors of friends and working groups in Berlin and Frankfurt."[2] Described by Adolf Löwe as Tillich's "most prophetic book," Tillich himself later records that of all the books he had written this was the one of which he was most proud.[3] In a penetrating analysis of political thought, particularly relevant to the situation in Germany in the 1930s, he issued a call for a renewed form of socialism. He hoped to influence not only existing socialists, but also the so-called National Socialists, who were in fact the enemies of socialism.[4]

Tillich's intention was to revitalize socialism by incorporating religious, emotional, psychic, cultural, and other elements that were currently finding expression only in reactionary forms. In doing so he hoped to provide the basis for an argument for socialism that would appeal to other social strata besides the proletariat, and thereby mobilize the social forces required to avert the impending disaster facing Germany. In truth, though, the tide had already turned long before 1933. Tillich's intervention was belated, and his book was quickly suppressed. Nonetheless, the relevance of his work was never solely contemporary, since it constituted an innovative attempt to confront some of the abiding problems that socialism must face.

The "Roots of Political Thought" and Their Significance for the Resolution of Socialism's Inner Conflicts

Tillich begins his analysis by considering what he called "the two roots of political thought," which "*must be sought in human being itself.*"[5] Human nature includes both being and consciousness, not as separable entities, but forming a unity. Making use of Martin Heidegger's terminology, Tillich refers to our having been "thrown" into existence. This situation means having "an origin which is not oneself," and from this arises the question of the "Whence?" of existence. In describing what he calls "the origin," Tillich writes: "Our life proceeds in a tension between dependence on the origin and independence....The origin brings us forth as something new and singular; but it takes us, as such, back to the origin again."[6]

The way in which everything living follows the course of birth, development, and death, finds expression, Tillich says, in all mythology. "Every myth is a myth of origin, that is, an answer to the question about the 'Whence' of existence and an expression of dependence on the origin and on its power." The origin must be viewed not in the abstract, but in terms of the various "*powers of origin,*" which Tillich associated with ties to blood, soil, and social group. From the myth of origin arises the first root of political thought: "*The consciousness orientated to the myth of origin is the root of all conservative and romantic thought in politics.*"[7]

Human beings are not, however, simply bound to the cycle of birth and death, but experience a demand that frees them from the origin, and forces them to ask the question, "Whither?" This demand is directed to "what ought to be," and confronts humanity as an "unconditional demand," the "*demand of justice.*" Although unconditional, the demand is not unrelated to our human nature, and is itself rooted in the origin. Out of it there emerges "something unconditionally new," which transcends the given. From all this Tillich identifies the second root of political thought: "*The breaking of the myth of origin by the unconditional demand is the root of liberal, democratic and socialist thought in politics.*"[8]

In the background to this admittedly rather forbidding anthropological analysis of political thought lie the categories of Tillich's philosophy of religion. This is suggested by his reference to the "unconditional demand," and his preoccupation with the problem of *meaning* implicit in the questions "Whence?" and "Whither?" In opting for the latter, he was in effect recasting the traditional existential question in a manner which gave it a particular political relevance, and his description of the demand, as the demand of justice, introduced a strong ethical content into his thinking. It would be wrong to infer too much from his use of Heideggerian terminology, since Tillich himself records that his own existentialism should be traced back to his reading of Kierkegaard and Marx, and that he always assumed a critical relation to Heidegger's thought.[9]

Unfortunately Tillich did not give a more detailed account of what precisely he meant by the "origin" and *"powers of origin."* His language certainly suggests the use of Freudian insights within his political theory (e.g., his reference to "the tie to the father" in his discussion of the origin).[10] The use of the word "powers" is characteristically Tillichian, and indicates the Platonic cast of his thought. The way in which the powers of origin engendered the ties and bonds that hold people together presents by no means a wholly negative picture, and in part suggests a rather Rousseauesque understanding of ideal primitive community. That the origin had its positive features is clear from the way in which the demand which breaks the bondage to the origin, is itself based upon the origin.

Tillich's reflections on this subject are perhaps best seen as an attempt to identify the more vital realm within human existence, testifying to its power, but insisting that it must be subordinated to proper ends. In human society the expression of vital needs and powers has been closely associated with the emergence of mythological beliefs, to which human beings in turn often become subject. For Tillich, the more elemental aspect of human nature must be channeled in directions consistent with true human fulfillment. Later, in *The Courage to Be*, Tillich spoke of the need for vitality to be combined with intentionality.[11]

Having outlined the two roots of political thought, Tillich proceeded to apply his interpretative framework. He argued that the break with the myth of origin occurred preeminently in Old Testament prophetism. Through its radicalizing of the "social imperative," Jewish prophetism freed itself from bondage to the origin with its ties to soil, land, and social group. In the expectation of a "new heaven and a new earth," time is elevated above space and directed toward an unconditionally new reality.[12]

The autonomous thinking of the European enlightenment is also interpreted as a breaking of the myth of origin. However, in contrast to prophetism, where the "father," understood as origin, remains "as bearer of the demand," autonomy breaks all ties with the father. The dangerous consequence of this autonomy is that it falls into an emptiness which becomes a "breeding-ground for a new outbreak of positive paganism."[13]

Tillich saw Western bourgeois society as the product of both a prophetic and humanistic break with the origin. In the prophetic break, which occurred in Protestantism, there was a freeing from the medieval bonds of origin upheld by the priesthood. The humanistic break of the enlightenment brought freedom from both religious and political absolutism. The growth of bourgeois society is also inextricably bound up with the rise of capitalism. The principle of bourgeois society is "*the radical dissolution of all conditions, bonds, and forms related to the origin into elements that are to be rationally mastered.*" This severing of all ties to the origin results in what Tillich describes as a situation of total "objectification."[14] *reification*

In bourgeois society two solutions are offered to the problem of how society can be rationally structured. The first is the liberal belief in natural harmony which affirms that "the free flow of human productive forces will lead inevitably to a rational formation of society." With the second solution, the subject, as the bearer of reason, rationally directs and shapes all aspects of society through central government. Insofar as this involves a liberal rather than an absolutist premise, this is democratic. Liberalism and democracy share a belief in harmony. This belief is of crucial importance for Western bourgeois society: "*If the belief in harmony is shaken, the bourgeois principle is shaken.*"[15]

Political romanticism derives its significance as a "*countermovement to prophetism and the enlightenment,*" attempting to restore the broken myth of origin, both spiritually and socially. It is based on a consciousness orientated to the myth of origin. Taking conservative and revolutionary forms, the conservative form seeks to defend past forms of bondage to the origin, and appears in groups not fully integrated into bourgeois society (e.g., aristocrats, peasants, and priests), while the revolutionary form attempts to find a new basis for ties to the origin, and appears in groups who have become part of the "rational system," but feel threatened by "complete absorption." This latter form finds expression in Nazism.[16]

To understand proletarian existence requires the recognition of the way in which the proletariat is the product of bourgeois society, with its drive toward "objectification" and the dissolution of all bonds to the origin, and

see p 130

also the fact that the belief in harmony is contradicted by the reality of class domination. Tillich considered socialism to be involved in an "inner conflict" that arises out of the proletarian situation. Explaining this, he writes: "While the bourgeoisie disclaimed for itself the radical implications of its own principle and allied itself with pre-bourgeois forces, it abandoned the proletariat completely to the dynamic of this principle." Yet for socialism and the class struggle to exist at all, the proletariat must be able to resist the bourgeois principle as a whole, and to do so, must still possess elements from the powers of origin. However, since these forces are also used by the bourgeoisie to consolidate class rule, the proletariat finds that it "*must deny that power by which it struggles against the bourgeois principle, namely, the power of the origin. And it must affirm that which it seeks to destroy, namely, the bourgeois principle.*" This inner conflict manifests itself at various levels. It emerges in socialist belief, view of human nature, concept of society, ideas of culture, community, and economics, and finally praxis.[17]

Since the inner conflict of socialism goes back to the proletarian situation, it can only be resolved if there are forces in the proletariat which transcend its situation. Tillich insists that there still exists an aspect of human being related to the origin which resists total objectification. The struggle of the proletariat is therefore explicable since "*there remains an element of proletarian being which has not been reduced to the status of a thing, and from this element there emerges the struggle against the bourgeois principle.*" He sought to resolve the inner conflict of socialism through the unfolding of the "socialist principle," which he defines as having three elements: "*The power of origin, the shattering of the belief in harmony, and an emphasis on the demand.*" Here the bourgeois principle and political romanticism, being partly affirmed and partly denied, are both fundamentally transcended.[18]

Tillich combined these three elements of the socialist principle in the symbol of "expectation" and argued that they are to be found combined in prophetism: "*Socialism is prophetism on the soil of an autonomous, self-sufficient world.*"[19] For Tillich, expectation is directed toward something unconditionally new. In contrast to political romanticism, the priority is given decisively to the future. Thus, expectation provides the break with the bond of origin, and an emphasis on the demand. Although realized in history, no particular time is considered to be the fulfillment, and therefore expectation is not utopian. The fulfillment which expectation looks for is a "nonobjectified" one. (This shatters belief in a present or future harmony.) Expectation also unites origin and goal—the goal is the fulfillment of the origin, and the origin provides the power to reach the goal.[20] Including both promise and demand, expectation is both independent of and dependent on human activity, and "in the tension of these two apparently contradictory factors lies the depth of the socialist principle."[21]

Socialist expectation combines prophetic substance and rational form. The prophetic aspect of expectation points toward the transcending of what is known, to the "wholly other," while rational expectation confines itself to the knowable and calculable: "*Prophetic expectation is transcendent; rational expectation is immanent.*" This tension is not necessarily destructive for socialism, and a false dichotomy between the prophetic and rational must be avoided: "*Human expectation is always transcendent and immanent at the same time.*" Even when expectation expresses itself in rational and immanent terms, it still makes use of transcendent symbols. Similarly, prophetic expectation uses materials from everyday life, and does not exclude concrete analysis.[22]

We must now consider the different dimensions of socialism's inner conflict, and the way in which the socialist principle of expectation makes possible their resolution.

The first inner conflict Tillich identified was in socialist belief. For socialism the idea of harmony becomes an eschatological expectation, and in consequence it "*must reckon with a leap that can in no way be explained in terms of present reality.*" This represents a break with the bourgeois principle, with its presupposition of a rational world order, and introduces a prophetic element in socialism. But this expectation must be formulated in a purely immanent manner to counter bourgeois society's use of transcendent eschatology as an anti-revolutionary ideology. Hence a situation of inner conflict is present.[23]

According to the socialist principle the expected classless society is not a complete break with the present. It is not cut off from the power of origin but is the true meaning of the origin, and is therefore in continuity with the prerevolutionary situation. Also the belief in harmony in classless society is rejected since opposition among the powers of origin will remain. Thus the need for an irrational leap is avoided, and the conflict thereby resolved.[24]

The second inner conflict is in the socialist view of human nature. Socialism follows bourgeois anthropology in considering human nature from the standpoint of reason, to which all its other aspects must be subordinated. This results in a loss of the level of human being which Tillich refers to as the "spiritual-vital center." Since socialism rejects belief in a present harmony, the idea of human nature being determined by reason, whether through natural harmony or progressive education, must be postponed til the future classless society in which reason rules. But this is problematic: *"There is nothing to mediate the leap from unreason to reason. Between reality and expectation lies an abyss."* If it is said that the new social situation leads to the transformation of human beings, there still remains the question of how such a changed situation is realized without the transformation of human nature. Adopting a different anthropology to avoid such difficulties is hindered by the way in which the prebourgeois view of human nature is ideologically misused by the bourgeoisie to reinforce class rule. In consequence of this, socialism must fight for "the bourgeois principle against the bourgeoisie and against itself as well."[25]

The socialist principle resolves this internal conflict through its recognition of the "spiritual and vital center" in human beings, and by affirming the powers of origin, though in terms in which the origin is subordinated to the demand. It also rejects the belief in harmony, and therefore excludes the idea of a future post-revolutionary situation in which reason alone is victorious. This affirmation of the forces of origin necessitates a rejection of the crude *"drive psychology"* of vulgar Marxism, which reduces the human person to the status of a mere mechanism determined by pleasure and pain reactions, and sees revolution as the outcome of the pain reaction of the suffering proletariat. This mechanistic psychology is an expression of the very objectification and dehumanization against which socialism must struggle. Responding favorably to the attempts at dialogue between Marxism and psychoanalysis, Tillich refers to the side of psychoanalysis which "dethrones" consciousness and points to the "psychic and vital center."[26]

For Tillich the third inner conflict, which is the one of most direct importance for politics, occurs in the socialist concept of society. He argued that socialism is undermined by its ambiguous attitude to the use of power. In the situation of class domination, power is used by socialism to achieve its goals, but as soon as this power is victorious it must be renounced. Here socialism is more radical in its belief in harmony than the bourgeoisie who took advantage of power to consolidate class rule, breaking with the belief in harmony, though still retaining it as ideology. Tillich rejected the idea that the proletariat should renounce power, and argued that the socialist belief in future harmony is undermined by the present experience of the absence of a unified proletarian interest. However, when socialism rejects the belief in future harmony and affirms the powers of the origin, the familiar inner conflict emerges, since the forces of origin have already been coopted by the bourgeoisie to reinforce class rule.[27]

In order to resolve this dilemma, Tillich insists that socialism must develop a positive understanding of power and a new theory of the state. When exercised in accord with the socialist principle, the use of power is informed by "the relationship of power to the origin and goal of human life," and is based upon "consent" and "justice." In criticizing socialism's attitude toward the use of power Tillich had particularly in mind the ineffectiveness and vacillation of German social democracy after World War I.[28]

Of the remaining manifestations of inner conflict, those in the socialist idea of culture and the socialist idea of community were perhaps the most significant. Tillich observes how the rejection of religion due to its authoritarian and reactionary use had blinded socialism to the religious roots within itself. Similarly, the evils of nationalism had forced upon socialism a stance which failed to recognize the rightful place of bonds to the land, nation, and social group. However, the socialist principle of expectation makes possible the incorporation of all these various origin related elements.[29]

Tillich's contribution to political theory in *The Socialist Decision* should be situated in the context of post-World War I Germany and the attempts to renew a socialist tradition that had become ossified and was unable to respond to the crises in bourgeois society. To the modern commentator it is somewhat surprising that Tillich did not devote more of his attention to the distortion of Marxist ideas (and practice!) in the Soviet Union. Although this would have risked the socialist unity for which he strove in the struggle of German workers against fascism, it was surely necessary for any fundamental analysis of socialism in this period. That said, Tillich clearly sought an alternative to the Soviet model of socialism, and his concern with the "roots" of political thinking, his analysis of fascism, interest in psychoanalysis, and preoccupation with relationship between religion and socialism were typical of the kind of theoretical study and reevaluation of Marxism promoted by the Frankfurt School.[30]

The intellectual milieu in which Tillich made his contribution also owed much to the rediscovery and publication of the *Paris Manuscripts*, which had been preceded by the critique of the "reification" in capitalist society offered by Georg Lukács. Tillich readily acknowledged the stimulus which Marx's early writings had given to his thinking.[31] Moreover, his frequent use of the term "Verdinglichung" (which would have been better rendered as "reification" rather than "objectification" in the English translation), suggests a strong Lukácsian influence.[32] In *The Religious Situation*, published in 1926, Tillich had used the term "self-sufficient finitude" when describing the unconditional dominance of economic activity which characterizes the spirit of capitalist society, offering a description of bourgeois society that had much in common with Lukács' treatment of reification, and which complements his account in *The Socialist Decision*.[33] Where Tillich departed from Marxism was in the way his concern with dehumanization and alienation extended to an indictment of capitalist society for its lack of any sense of ultimacy, that is, of the relation to the divine in human life.

Although Tillich's socialist vision was to remain unfulfilled, much of his analysis retains its force, since he effectively diagnosed many of the ills that continue to afflict Western capitalist societies. The dominance of the bourgeois principle has resulted in fragmentation and a weakening of the sense of community, and a banal consumerism has often replaced the search for what might constitute a meaningful existence. The more Freudian component and emphasis upon the vital and instinctual within Tillich's analysis was to find an echo in the 1960s in Herbert Marcuse's deeply pessimistic essay in cultural analysis, poignantly entitled *One-Dimensional Man*.[34]

Undoubtedly, the main source of Tillich's inspiration was prophetism, which provided him with the organizing principle around which he endeavored to reshape socialism. The prophetic tradition constituted a vital heritage which Marxism rejected at its peril and needed if it was to transcend its bourgeois captivity. The inner conflicts Tillich diagnosed were real enough, and pointed to crucial unresolved tensions in socialist thinking. Without prophetism's capacity to enlist the forces and energies within the deeper dimension of human being, socialism would be unable to command the loyalty of the proletariat and other social groups potentially able to oppose capitalism. This appeal was widened further by Tillich, through stressing the universal aspect of socialism, and arguing that the particular element of proletarian existence must be combined with the vision of a classless society.[35]

Thus emerged the basis of a strategy for socialist transition that was comprehensive enough to avoid the impasse of previous revolutionary politics, which tended to dogmatically insist on the proletarianization of other strata.[36] Included within this overall reassessment was the prospect of an alliance between socialism and Christianity, since socialism's recognition of its own prophetic element would open the way for a rapprochement with the prophetism so integral to the history of Western Religion.[37]

The prophetic element which Tillich discerned in socialism was likewise present in Marxism. This prophetic passion goes back to Marx himself. Thus elsewhere he writes: "We cannot miss the messianic note in Marx's writings. Especially in the earlier writings we hear the voice of a modern secular prophet."[38] Tillich recognized a structural analogy between the Marxist and prophetic interpretations of history. Both are historical rather than naturalistic interpretations, and see history as having a meaning of its own, an aim toward which it is moving.

> Both prophetism and Marxism attack the existing order of society....They passionately challenge concrete forms of injustice, threatening those responsible for it, especially the ruling groups, with the judgement of history....Both prophetism and Marxism believe that the transition from the present stage of history into the stage of fulfillment will occur in a catastrophe or in a series of catastrophic events, the end of which will be the establishment of a kingdom of peace and justice....Freedom and historical destiny are not contradictory for prophetic and Marxist thinking.[39]

These parallels which Tillich describes should in fact come as no surprise, since Marx was deeply influenced by both utopian socialism and Hegel's philosophy of history, with its rational and secularizing reinterpretation of Christianity.

While Tillich was right in stressing the prophetic character of Marxism, his exclusive emphasis on this point was in danger of eclipsing other aspects of socialism. In particular, political economy, which had been central to the synthesis that Marx achieved, received insufficient attention in Tillich's work. Although he clearly accepted the main features of Marx's analysis of capitalism, and had an interest in economics generally, he tended to avoid detailed discussion or even to recognize the significance of Marx's economic theory, and it was to be no different in his treatment of economic questions in *The Socialist Decision*.[40] This failure constituted one of the major inadequacies of his religious socialism. Ernst Bloch struck a better balance when he at least insisted on the unity of the "warm" and "cold" stream in Marxism, and thus gave due weight to Marxism's rigorous scientific analysis.[41] To avoid this criticism Tillich would have had to give much greater attention to the *rational* side of expectation.

The particular definition which Tillich gave to his category of expectation was intended to preserve the understanding of the Kingdom of God as transcendent, while still positively relating socio-political realities to the manifestation of the Kingdom of God within history. In speaking of expectation as "nonobjectified," he avoided a utopianism which saw the Kingdom as fulfilled in history. However, equally vehemently, Tillich rejected the attempt of political romanticism to distort expectation by limiting its application to the destiny of the individual soul, and thus excluding its world-transforming aspect.[42]

The real shortcoming in the doctrine of expectation, as Tillich expounded it, lay in his attitude toward utopianism. Although he rightly rejected the excesses of millenarianism and insisted that the Kingdom is never completely fulfilled in history, he was unwise in distancing himself from utopianism by so often equating it with the unrealizable. It was not just theological considerations which led Tillich toward this negative assessment, since he seems also to have been influenced by Marx's critique of utopian socialism.[43]

If Tillich had been prepared to describe in more directly utopian language the qualitatively new society to be ushered in by socialism, his whole perspective would have assumed a much greater clarity, and his conception of prophetism would have had much more resonance with both religion and socialism. Such a stance presents no theological difficulties since the Kingdom, though not fulfilled, is manifest in history. Hence Tillich's advice in his article, "The Church and Communism," written in 1937: *"The Churches have to accept the communist hope for a new future as representing, although in a secularized way, the Christian hope for the coming of the kingdom of God in history."*[44]

Despite all his protestations, Tillich's work is in fact best viewed in utopian terms. Indeed, the very vehemence of his critique serves to betray his deep inner attachment and affinity with utopian thinking. What he feared most was that unrealistic and impractical expectations would only lead to disappointment and disillusionment.[45] By virtue of their being too utopian, such expectations only served to undermine hopes for the new society, and in a sense Tillich was opposing them in the name of utopia. That Tillich's view of utopianism was in fact by no means wholly negative is clear from an essay of 1931, where he writes:

> The spirit of utopia (a coinage of Ernst Bloch) is the power which changes reality. It is the spring (*Triebfeder*) of all historical movements; it is the tension which thrusts humanity beyond every calm and security into new insecurity and unrest. Utopia is the power of the new.[46]

Similarly, in an essay entitled "The Political Meaning of Utopia," written in 1951, Tillich explicitly acknowledged that utopia also has a positive dimension. In particular, he refers to the power of utopia "to transform the given." Referring back to the period after World War I, he says that we "affirmed the idea of utopia," but adds "we did not dare affirm it as absolute." This tension is resolved by conceiving of utopia in both "immanent" and "transcendent" terms. With the former, "fulfillment is realized in time and space," though only in 'an anticipatory, fragmentary way.'"[47]

Throughout *The Socialist Decision*, in stressing the crucial importance of an attitude of expectation, Tillich was essentially calling for a utopian orientation in thinking and practice, without which social revolution would prove impossible. It was this orientation that provided the answer to socialism's conflicts, and inspired a *power of being* that would secure socialist advance:

> The success of the revolution depends on the inspiring power of an expectation in which all aspects of human existence find a new fulfillment; and the success of the revolution requires persons whose being and consciousness is formed through their anticipation of the coming fulfillment.[48]

It is unfortunate that Tillich seems to have allowed his tendency to equate utopianism with that which is unrealizable to prevent him from making the utopian content of this thinking more explicit. Just as his treatment of theonomy, kairos, and the demonic, and his category of expectation, expressed an essential and vital aspect of his thinking, so too did his treatment of *utopia*.

To have formally embraced utopianism need not in itself have required from Tillich any muting of the force of his critique of socialism. In its view of human nature and its often unqualified belief in future harmony, Marxism, particularly that of the Second and Third International, was much too optimistic. In "The Political Meaning of Utopia," Tillich pinpoints what he describes as the fundamental failure of utopianism: "It forgets the finitude and alienation of man."[49] This was certainly a legitimate criticism of much of Marxism, and Tillich's discussion of the inner conflict in socialist anthropology was an attempt to resolve the difficulty.

Elsewhere in his writings he refers to the conflict between Christianity and the Marxist assessment of human nature.[50] Tillich regarded socialism in this respect as basically dependent on bourgeois thinking, a point of view which was also shared by Reinhold Niebuhr who writes: "Marxism expects man to be as tame and social on the other side of the proletarian revolution as Adam Smith and Jeremy Bentham thought them to be tame and prudential this side of the revolution."[51] By insisting on the continuance of disharmony and maintaining more realism in his view of human nature Tillich provided a valuable corrective for socialism. The contrast he presents is in fact too sharp–Marx himself stressed the different stages of communist society and only envisaged a progressive disalienation—as we shall discuss in the final chapter below (p. 175). Nonetheless, Marx paid too little attention to questions such as the organization of the state in post-revolutionary society, and tended to speak as though the alienation of capitalism was the only alienation afflicting humankind.

All this need not—and did not for Tillich—lead to a rejection of socialism, but simply suggested the lines upon which it must be transformed and renewed. Tillich's discussion of power and his call for a new theory of the state, in particular, indicate an important area where fresh thinking among Marxists is required.

Historical Materialism and the Historical Dialectic Reconsidered

Tillich regarded Marxism as basic to the self-understanding of the socialist movement, and this is reflected in the consideration of the problems posed by historical materialism and the historical dialectic to be found in *The Socialist Decision.*[52]

Historical materialism, Tillich insisted, is in the first instance a polemical concept ("*kampfbegriff*"), "developed in opposition to the idealist interpretation of history." Accordingly it abandons the idealist notion of a directing logic within history, and looks for "the real causes of the historical process." However, equally keen to avoid a metaphysical materialism, he writes that the "*matter*" of history is "*humanity that seeks to satisfy its needs through a common productive enterprise.*"[53] Aware that the materialistic interpretation of history affirms the primacy of the economic over other functions, Tillich points out how Marxism has been vigorously attacked for this view, which is regarded as a rejection of all higher values. He accepted that the later deterministic distortion of historical materialism was in part attributable to the way Marx had expressed his position, but he contended that the image of substructure-superstructure should not be interpreted as meaning that "a discrete factor called 'spirit' [*Geist*] is causally dependent on another discrete factor, 'economics.'" He considered such a cause-effect relation inappropriate to the image and to the reality of the situation: "Economics is not a thing.... *All aspects of human being must be considered when economics is considered.*" Economics includes the spiritual dimension, and likewise spirit also cannot be isolated: "*Spirit is never something in itself; it is always the spirit of something.*" When being is made cause and spirit the effect, the unity of being and consciousness is lost—a unity which Marx himself had emphasized.[54]

Tillich did challenge Marx's architectural model, implicitly at least, and his use of historical materialism was always a critical one. In an essay written in 1924 Tillich employed the term "gestalt" (living structural whole), in order to modify Marx's static metaphor of a building. He was intent on interpreting Marx's model more dynamically, and argued that the economic base is not severed from other levels, with which it has a causal relationship, but exists in immediate relation to the whole structure. This suggests a more dialectical and organic approach to understanding Marx's materialism, and it is to be regretted that Tillich did not develop the point in *The Socialist Decision*.[55]

In his assessment of the historical dialectic, Tillich singles out two major misconceptions. Under the influence of nineteenth-century positivism, vulgar Marxism had reduced necessity to a matter of cause and effect. Here belief in the inevitability of the transition to socialism had "shattered the power of socialist action." Despite some success in predicting the technical development of capitalism, "the human response to these developments was judged wholly inaccurately." The proletariat, the bourgeoisie, and the adherents of political romanticism behaved in a different manner than had been anticipated on the basis of a primitive anthropology. In reaction to this form of Marxism, there emerged an "ethical socialism" which made human action the decisive factor, and where "freedom took the place of necessity."

Tillich considered that in both these interpretations the dialectical method is seriously misunderstood. Against the mechanistic view of necessity he argued that humanity and history cannot be understood according to the model of a *"thing"* which thereby excludes human freedom. The movement of history must never be separated from human action. However, equally importantly, this action must always be related to the impetus of history. Thus he regarded ethical socialism as lacking in power since "it presents a demand that is unrelated to being and is not one with the impulse of history." Tillich saw human action and the knowledge of the dialectical movement of history linked together in the proletarian situation. Unlike other groups, the proletariat directly experiences the injustice of the social structure, "and lives directly in the expectation of, and experiences the tension toward a new order of things, toward justice."[56]

The historical dialectic was a theme that Tillich also considered in earlier essays. In "The Protestant Principle and the Proletarian Situation" (1931), he specifically links Marx's dialectic with the Christian doctrine of providence and predestination. Transcendent necessity, he insists, should not be understood as a caused or mechanical necessity. "Man," he writes, "never becomes a 'thing,' a mere object, deprived of his psychological freedom." Accordingly, the necessity with which capitalism leads to a classless society does not "give to the proletariat the right merely to watch the process but rather makes the demand that the dialectical necessity be materialized by means of revolutionary effort."[57]

The kind of corrective that Tillich sought to introduce in his treatment of both historical materialism and the historical dialectic was one that was consistent with a return to Marx. His insistence upon the unity of being and consciousness and distaste for metaphysical materialism only implied a rejection of the Marxism of the Second and Third International. Similarly, his attempt to restore the unity between freedom and necessity in the movement toward socialism simply constituted a recovery of the Hegelian perspective that informed Marx's understanding of historical change. Tillich's main deficiency here was in the way in which he failed to relate these issues to an economic analysis, and thus introduced a level of abstraction not present in Marx. Furthermore, given the importance for the socialist movement of the interpretation of these central aspects of Marxist theory, a critical treatment of Engels, Kautsky, and Lenin would have given Tillich's attack upon the reigning orthodoxy an added force.

Conclusion

Although much modern political theology is indebted to Marxism, the kind of detailed and explicit assessment which Tillich offers is all too rare. The growth of liberation theology in the 1960s and 1970s in the third world has been a welcome development, but here Marxism has been used more as a method of analysis, and practical exigencies have tended to inhibit the kind of sustained dialogue in which Tillich was engaged. Unfortunately, although Tillich is widely known, the significance of his social theology has been neglected.[58] To understand the reasons for this we must briefly consider the development of his thought from 1933 onward.

Following his emigration to America, Tillich's attention turned to more traditional theological issues, and an interest in existentialism and psychoanalysis. However, the existentialist emphasis within his theology always remained sufficiently critical to avoid a subjective individualism which excluded corporate and political concerns.[59] Justice cannot be done to Tillich by separating his thought into two distinct periods; existentialism was important prior to 1933, and it would be wrong to claim he completely rejected his earlier socialist vision when in America. J. Wogaman refers to a lecture in 1957 where Tillich was asked if he still supported socialism. He replied quickly: "That is the only possible economic system from a Christian point of view."[60]

However, Tillich did undergo a definite change in perspective, insofar as he came to regard the more revolutionary socialism he subscribed to in Germany as no longer appropriate in the context of the economic prosperity and less polarized conditions in the United States. Thus in an article in 1943 Tillich sharply distanced himself from the classical Marxian position on the proletariat:

> In Marx's vision of the present world it is the proletariat which has the favored place for truth and action because it is at the edge of complete dehumanization, where no more ideology is possible. Religious Socialism also asks the question of the "favored place" or of the "liberated finitude" without being able to identify it with a special sociological group. Religious Socialism is inclined to believe that "broken" people in all groups are the "favored place" in our present historical situation.

And in 1949 he makes the judgment:

> I do not doubt that the basic conceptions of religious socialism are valid, that they point to the political and cultural life by which alone Europe can be built up, but I am *not* sure that the adoption of religious-socialist principles is a possibility in any foreseeable future.

However, in 1952 Tillich said that he was not happy with the title "Beyond Religious Socialism," which the editors had given his 1949 article, and wrote: "If the prophetic message is true, there is nothing 'beyond religious socialism.'" At the end of his life, Tillich spoke again on this subject. He confined the relevance of the detailed analysis of his Religious Socialism, with its strong emphasis on the dehumanization and revolutionary role of the proletariat, to Germany after World War I, but still wished to affirm some of the principles behind Religious Socialism. Thus he speaks of the "basic principles of justice, including economic justice, that underlay Religious Socialism and, I believe, should underlie every social system." Commenting on the evolution of Tillich's political thought, J.L. Adams says that Tillich insisted "that the Neo-Marxist formulations of Religious Socialism did not fit the American scene," and "came to believe in the necessity and rightness of a dispersion of power in a mixed economy."[61]

The trajectory of Tillich's thought was a familiar one. Like many socialist intellectuals of his generation, he responded to the deformation of socialism in the Soviet Union, and the genesis of a more liberal form of capitalism in the West, by abandoning his earlier Marxism and embracing a reformist social democracy. Furthermore, although he had been involved in helping fellow emigres, took part in wartime propaganda, and served as chair of the Council for a Democratic Germany, he became much less politically active after the war. There was some participation in the Fellowship of Socialist Christians, but this group became increasingly more reformist in its leanings and less concerned with Marxism.[62]

In a sense Tillich fell victim to the consequences of his own theology—he had announced the socialist kairos that never came. Rather than developing a Marxist analysis and theological response appropriate to this new situation, he devoted himself to writing his *Systematic Theology*. Despite its indebtedness to his earlier theology, when it finally appeared his "System" proved very different from the more political work envisaged when he announced the first volume back in 1927.[63] Tillich had largely retreated from the terrain of political theory, and we do not find in his later work anything comparable to the edifice which Reinhold Niebuhr constructed in defense of a reformist agenda for social change and commitment to a mixed economy.

Still, it must be said that Tillich's achievement in *The Socialist Decision*, in defense of his earlier socialist vision, was a considerable one. His work passes two important tests. It provided both an original contribution in terms of its political theory and an assessment of socialism that challenged the generally held notion that Marxism and Christianity are completely hostile and irreconcilable. To be sure, the belief in transcendence separates Christianity from Marxism, but Tillich rightly pointed to the way in which, when understood correctly, eschatology and prophetism have much in common with socialism. In terms of its application to the present, despite Tillich's own later change of perspective, those conscious of the limitations of reformist social democracy and committed to a humanist form of Marxist socialism will find much on which to ponder in this book. Indeed, given the recent demise of the Stalinist heritage in Eastern Europe, if the premature talk of a post-Marxist era and the consequent abandonment of the socialist project is to be challenged, an analysis of the kind Tillich offered is a necessary part of the search for a renewed and democratic socialism. This analysis suggests the need for a fundamental reorientation of socialist thinking and strategy based upon a more holistic anthropology, an acceptance of the vitality and centrality of the prophetic dimension within socialism, and a willingness to recognize the need for cooperation with non-proletarian strata.

This agenda need not imply any surrendering of socialist objectives and principles, since it is these which still form the basis of socialism's appeal. Although self-evident, the fact has often been ignored that socialism must find expression in terms which positively relate to the more deep-seated needs and aspirations of people, if it is to be effective in mobilizing support. The tragedy is that in its mechanistic and determinist forms, Marxism has failed to recognize this, and it has paid the price for not doing so. A viable socialist strategy must embrace cultural, national, and religious questions, and especially the innate utopian propensity and aspirations within people. Although the changes in the sociological structure of society in the advanced capitalist countries since the period in which Tillich was writing mean that we face a different set of problems, their resolution will still need to be upon similar lines.

The failure of existing so-called socialist countries to escape from relative economic backwardness and advance toward a genuinely democratic socialism, coupled with the fact that capitalism managed to extricate itself from the crises of the 1920s and 1930s and has proved to have a much longer course to run, does not mean that the death knell of socialism has been sounded. Marx himself, especially in his later economic writings, stressed that capitalism must first develop to full maturity before conditions would be ripe for socialism. If the reports of socialism's death are therefore greatly exaggerated, Tillich's work in Weimar Germany, whatever its limitations, retains its relevance.

Chapter 8

Eschatology and Politics:
Jürgen Moltmann's Political Theology

Recalling his childhood, Jürgen Moltmann describes how he would gaze out of the window of his parents' home in Northern Germany: "There the horizon is a boundary which does not confine but rather invites one to go on beyond." At the age of seventeen, in 1944, he went to war, and after capture in 1945 was imprisoned for three years. As a prisoner of war his "horizon" was a barbed wire fence. It was here, he tells us, that he learned what it meant to "hope against hope."[1] On his return to Germany in 1948, Moltmann became a student of theology at Göttingen. For those of his generation who had survived the war, a liberal bourgeois theology held no attraction, and he came under the influence of the theology of the Confessing Church inspired by Karl Barth.[2]

For a time Moltmann was doubtful whether progress could be made beyond Barth's *Church Dogmatics*, but this was all to change with his discovery of the centrality of eschatology. In making this new departure Moltmann stresses his indebtedness to Ernst Bloch, enthusiastically acknowledging Bloch's Marxist humanism, which identifies a "warm stream" in Marxism that goes back to the pre-Marxist sources of prophetic history and later messianic thinking in the West. It was in constant and critical dialogue with Bloch's *Das Prinzip Hoffnung* (*The Principle of Hope*) that he developed his own eschatological thinking, using an amended version of Bloch's utopian philosophy as a means of both theological criticism and theological construction. Thus Moltmann took up many of Bloch's categories, such as *novum*, *front line*, and *docta spes*, and pressed them into service in his own theology.[3]

Political Theology and the Theology of Hope

Along with Johannes Metz, in the late 1960s, Moltmann began to describe the task of an ethics of Christian hope as "political theology." Political theology is not so much a branch of theology as a statement about the nature of theology itself. For Moltmann, all theology is political, whether it is conscious of it or not. There cannot be an apolitical theology. Nor can political theology be reduced to a political ethics, since theology must engage in self-critical reflection upon its own ideological and institutional standpoint. It must ask for whom its theology is intended, and whose interests it is serving. Accordingly, political theology stands opposed to political religions of society that legitimize the existing social order (e.g., Christianity after Constantine).[4]

To understand Moltmann's political theology we must begin with his first major work, *Theology of Hope* (1964), translated into English in 1967, which represents a comprehensive attempt to present theology in eschatological perspective. Thus in the introduction he writes:

> From first to last, and not merely in epilogue, Christianity is eschatology, is hope, forward looking and forward moving, and therefore also revolutionizing and transforming the present....The God spoken of here is no intra-worldly or extra-worldly God, but the "God of Hope" (Rom. 15:13), a God with "future as his essential nature" (as E. Bloch puts it)....[5]

Moltmann regards the rediscovery of eschatology at the end of the nineteenth century by Johannes Weiss and Albert Schweitzer as one of the most important developments in modern theological scholarship. The effect of this was to seriously question the reduction of eschatology to ethics in nineteenth-century Liberal Protestantism. Unfortunately, Weiss and Schweitzer never really followed through the implications of their discovery. Following World War I, "dialectical theology" showed a renewed interest in eschatology, but here eschatology was understood in Greek thought forms. For Moltmann, the real language of eschatology "is not the Greek *logos*, but the *promise* which has stamped the language, the hope and the experience of Israel."[6]

In his *Theology of Hope*, Moltmann includes a detailed interpretation of the Old Testament, demonstrating how promissory history forms its central and unifying theme. The passage from semi-nomadic life to the settled life of Canaan did not involve abandoning the God of promise for epiphany gods. Appearances of Yahweh were linked with the divine word of promise, and not the hallowing of times or places. Even the cyclical festivals were historicized and interpreted in the framework of promise. Israel came to owe its very self-identity to major promises such as those associated with Abraham, the Exodus, and Sinai. The religion of promise makes possible the experience of reality as history, events within the horizon of promise being experienced as "historic." Discussing the tension between promise and fulfillment, Moltmann quotes von Rad: "Only where Yahweh had revealed himself in his word and acts did history exist for Israel."[7]

Moltmann begins his discussion of promise in the prophets by noting that the concept of eschatology has become rather vague, and offers the following definition: "Promises and expectations are eschatological which are directed toward an historic future in the sense of the ultimate horizon."[8] The concept of "horizon," as the moving boundary of expectation, ties in closely with an understanding of promise, and prophetic eschatology was in fact developed from this earlier faith in promise. It was through the experience of the Exile, that faith as promise was expanded to become prophetic eschatology. In the situation of possible annihilation, the covenant is interpreted as null and void, and salvation becomes dependent on the future action of Yahweh. The prophetic message becomes fully eschatological through its application to all nations, and the overcoming of even the boundary of death. Moltmann goes on to suggest that apocalyptic should be considered as an eschatological and historic interpretation of the cosmos. Although apocalyptic conceives of its eschatology in cosmological terms, this is not the end of eschatology, but the start of an eschatological cosmology and ontology.[9]

In his treatment of the New Testament, Moltmann criticizes approaches to christology from a Greek metaphysical view of God, or from the perspective of the anthropology of modern existentialism. If Jesus was a Jew, and it was Yahweh who raised him from the dead, then Israel's history of promise should form the foundation of our understanding of christology. In the New Testament God is in fact described as the "God of promise." Paul gives Abraham, as the father of promise, a central place in his exposition of the Gospel. The promissory character of the Gospel is also seen in Paul's conflicts within the primitive Church and his criticism of the Hellenistic "ecstasy of fulfillment," which reduced the eschaton to the presence of the eternal.[10]

On the question of the resurrection, Moltmann regards historical and existentialist approaches as inadequate, and insists that the resurrection must be seen in the light of the horizon of the promised future.[11] Hegel's interpretation of modern atheism's experience of the "death of God" in terms of a universal Good Friday of godforsakenness, suggested to Moltmann a dialectical understanding of cross and resurrection, in eschatological openness to "the future of God and the annihilation of death."[12]

In the Easter appearances the crucified one is identified with the risen and coming one, an identity that "points the direction for coming events and makes a path for them." In this "identity in total contradiction," cross and resurrection form an open dialectic, which finds its resolving synthesis in the eschaton.[13] Amidst the unredeemedness of the world there can therefore be hope for "the fulfillment of the promised righteousness of God in all things, the fulfillment of the resurrection of the dead that is promised in his resurrection, the fulfillment of the lordship of the crucified one over all things that is promised in his exaltation."[14] The universal scope of the promise of the coming Kingdom leads us to hope and to suffer under the present forsakenness of the world: "The *pro-missio* of the kingdom is the ground of the *missio* of love to the world."[15]

In the final chapter on the "Exodus Church," Moltmann considers the role of the Church in modern society in the context of its eschatological hope. As a community orientated toward a horizon of eschatological expectation, the Church's work and action in the world is determined by the "open foreland of its hopes for the world."[16] The Church is nothing in itself, but exists for others. It is a Church for the world, not in the sense of conforming to the world's expectations, but in that of taking up society into its own horizon of expectation for the coming Kingdom. Accordingly, the Church can no longer confine itself to the social roles which society ascribes to it. Thus Christianity must avoid the role of helping to stabilize existing institutional life, and should never allow itself to become a religion of society ("cultus publicus").

Nor, in the situation of modern industrial society, should Christianity restrict itself to the sphere of individual subjectivity ("cultus privatus"). It should not content itself with creating community as a means of refuge from the pressures of the existing world, and thereby withdraw from any responsibly for the social order, but rather should inspire women and men with a world-transforming hope. The breadth of this eschatological hope requires a corresponding understanding of salvation, which must be interpreted as shalom in the Old Testament sense. Thus God's saving action relates not just to the individual and personal dimension, but includes the eschatological hope of peace and justice. Christian mission is therefore directed to the whole of life, and must embrace the concrete social and political existence of humankind.

Moltmann's *Theology of Hope* has powerfully reinstated eschatology as the unifying core of Christian theology, and identified the utopian impulse that lies at the heart of the Christian message. The Church has always fought against the disturbing implications of such a perspective, and eschatology has often been fatally weakened through adopting an alien metaphysics that reinterprets transcendence in ahistorical terms. The priority which Moltmann insists should be given to eschatology is a prerequisite for political theology. In its directedness toward the future his treatment of promise assumes utopian proportions. Promise, we are told, "announces the coming of a reality that does not yet exist," it "bores like a thorn in the flesh of every present and opens it for the future."[17]

The main deficiency in Moltmann's analysis is that it is not sufficiently related to human action. As his understanding of cross and resurrection indicates, the emphasis is upon "total contradiction." "The expected future," he writes, "does not have to develop within the framework of the possibilities inherent in the present, but arises from that which is possible to the God of the promise."[18] This undermines the centrality of human action, and the role of promise in motivating such action, and presupposes a conception of transcendence that is in fact undialectical. Although, as we have seen, Moltmann links together promise and mission, his insight into their intimate relation is left without adequate foundation.

The implications for politics of Moltmann's attempt to renew the eschatological dimension within the Christian faith are drawn only in a minimal way in the *Theology of Hope*, and it is significant that his concluding chapter should be concerned exclusively with the role of the Church. Through so strongly emphasizing divine action mediated through the word of promise to Israel and the Church it would seem that a positive assessment of the purely secular is inhibited. Thus when Moltmann envisages the Church taking up the world into its horizon of expectation we are in fact presented with a rather conservative perspective that hardly assists in any evaluation of the contribution of political movements.[19]

These strictures aside, what Moltmann says on the Church's role represents a forceful critique of the prevailing patterns of its accommodation and conformity to modern society. It must also be acknowledged that his eschatology brings an openness to his theology that makes possible a far more politically responsible attitude to the world and its future than much of previous Christian theology. Hence his justified critique of Bultmann's reduction of eschatology and revelation to anthropology: "Is any self-understanding of man conceivable at all which is not determined by his relation to the world, to history, to society?"[20]

Finally, it must be asked whether Moltmann is radical enough in pursuing the implications of his demand for the re-eschatologizing of the Christian faith. In particular, should not the kind of criticism of the theological tradition which Moltmann offers be applied to the Bible itself? Jesus was an apocalyptic prophet, but did not the evangelists in varying degrees seek to moderate his eschatology and politics? Although Paul maintained a tension between retaining a certain eschatological thrust and accommodation to the existing social order (e.g., his attitude to slavery, the state, and women), it is the former on which Moltmann chooses to concentrate, and yet the implications of his theology surely question much of Paulinism.

Moltmann is in fact very selective in the use he makes of scripture, as is illustrated by the fact that *Theology of Hope* does not contain a single reference to John's Gospel. If it had he would have had to distance himself from its realized eschatology.[21] In his critical treatment of the biblical material Ernst Bloch was commendably more consistent. Not that this implies an acceptance of Bloch's *atheistic* messianism, since a *Christian* messianism could be just as readily used as a criterion for biblical critical work. Had Moltmann more consistently carried through his program of re-eschatologizing the Christian faith, the political liberation implied in the theme of "Exodus" would have acquired a much more comprehensive application.

Moltmann's "Theologia Crucis"

The roots of Moltmann's theology lay much deeper than the prevailing mood of optimism of the 1960s, and in his book *The Crucified God* (1972), translated into English in 1974, he turns his attention toward a theology of the cross. This work was intended to complement his earlier *Theology of Hope*, the emphasis moving away from the resurrection back to the cross itself. In philosophy, the inspiration has moved away from Bloch's philosophy of hope, and, in line with his increased concern with the theodicy problem, toward the "negative dialectic" and "critical theory" of Theodor Adorno and Max Horkheimer. Moltmann views his own attempt at a theology of the cross as in continuity with tradition, though his intention was to take this theology further. In particular, the theology of the cross must not be restricted to criticism of the Church, as in the reformation, but must also be expounded as a criticism of society. In his "theologia crucis" he wants to "go beyond a concern for personal salvation, and enquire about the liberation of man."[22] The cross raises the question: "What are the economic, social and political consequences of the gospel of the Son of Man who was crucified as a 'rebel?'"[23]

Discussing the christological titles, Moltmann concludes that the titles change in different situations, but that in this variability there is a factor which is constant—the name Jesus and his history. Within this history, it is the end of Jesus' life in the cross and resurrection which is of particular importance. He consequently quotes with approval Martin Kähler's comment that the cross requires a christology.[24] It is the cross which calls into question all christologies and makes them in constant need of revision. Moltmann is highly critical of the christology of the early fathers, which begins with the question: "How can the intransitory God be in a transitory human being?"[25] The conception of God as unchangeable and incapable of suffering created serious difficulties for any attempt to understand the abandonment and death of Jesus. Modern christologies which take existential problems as their starting point are also inadequate. Reducing Jesus to a moral example (Kant), or a redeeming archetype (Schleiermacher), simply makes the cross and resurrection an embarrassment. For Moltmann, the person and history of Jesus should be considered in the light of the language of Jewish expectation. Here the question asked of Jesus is: "Are you the one who is to come, or shall we look for another?" In answer to this question, his office should not be seen as upheld by the incarnation, or by his being the archetype of true humanity, "but by the future of the kingdom which is inaugurated in and around him."[26]

Moltmann considers the relationship between the Christ of faith and the historical Jesus to be of the utmost importance. Although he does not intend anything like a return to the ill-fated quest for the historical Jesus, he emphasizes the connection between Jesus' preaching and his person, and the significance of his death abandoned on the cross. Jesus' proclamation of the imminent arrival of the Kingdom of God meant that his preaching was inextricably bound up with his own personal destiny. With message and person thus identified, the disaster of Jesus' death implies the end of his eschatological message: "If his preaching is inseparable from his person, then his preaching dies with him on the cross." Moltmann himself, however, saw an alternative to such a conclusion. In the light of his vindication in the resurrection, Jesus' message of the Kingdom could now be proclaimed on a new basis, as the "word of the cross." Here the Jesus who preached becomes the Christ who is preached—the continuity lying in the identity of the crucified and risen one.[27]

Jesus' death must be interpreted in the context of his life and ministry, and in particular his conflict with the guardians of the law and the political religion of the *Pax Romana*.[28]

In his proclamation of the eschatological law of grace, Jesus placed his preaching and person above the authority of Moses and the Torah. His acts of forgiveness of sin would have been understood as the blasphemy of self-deification. Unlike the Jewish expectation of the Son of Man coming to judge sinners and redeem the righteous, "Jesus actually turned toward the sinners and the lost." With John the Baptist, Jesus preached the imminence of the Kingdom, though unlike John, the Kingdom does not come as judgment, but as the unconditional grace of God for the poor and for sinners. Jesus' authority was not derived from tradition, but came directly from the God whom he called "My Father." The discrepancy between his claim and his vulnerability meant that Jesus' preaching was open to refutation by crucifixion, and his death should be seen in terms of his provocation of the custodians of the law.[29]

The conflict with the custodians of the law was only part of Jesus' offence, as is evident from the fact that he was not punished by stoning, the prescribed treatment for blasphemers, but underwent crucifixion, a punishment reserved for crimes against the state. The *Pax Romana* was associated with the emperor cult, so Jesus would have been dealt with in the name of the state's gods. Moltmann takes up Oscar Cullmann's suggestion that it was the Roman authorities who captured Jesus for fear of revolt. The hearing before the high priest was merely a moral consultation to ensure his execution would not start an uprising of the Jews. The real trial was a political one, with the Sanhedrin acting in collusion with Pilate. The inscription "King of the Jews" was much too dangerous to have been simply invented by the primitive Church. Moltmann rejects Bultmann's view that the death of Jesus as a political offender was due to misunderstanding, and after a careful examination of Jesus' relationship with the Zealots concludes that Pilate's condemnation of Jesus as a rebel was not without some foundation. Although Jesus was no Zealot, his message did challenge the political religion of the Roman state.[30]

Even more significant than Jesus' death as a "blasphemer" and "rebel" was his complete abandonment by God. Discussing the New Testament evidence for this, Moltmann concludes: "Jesus died with the signs and expressions of a profound abandonment by God."[31] Jesus' proclamation of the imminence of God's Kingdom of free grace, his intimate relation with

God, whom he called "My Father," and his association of the decision of faith with his own person, all meant that he experienced the cross as a rejection by God. His message was so closely bound up with his own person that his death also inevitably meant the death of the cause for which he had lived. In his cry of dereliction, it is not his personal existence which is at stake, but his message of the Kingdom, and indeed the very deity of his God and Father.

What took place in the crucifixion can only be understood in trinitarian perspective. Rejecting the traditional distinction between the immanent and economic Trinity (i.e., God in himself and God as revealed in the economy of his saving acts), Moltmann sees the abandonment of Jesus upon the cross as the origin of the doctrine of God as Trinity.[32] The cross should not be understood as the "death of God," but "death *in* God," and along with Jesus' separation from his Father ("God against God"), requires the development of a trinitarian theology.[33] With the theodicy question firmly in view, Moltmann's emphasis is now not so much on God's futurity, but becomes radically incarnational: "God allows himself to be forced out. God suffers, and allows himself to be crucified and is crucified, and in this consummates his unconditional love."[34] In this identification with the forsaken, the Son gives himself up to abandonment, and the Father suffers the death of the Son in the "infinite grief of love."[35]

In Jesus' death, "Father and Son are most deeply separated in forsakenness and at the same time are most inwardly one in their surrender. What proceeds from this event between Father and Son is the Spirit which justifies the godless, fills the forsaken with love, and even brings the dead alive."[36] The inspiration behind Moltmann's theology of the cross is in a large measure Hegelian. Already in *Theology of Hope*, making use of Hegel, Moltmann had spoken of the "universalizing of the historic Good Friday of the god-forsakenness of Jesus, so that it becomes a speculative Good Friday of the forsakenness of all that is."[37] In *The Crucified God*, this insight is more fully explicated:

> The cross stands between the Father and the Son in all the harshness of his forsakenness. If one describes the life of God within the Trinity as the "history of God" (Hegel), this history contains within itself the whole abyss of godforsakenness, absolute death and the non-God....The concrete "history of God" in the death of Jesus on the cross on Golgotha therefore contains within itself all the depths and abysses of human history and therefore can be understood as the history of history. All human history, however much it may be determined by guilt and death, is taken up into the "history of God," i.e., into the Trinity, and integrated into the future of the "history of God."...the Trinity is

no self-contained group in heaven, but an eschatological process open for men on earth, which stems from the cross of Christ.[38]

The cross must also be viewed in the light of the resurrection and from an eschatological perspective.[39] Moltmann points out that the symbol of resurrection comes from Jewish apocalyptic expectation, the dominating theme of which is the question of the triumph of God's righteousness in the midst of suffering. Belief in the resurrection was a consequence of the realization that death sets no limit to God's justice. The issue of Jesus' resurrection is not simply a matter of whether it is a possible or conceivable event, but is primarily concerned with the question of the righteousness of God: "If God raised this dishonored man in his coming righteousness, it follows that in this crucified figure he manifests his true righteousness, the right of the unconditional grace which makes righteous the unrighteous and those without rights."[40]

Having summarized Moltmann's overall argument, we can now consider the political implications which he draws from it. For Moltmann, the death cry of Jesus means that Christian theology must hearken to the death cry of the wretched and suffering of this world.[41] Moreover, if the one crucified by the state has been vindicated in resurrection, then Christianity must accept the consequences of this for politics.[42] Although Jesus died the death of a political offender in dishonor and shame, the raising of the crucified one brings a reversal of values: "What the state has determined to be disgraceful is changed into what is supreme."[43]

Since God's being is manifested in the helplessness and death of Jesus "the gods of the power and riches of the world and world history then belong on the other side of the cross, for it was in their name that Jesus was crucified....If the crucified one is Kyrios, then the Caesars must renounce the title."[44] Thus, the authority of God no longer rests with the powerful and rich, but with the outcast Son of Man. All this means that Christian political theology must reject the political religions of society which uphold unjust social orders through giving them religious sanction. Since Constantine this has been the dominant form of Christianity, and even where there is a separation of church and state, modern "civic religion" performs a similar integrative function. The churches must become "institutions for the free criticism of society," and it must be recognized that in the death of Jesus God has shown himself to be "the God of the poor, the oppressed, and the humiliated."[45]

Moltmann maintains that Christian theology finds its relevance only through identification with the crucified Christ, and in solidarity with the suffering and oppressed. He describes his theology of the cross as "a critical and liberating theory of God and man."[46] This liberation must be effective amid the various dimensions of oppression that afflict humanity, of which he identifies five: (1) poverty in the economic sphere; (2) force in the political sphere; (3) racial and cultural alienation; (4) pollution; and (5) the "deeper" problem of "senselessness and godforsakenness." Within these different forms of oppression there exist "vicious circles," which are interlinked. For example, poverty leads to force, and force begets counter-force. Since these vicious circles compound one another, liberation must be active in all five dimensions. The vicious circle of poverty can be overcome through socialism. In political life the answer is democracy and human rights. With the problems of racial and cultural alienation, liberation "means identity in the recognition of others." With pollution the antidote lies in "peace with nature." In the existential problems facing all societies, liberation comes through the presence of meaning in life, with knowledge of God's presence in the godforsaken Christ bringing the "courage to be."[47]

To assess properly *The Crucified God* would require detailed exegetical and historical work. Moreover, the extent to which Moltmann's whole argument relies upon historical evidence lays him open to the charge that his basic methodology is flawed. Here I can only hope to briefly touch upon these issues.

The spectacular failure of the various nineteenth-century attempts to reconstruct the life of the historical Jesus—which tended to say more about the inquirer than the subject—has resulted in a near total skepticism concerning the Jesus of history in the present century. Yet the danger of reading into the Christian message our own preoccupations is in no way lessened by a retreat to "the Christ of faith," as Bultmann's existentialist reductionism demonstrates. Through the work of scholars such as Ernst Käsemann, the limited use of critical historical analysis of the Gospel accounts of Jesus is now more widely accepted as forming an important part of a responsible attempt to discern the scope and content of the Christian message and its continuity with the historical Jesus.[48] It is in this context that Moltmann's insistence on the relevance for Christian theology of what can be known—albeit only in bare outline—of Jesus' message and the manner of his death must be judged. His historical account of Jesus as an eschatological figure is one that is in line with the prophetic, apocalyptic, and utopian origins of the Christian faith, and since Schweitzer has become widely accepted.

The vexed question of the degree to which Jesus' ministry had a political nature is more complex—though Moltmann puts up a strong case that Jesus' message was seen as constituting a political threat to the established order.[49] Be that as it may, the task of relating political theology to its Christian origins is an essential one, which for all its difficulties Moltmann is right at least to attempt.

Moltmann's rejection of political religions of society on the basis of his theology of the cross, offers an instructive critique of the Church's cooption into the state, whether formally, with all the accoutrements of establishment status, or informally, through its accommodation to the dominant ideology in civil society. This rejection challenges the Church on its faithfulness to its mission. The conflictual character of Christ's ministry remains but a painful memory to the Church today, whose conscience too readily acquiesces in what amounts to its accommodation to the prevailing structures of society and the neglect of its prophetic responsibility. However, it is not sufficient to merely identify this problem; detailed social and political analysis is also required if the Church is to discern what its role in society should be.

But Moltmann does not examine in any depth the nature of the state in modern capitalist society or consider the ideological means it employs to secure allegiance and hegemony. Nor do we find any real consideration of the specific social forces that stand in opposition to the oppressive institutions of the state. Perhaps such an expectation is unrealistic, but it would at least be reassuring if he was more ready to indicate the need for such work.

Along with his observations on political religion, Moltmann also draws a number of specific political conclusions. Although these can be summarized as a call to take up the cause of the poor and oppressed, the particular objectives he avows are not especially revolutionary. Thus his program for dealing with the various dimensions of oppression is somewhat abstract and does not go far beyond a reformist social democratic framework. It is therefore not surprising that he should be criticized by advocates of "liberation theology," such as José Míguez Bonino and Enrique Dussell.[50] Although major reforms would undoubtedly do much to attenuate social division and other destructive features of capitalism, the utopianism within Christian theology surely suggests a higher objective than the possible achievements of welfare capitalism—the sustainability of which is in any case questionable. Moltmann might no doubt concede the point, but in the absence of any sustained reflection upon a more avowedly socialist politics, or analysis of class forces and the question of agency, it is difficult to avoid the conclusion that his work remains within a liberal and reformist perspective. It is to be regretted that in his more recent books he has occupied himself with more doctrinal matters, and insofar as he has continued to deal with political issues his preoccupation with ecology seems to have eclipsed all else.[51]

Contrasting liberation theology's "option for socialism and a Marxist analysis," Míguez Bonino rightly asks of Moltmann: "Can we remain satisfied with a general description of 'the demonic circles of death,' without trying to understand them in their unity, their roots, their dynamics, i.e., without giving a coherent socio-analytic account of this manifold oppression?"[52] Although Moltmann rightly insists that a critical distance must be maintained toward historical movements, since the Kingdom of God can never be identified with any given historical reality, this does not preclude a critical solidarity with socialist movements—as his own predilection for the reformist variety suggests. In an open letter to Míguez Bonino, Moltmann stresses the difference between European and Latin American conditions. This is perfectly true, but does the absence of a revolutionary or even pre-revolutionary situation in Europe warrant the abandonment of Marxian analysis and the hope for a classless society?[53]

One invaluable contribution which Moltmann's theology of the cross does make to political theology lies in its serious attention to the reality of evil and of suffering. A political theology which simply baptized the hope for a future classless society, and did not have anything to say concerning previous generations would be ultimately dehumanizing. The hope for God's salvation is that it should be seen on this earth, but even its eventual triumph still leaves us with the plight of those untouched by it. The knowledge of God's participation in human suffering and the victory of his love over even death itself does at least begin to address the question of the tragedy of history. The future must not become a "Moloch" to which the memory of previous generations is sacrificed, since to suppress such a memory would be to demean ourselves.

The particular trinitarian theology which Moltmann expounds in his theology of the cross is more problematic. In conflating the economic and immanent Trinity, and making the cross constitutive for the inner life of the Trinity, the divine essence becomes subject to temporality and loses its independence from creation.[54] Moltmann's later thinking on the Trinity was similarly inadequate. Thus in *The Church in the Power of the Spirit*, although widening the scope of his discussion beyond the cross, he again understands the trinitarian being of God in historical and eschatological terms, drawing a distinction between the "Trinity in the origin" and "the Trinity in the glorification."[55] In *The Trinity and the Kingdom of God*, he speaks of "interaction" between the immanent and economic Trinity, and argues that as a completed reality the immanent Trinity has its locus in the future.[56] Thus Moltmann's strong emphasis upon the incarnation, and the trinitarianism associated with it, remains in continuity with his futurist eschatology. This eschatological understanding of the mode of God's being was central to Moltmann's political theology, and a theme which he developed in a number of essays to which we must now turn, in order to fully consider its significance.

Eschatology and the Future

Moltmann rejects both traditional theistic and modern anthropological conceptions of God, and argues that God should always be considered in relation to the future. Classical theism, where God is thought of as "the absolute," "the universal," has been completely undermined by the present-day scientific and technological worldview.[57] The cosmological proofs for the existence of God have lost their power "since modern man no longer understands himself as a part of the cosmos, but has placed the world as material of his scientific and technical possibilities over against himself. He no longer lives in the house of ordered being but in the open history of a technical transformation of the world." In reaction to this collapse of traditional metaphysics anthropological theology turns its attention to human subjectivity and the "identity question," "the question of man as to his authenticity."[58]

Behind the theistic worldview, Moltmann argues, lies the theodicy question, which classical theism attempts to answer through its vision of an orderly cosmos. Today this question presents itself in an even more pressing form, and instead of being an indictment against God becomes an accusation against ourselves that demands a political theology concerned with establishing God's righteousness in the world. Existential theology must similarly look toward a political theology, since the identity question must be considered in relation to the social and political dimension of human existence, and identity cannot be found without participation in the struggle for justice and a more human world. Thus the former ways in which the divinity of God has been understood must be taken up into the question of the coming of God's Kingdom amid injustice and suffering: "Political theology unites cosmological theology and the theology of existence in the eschatological understanding of the history of man and the world."[59]

For Moltmann, the future must not be seen merely as the extrapolation of the present, but as the anticipation of the new reality and liberating future that God will bring.[60] Nor must transcendence be perceived in terms of the "finitude of all things" or the "subjectivity of man," but rather as "a qualitatively different, transforming and new future." Here transcendence is concerned with "revolutionary consciousness" and the transformation of existing social conditions. Thus, rejecting metaphysical and existential interpretations, Moltmann speaks of "the future as a new paradigm of transcendence."[61]

This ontological primacy of the future is only assured if the future is understood as the "mode of God's being." Here the reality of God is no longer sought "beyond us" or "in us," but "in front of us." Moltmann uses the words *"Futurum"* and *"Adventus"* to further elucidate his own response to the question of the priority of the future in eschatology. He points out that the original meaning of the German word *"Zukunft,"* which is the translation of the Latin *"adventus,"* is "the 'arrival' or 'coming' of something other, something new and transforming, which had not yet been present in that form and is still not present as yet." Future in the sense of *adventus* does not emerge from the present, rather "the present springs from a future which one must be expectant of in transience." In contrast, *"Futurum* means that which will be, what is going to arise from the becoming of being." Thus he arrives at the distinction between *Futurum*, meaning the temporal prolonging of being, and *Zukunft*, which is "the soul of time." "The *adventus Dei,*" he writes, "takes the place of the *futurum* of being."[62]

In his understanding of the mode of God's being Moltmann is heavily indebted to the ontology of Ernst Bloch. For Bloch, utopian being replaces the static notion of being in Greek metaphysics. This change in emphasis is welcomed by Moltmann, who enthusiastically accepts Bloch's category of "that-which-is-not-yet," describing it as a "magnificent conception." However, although Bloch's ontology provided Moltmann with certain formal categories, it was not definitive for his doctrine of God. Thus, with Bloch's speculative metaphysics and process theologies in mind, he contends, "God's being is coming," and "does not lie in the process of the world's becoming."[63]

Moltmann stresses repeatedly that eschatology must be conceived as the arrival of that which is a new reality. Future as *adventus* must not be confused with the *futurum* of being, since it brings "something which is principally new and radically transforming, which is neither in its reality nor in its potentiality already in existence."[64] To express this he speaks of a *"novum ex nihilo,"* where that which is new arises "not out of the possibilities which we possess," but through "God's creative act."[65]

Moltmann's understanding of eschatology in terms of the arrival of the future rather than simply the extrapolation of the present does help express the element of transcendence in history. However, the language he uses suggests an unhelpful severing of the relation between past and future insofar as he understands transcendence as not bearing any relation to the immanent processes of history. Indeed so strong is his emphasis on the "novum," that he falls into a form of quasi-supernaturalism, in the sense that the activity of God is presented in opposition to the workings of the created order. Although Moltmann was right in rejecting Bloch's speculative doctrine of entelechy, with its conception of the future being processed out of the womb of matter itself, he should have left room for an understanding of the future as the product of *human* endeavor and striving.

Rubem Alves perceptively describes Moltmann's position as "a 90-degree rotation of the idea of transcendence of the early Barth." Alves goes on to correctly observe that the "structure of transcendence" is "always dialectical and historical, and never undialectical and ahistorically related to the transcendent hope."[66] Such a perspective includes the possibility of that which is genuinely new and not merely unfolding, but still sees it as emerging from the present. By not placing an adequate emphasis upon the role of human participation, Moltmann undermines the motivation for the human action which is necessary to secure change. He also precludes the possibility of a positive assessment of secular political movements, since if divine action is unrelated to historical realities it is difficult to see how such movements can be ascribed any significance. Although Moltmann does sometimes mention the need for cooperation with secular movements, he provides no theological basis for it. His perception of transcendence must therefore be judged as unproductive for the development of a political theology.[67]

Equally unsatisfactory is Moltmann's notion of the future as God's mode of being. Such a position denies God's independence from created reality, and thereby destroys the foundations of a Christian doctrine of creation. There is also a problem of consistency, since if the deity of God is confined to the future, how can we speak of divine activity in the present? That Moltmann clearly wishes to do so, at least in some form, is clear from his somewhat vague assertions that "God is already present in the way in which his future masters the present," and "as the power of the future, God works into the present." Concerning the incarnation, he offers insights in line with his argument in *The Crucified God*, and speaks of "the presence of the future of God in this particular person," and says plainly that "in passion and resurrection God acts in Jesus."[68] Similarly, he writes that in Christ is found

resurrection," fails to recognize the significance of the human emancipation that is *possible* within human history.[77] The socialist hope offers us the prospect of a society free from the inequality and alienation of capitalism, with democratic rights established not just in the political but also in the economic sphere, and with advanced productivity providing the material basis for the full development of the individual. This hope constitutes a social utopia which could become an increasingly realizable goal if the inherited productive and technical wealth of humankind were to be subordinated to truly human ends and more justly distributed. Does not Christian theology have to situate itself in relation to this prospect of a period of history, which although not the ultimate Kingdom of God, is qualitatively different from all previous history? Is not the hope of this immanent utopia even more of a driving force for human motivation and aspiration precisely because it is radically *this*-worldly? Important as the hope and solace of the eschatology of the resurrection may be, it becomes escapism if it leads us to abandon our hope for this earth.

Behind Moltmann's critique of Bloch is his antipathy to some central features of Marx's thought. In his book *Man: Christian Anthropology in the Conflicts of the Present*, Moltmann discusses Marx's account of alienation and its overcoming in "the utopia of the total man." He criticizes Marx for failing to distinguish alienation under capitalism from industrial alienation, which the elimination of capitalism will not bring to a close. Nor will communism resolve existential alienation or provide the answer to mankind's religious and metaphysical needs. When Marxism rejects religion, the "authority of the absolute" is identified with "the future total man," and this Moltmann sees as leading to totalitarianism: "If 'God' is only man's idea of his humanity, then this category, which means the future society of mankind, and so in concrete terms the future of the party which represents that mankind as its *avant-garde*, takes over the functions of divine authority."[78]

In *Theology and Joy* Moltmann rejects as essentially Aristotelian Marx's emphasis on free productive activity as the means by which human individuals find their humanity. This he argues does not break with capitalism's "compulsion of works," which is simply reordered "so that labour for the sake of others is changed into activity for its own sake and outside determination is replaced with self-determination."[79]

As a criticism of the Marx of the *Paris Manuscripts*, Moltmann's insistence on the continuance of existential alienation is perfectly valid. However, his other observations are more questionable. Marx's vision of a society controlled by the producers themselves, with vastly reduced labor time, and where the skills associated with a high degree of automation make even necessary labor fulfilling, would largely remove alienation from the sphere of work. The continuance of alienated labor only applies to bureaucratic collectivist states prior to such advanced conditions. The notion that in socialism workers would be tied to a "compulsion of works" hardly squares with Marx's idea of socialism as being based upon productive conditions which abolish scarcity and where necessary work becomes marginal. Work is the very thing people are not tied to—they are free as never before to develop as artistic, scientific and social individuals. The charge of totalitarianism is equally incorrect since for Marx (and Bloch) political freedom was a prerequisite for socialism. Existing states based on collective ownership, which deny political rights, should not be confused with future communist society. In suggesting that totalitarianism is inseparable from Marxism, Moltmann reveals very strikingly the gulf between his political theology and the liberation theologies of the third world. Although elsewhere Moltmann stresses the relationship between socialism and democracy, his treatment of this question is too cursory to remove the inconsistencies in his position.[80]

Had Moltmann taken a more positive view of the Marxian utopia his theology would not have provided him with any framework in which to interpret its significance. For him the Kingdom belongs to the future and is fulfilled when God is all in all—in history there are only anticipations of the future Kingdom. How these anticipations relate to each other and whether history leads to a specific manifestation of the Kingdom that is qualitatively different from all that precedes it is not a question that Moltmann particularly addresses. This is surprising, since the issue is surely raised by any faithful wrestling with Bloch's idea of "concrete utopia"—the realm of human freedom on this earth. Moltmann is entitled to criticize the more extravagant features of Marx's and Bloch's utopias, but in dismissing them completely he reveals how uneschatological his theology has become.

Moltmann rightly recognized that Weiss and Schweitzer have thrown down the fundamental challenge to twentieth-century theology. But like Barth, who also made eschatology his starting point, Moltmann ends up by abandoning a radical this-worldly perspective in terms of his perception of the Kingdom. To replace Barth's "Wholly Other" with the "Wholly Future" makes it no less of a transcendent irrelevance. If eschatology is not about God's Kingdom on this earth, it is not eschatology in the way Weiss and Schweitzer understood it. This does not mean rejecting ultimate and transcendent fulfillment, but simply affirming—with Jesus, the prophets, and medieval chiliasm—the utopia of the kingdom of human freedom *in* history.

The way in which Moltmann so substantially parts company with Bloch raises questions about the use he makes of Bloch's philosophy. To take the central categories of Bloch's utopian philosophy while jettisoning its core is to wrench them out of context and deprive them of their original meaning and creative power. Moltmann may have been inspired by Bloch's philosophy of hope but in the most crucial respect his theology is in fact its antithesis. It is therefore no surprise that, referring to a meeting he had with Bloch, Gerald O'Collins should record: "Bloch seemed to fear that the theologians might blunt the revolutionary edge of his philosophy."[81]

Despite the criticism in much of this chapter, it should still be acknowledged that Moltmann's political theology constitutes a considerable achievement. His enterprising attempt to view the whole of theology in an eschatological light presents us with an interpretation of the Christian faith that acknowledges its social and political implications. He also usefully delineates the necessarily comprehensive scope of political theology. If political theology is to be more than simply a branch of theology, then the kind of restructuring of our perceptions of the Christian faith, at least in part along the lines Moltmann suggests, is essential. Yet his work leaves us with a suggestive but unfinished agenda. How does future social and political liberation relate to the present movements and developments in human history? To what extent should political theology engage in detailed sociopolitical analysis, and what use must it make of Marxist theory? How should a political theology relate to traditional theism and modern existentialist theology? What sort of ontology is required in understanding God in relation to the future and the prospect of liberation which it holds? Is there yet more that Christian theology must learn from Bloch's perception of the kingdom of human freedom as a possibility within human history? How can our hopes for the future be reconciled with the tragedy of the past?

Moltmann would be the first to concede the provisionality of all Christian theology. It is in that spirit that the criticism and development of his political theology must proceed.

Chapter 9

Political Theology in Union with Socialist Utopianism

Still casting its shadow over any attempt to construct a socialist political theology is the conference held at Tambach in 1919, where Karl Barth distanced himself from the continental religious socialist movement on the grounds that the Kingdom of God must never be identified with any human political movement.[1] As a motive for complete withdrawal from, or a much more restrained commitment to, the socialist movement, this reservation has exerted a powerful influence upon individuals and the life of the Church in our present century.

Barth's criticism must be accepted, but not the corollary that is often drawn from it, which justifies disengaging adherence to the Christian faith from political commitment. Although the Kingdom of God cannot be unequivocally identified with any political ideology or movement, the Church cannot remain neutral in a world of conflicting and competing ideologies. A socialist political theology represents an attempt to enter into *critical* solidarity with the socialist movement, based upon the belief that socialism represents the political option that in our time expresses the demand of the Kingdom.

Given the many variants of what is commonly thought to constitute socialism, it is necessary to be clear about the kind of socialism here envisaged. Certainly it is not communism as it has hitherto existed, where the absence of democracy and entrenched bureaucracy stifles human freedom. Nor is it the kind of mixed economy associated with Keynesianism and the advent of welfare capitalism, where socialism is reduced to a concern with only the amelioration of social conditions under capitalism. It is to the vision of a classless society, with democracy and social justice, made possible through the communal ownership and control of society's productive resources, which are sufficiently developed to remove all want, that we must turn.

In the Western world, for most of the present century Marx has been seen through the eyes of the official ideology of Marxism-Leninism, and regarded as a determinist and scientific thinker whose ideas formed the basis for Soviet society and polity. Explicating the humanist vision that motivated Marx, and inspired his notion of a society of human emancipation and freedom, reveals a very different picture. Here social harmony, justice, human fulfillment, and the conquest of the alienation that pervades capitalist society are the hallmarks of what is an essentially utopian credo.

Against such a project, how can religious withdrawal be justified? Is not Christianity itself, in its own vision of the Kingdom, striving for such an end? Although the extra-historical fulfillment of the Kingdom has often been emphasized at the expense of its inner-historical manifestation, there are today indications of a recovery of temporal expectations. Once the utopian content of Christianity is recognized, the community of interest and purpose with the Marxian hope for the future classless society, or as Ernst Bloch puts it the "*regnum humanum,*" is evident.

The inner-historical and extra-historical dimensions of the Kingdom of God in this perspective must be seen within the wider context of the manifold relationship of the Kingdom of God to history. The socialist utopia of a stage in history that can be characterized as the *realm of human freedom*, represents a manifestation of the Kingdom of God within history, which must be distinguished from both previous historical anticipations of the Kingdom and the Kingdom in its ultimate fulfillment. Tillich and Moltmann did not place the anticipations of the Kingdom in such an eschatological framework. To do so requires that the socialist utopia be accorded a special status, and it is here that the idea of the *millennium* makes it possible to interpret theologically the socialist hope for a qualitatively new society. Here it is not the pre-millennialist 1000-year mystical reign of Christ and the Saints that is envisaged, but the idea of a final, more liberated stage of human history which is distinct from all that precedes it.

Suggesting the need to revive the tradition of millenarianism may be thought fanciful, but is it not precisely this tradition which provides the best means of expressing the hopes for a classless society, with which a socialist political theology identifies? To argue in this way raises the issue of what might be an appropriate ontology for a theology which sought to reject the complete demise of the idea of the millennium through its identification with the Church, and wished to restore its original more revolutionary intent.

One of the major criticisms of both Tillich and Moltmann made in the present work concerns the ontology that formed the basis for their eschatology. In the case of Tillich, his eschatology was undermined by the Platonic structure in which it was so often expressed. The difficulty with Moltmann's ontology was that in his legitimate desire to give the primacy to the future in eschatology, he introduced an understanding of the mode of God's being and reverse causality which proved contradictory, and made the Deity itself subject to temporality, so that God's divinity and independence from creation was no longer assured.

In the light of such precedents, it might reasonably be thought that the wisest course for political theology would be to avoid ontology altogether. It is not only the problems of eschatology which raise the question of whether theology should occupy itself with ontological considerations. The logical difficulties of "two nature christology," which has its basis in Greek metaphysics, is another example. Moreover, since Kant, should not all forms of metaphysical reflection be abandoned?

Few would advocate the more speculative type of metaphysics. However, not everyone is prepared to concede that the logical positivists should have the last word on this issue. John Macquarrie defends a limited role for ontology in his discussion of existentialist metaphysics, which he describes as descriptive rather than speculative:

> No ontology is final or adequate. The flash of ontological insight, however, may be reckoned the most precious knowledge which we have. And although its truth cannot be established objectively, it is true to the extent that it yields a fuller interpretation of the existence of the persons who adhere to it....It supplies a basis for an ever-widening structure of intelligibility and meaning; and with widening of this structure, the ontology itself gets confirmation.[2]

Macquarrie's discussion develops the notion of "experiential verification" from Tillich's *Systematic Theology*.[3] Both correctly maintain that logical positivism is not necessarily a veto on ontology. Theology must be prepared to make statements and ask questions about both the infinite Being of God and our finite human being, and this will surely require some sort of ontology. But this still leaves us with the need to decide what might constitute a valid ontology for a political theology which shares socialism's utopianism.

Within the Christian tradition extensive use has been made of Platonism. However, the adequacy of Platonic metaphysics is now widely questioned, and a variety of attempts to develop alternative ontologies have been made, such as "process" theology and the "futurist" theologies of Moltmann and Pannenberg.[4] One difficulty with these alternatives—as we have shown in the case of Moltmann—is whether in a doctrine of God it is permissible that God should be made subject to temporality. Platonism avoided this problem, though only at the expense of a loss of historical consciousness. A suitable solution might be to maintain—with Platonism—a conception of God's being as independent of the modes of time, but to insist that the way God works in history is such as to give priority to future. Here a historical understanding of reality and the idea that history itself has a goal and purpose is affirmed, without vitiating divine transcendence. In terms of a trinitarian theology, this would involve the belief that prior to creation the divine life is complete within itself. Creation and the world process add nothing essential to the divinity of God, but do represent the overflowing of the fullness of the divine life in love—with the objective of fulfilling a definite purpose and goal *within* human history as well as beyond it. Hence the importance of the traditional distinction between the immanent and economic Trinity— rejected by Moltmann—which affirmed the love of God for creation as a matter of grace and not necessity. Relating all this to our theme, the possibility of the unfolding of history leading to the arrival of a qualitatively new society is thus placed within a theological context.

To interpret the socialist hope for universal peace, economic justice, and an end to the alienation within capitalism as the fulfillment of Christianity's millennial dreams, is undoubtedly controversial. Most theologians either equate the idea of the millennium with the Church or relegate it to mythology, whereas here it is identified with the outcome of an existing secular historical movement. However, it seems a strange irony that Karl Rahner in his introductory essay to Roger Garaudy's *From Anathema to Dialogue*, should offer the following singularly unhelpful contribution to that dialogue:

> *Christianity does not promise any intra-mundane future utopia.* It does indeed declare that the decision for the individual human being is realized with his *death*, whether he has made himself open to God's absolute future or not by his actions. But in regard to the collective history of mankind as such, it has yet no indication of how long this intra-mundane collective history is to last. And in regard to the material *content* of this future, it is likewise neutral. It does not set up any ideals of the future with a particular content, makes no prognoses about these and does not impose on man an obligation in regard to any particular goals of his intra-mundane future.[5]

Rahner partially qualifies this in subsequent paragraphs, but it is difficult to resist the jibe that here the "absolute future" is in danger of becoming absolutely irrelevant. Why the prospect of history unfolding toward a future of greater human freedom should be greeted with such agnosticism is far from clear. Although the potential for the abuse of human freedom—which in a nuclear age is painfully evident—makes the millennium only a hope and possibility, that in itself would hardly be a reason for adopting a "neutral" stance in relation to it. Rahner is rightly anxious that no finite future should be confused with the absolute future, but is this a justification for abandoning mankind's temporal hopes or evacuating history of "content"?

It is of course true that there are some weighty objections to a political theology which adopts a favorable stance toward Marxism and socialist utopianism. In particular, three questions need to be considered: (1) Does not the antipathy of Marxism toward religion undermine such a project? (2) Is not utopianism incompatible with the Christian doctrine of human nature? (3) What does Marxism have to say with regard to existential concerns and the problems of death, evil, and suffering?

The Implications of the Marxist Critique of Religion

The background to the formulation of Marx's critique of religion was the criticism of religion in Germany among the Young Hegelian School, beginning with Strauss' *Life of Jesus* in 1835. When Marx moved to Berlin in 1837, he joined a discussion group of Young Hegelians, forming a close friendship with Bruno Bauer, a leading member of the group. Bauer's critical work on the Gospels, and his strident attack upon Christianity, had quickly earned him a reputation, and many of the metaphors Marx was to use in his critique of religion were adapted from Bauer.[6] The other dominant figure in the growing controversy on religion was Ludwig Feuerbach, whose critical study of the Christian faith, *The Essence of Christianity*, was published in 1841. Marx's atheism (like Bauer's) was of the militant variety, and he did not think religion could be purified or humanized as did Feuerbach. Nonetheless, when Marx came to outline his views on religion Feuerbach's influence was unmistakable.

According to Feuerbach, religion has no objective content, but is merely a fantastic projection and distortion of human nature: "Man—this is the mystery of religion—projects his being into objectivity, and then makes himself an object to this projected image of himself thus converted into a subject....Thus in God man has his own activity as an object...God is, *per se*, his relinquished self."[7] Religion arises when human beings objectify the essence of humanity—the divine qualities of goodness, justice, and love being objectified qualities of the human race. In this process of projection people dehumanize themselves and become the victims of a self-inflicted alienation. If all the riches of the human essence are to be bestowed on an imaginary God, then human beings are denied them: "To enrich God, man must become poor; that God may be all, man must be nothing."[8] For Feuerbach, the secret of theology is anthropology: "The beginning, middle and end of religion is MAN."[9] In his later writings he locates the origin of religious projection in human feelings of helplessness and dependence on nature, as well as in fear of death.[10]

In the opening pages of his *Critique of Hegel's Philosophy of Right: Introduction* (1844), Marx takes up the Feuerbachian themes of religious projection and alienation: "Man who looked for a superhuman being in the fantastic reality of heaven and found nothing there but a *reflection* of himself, will no longer be disposed to find the *semblance* of himself, only an inhuman being, where he seeks and must seek his true reality." Summing up his argument he writes, "*man makes religion*, religion does not make man."[11]

Like Feuerbach, Marx understood religion as necessarily detracting from personal freedom and humanity, since what is given to God must be taken from the individual. As early as his doctoral thesis he writes: "Philosophy makes no secret of it. The confession of Prometheus: 'In simple words, I hate the pack of gods' is its own confession, its own aphorism against all heavenly and earthly gods who do not acknowledge human self-consciousness as the highest divinity. It will have none other beside."[12] Religion must therefore be rejected, and humankind must become the center of its own universe: "Religion is only the illusory sun which revolves round man as long as he does not revolve round himself."[13]

For Marx, religious self-alienation is a product of political and economic alienation—it is the fantasy of alienated humanity. Thus he speaks of religion as the "sigh of the oppressed creature," and "the *fantastic realization* of the human essence because the *human essence* has no true reality." Here Marx moved beyond Feuerbach, since his primary concern was to expose the social roots of religion: "This state, this society, produce religion, an *inverted world-consciousness*, because they are an *inverted world*."[14]

Marx assigned to religion the function of legitimizing the political and economic status quo. Religion sees the political order as divinely ordained, and gives it moral sanction. Religion also provides an illusory hope for people which becomes a compensation for suffering. This provoked perhaps Marx's most famous aphorism on religion as "the *opium* of the people," though the idea of religion as an opiate was by no means original to Marx. Religion decorates the chains of oppression with "imaginary flowers" of consolation. It turns its adherents' attention to an illusory heaven, distracting them from the real world where change is possible, and reinforcing their trapped situation. It thus contributes further to human alienation, by confirming oppressed humanity in its predicament.[15]

Since religion has a social origin, Marx insisted that the criticism of religion must lead on to the criticism of society. Thus he gave his critique a definite revolutionary twist:

> The immediate *task of philosophy*, which is at the service of history, once the *holy form* of human self-estrangement has been unmasked, is to unmask self-estrangement in its *unholy forms*. Thus the criticism of heaven turns into the criticism of the earth, the *criticism of religion* into the *criticism of law* and the *criticism of theology* into the *criticism of politics*.[16]

It was Marx's essentially humanist orientation which convinced him that revolutionary activity and the realization of human freedom must form the necessary complement to the critique of religion: "The criticism of religion ends with the teaching that *man is the highest being for man*, hence with the *categorical imperative to overthrow all relations* in which man is a debased, enslaved, forsaken, despicable being."[17]

Marx's view of the way in which religious consciousness and ideas are related to the material and social situation was further elaborated in 1845-46, when he outlined his materialist conception of history in his *Theses on Feuerbach* and in *The German Ideology*. Rejecting Feuerbach's purely contemplative materialism, Marx emphasized human interaction with nature and the basic importance of economic life. Given that "religious sentiment" was "a social product," as he puts it in his seventh thesis, he insisted that the approach to the study of religion must be via an examination of actual material circumstances. Thus in *The German Ideology*, he recommended taking material production and the associated mode of cooperation as the starting point, and attempting to "explain all the different theoretical products and forms of consciousness, religion, philosophy, ethics, etc. etc. and trace their origin and growth from that basis."[18] Here religious ideas are considered alongside other forms of ideology, and are denied any autonomy. This more detailed explanation of religion complemented Marx's earlier assessment of religion as the projection of alienated humanity. It also—at least in theory—opened the way for an account of the specific forms of religion under different socioeconomic conditions. Marx himself only occasionally ventured such judgments in the course of dealing with other questions. A notable example occurs in his treatment of commodity fetishism in *Capital*, where he observes that in capitalist society: "Christianity with its religious cult of man in the abstract, more particularly in its bourgeois development, i.e., in Protestantism, Deism, etc., is the most fitting form of religion."[19]

We must now consider the question of the extent to which Marx's theory of religion constitutes a refutation of the claims of Christianity.

People may indeed project religions, but that does not mean that all religion is therefore just projection. It is quite fallacious to argue that psychological and social explanations of the origin of religion thereby justify ontological statements concerning the reality of God. Christian revelation, which takes place in and through ordinary human experience, will always be susceptible to this sort of interpretation. However, such explanations do not refute the theological claims made concerning the reality of God, but merely say something, at the psychological and sociological level, about the way in which such claims have been arrived at. People may well make religion, but the question still remains whether the religion they make also becomes "a structure of discovery," to use Nicholas Lash's phrase, in and through which divine disclosure takes place.[20] Marx is guilty of the genetic fallacy, in thinking that in explaining the origin of something he has thereby explained it away. The idea of religion as projection is open to a religious as well as a naturalistic interpretation.

Marx is also mistaken in his belief that the notion of God excludes human freedom. For him, Prometheus becomes the hero of the human struggle for freedom against the gods. But here Marx speaks as though God and humanity were of one and the same essence. However, in the Christian tradition God is not a being beside other beings, but is, to use Paul Tillich's expression, "being-itself." Nor does divine agency contradict human freedom, since the divine purpose is operative in and through human freedom. For Marx, it is essential to human freedom that people become the center of their own universe, and cease to revolve around the "illusory sun" of the God of their imagination. Yet this presents us with a false dilemma, since if the affirmation of God is also an affirmation of humanity, then in living in relationship with its Creator humanity is true to itself.

In his basic anthropology Marx develops themes from renaissance humanism and enlightenment philosophy, incorporating them into his own particular form of radical atheism. It is possible to accept much of Marx's positive and affirmative view of humanity, while repudiating the atheism which distorts his perspective. Christianity too, despite its realism regarding the human capacity for sin, also has a high doctrine of human nature. Thus the creation account introduces the idea of *imageo Dei* (Genesis 1:26), placing humankind at the very summit of the created order.

The creation ordinance (Genesis 1:28 and 2:15) confers a divine commission to take responsibility for the world and exercise dominion over it—a call to creatively shape and transform the real world of society and politics. Thus José Míguez Bonino writes: "Creation is the installation of a movement, it is an invitation and a command to man to create his own history and culture, creatively to transform the world, and make it into his own house and to explore the configurations of human relationships available to him."[21] Christian theology can therefore welcome the Marxian injunction to "overthrow all relations in which man is a debased, enslaved, forsaken, despicable being." Marx was right to place human liberation at the center of his thinking, but rather than viewing this as a commission from God, he mistakenly regarded the very notion of God as antithetical to the realization of human freedom.

Although Marx was clearly criticizing religion as such, it is also true that in part he was attacking the form which religion took in his day. He was faced with an institutionalized form of religion which favored the interests of the ruling class, and which was preoccupied with other-worldly concerns. This critique of the negative social role of the Church was entirely justified and retains its relevance. The only way the Church can effectively respond to Marx's criticism is through transforming itself and placing itself in the vanguard of human freedom. As the heretical sects of the Middle Ages, continental religious socialism, and present-day political theologies clearly testify, Christianity is not without its revolutionary potential. For Marx, religion gives only an illusory hope for the future. But if the Christian hope of the coming Kingdom of God implies a power which is also manifest *within* human history, then far from hindering the revolutionary process, this hope provides the power and impetus for the transformation of historical conditions. This point must surely be conceded by Marxists, since even if belief in God is regarded as idealist nonsense it is still possible for certain forms of religion to exercise a positive influence on revolutionary consciousness.

Marx in fact recognized that religion was in part a *"protest* against real distress," though for him this aspect of religion was outweighed by the misguided form which the protest assumed.[22] But the idea of religion as protest was to bear fruit with the work of Ernst Bloch, who saw the value for Marxism of the utopian content of religion.[23] "True materialism," he writes, "while voiding the transcendence and reality of any divine hypostasis, does so without stripping the final qualitative contents of the process, the real utopia of a realm of freedom." Speaking of religion as "a *total hope*, and an explosive one," Bloch associates the origin of religion with the projection of a kingdom that lies ahead, and not beyond. Here religion is a protest against and rejection of existing conditions, and the herald of a new future of human freedom. Seen in the light of the Exodus, and through the social utopias of the prophets, religion is no opiate, but evokes discontent and stimulates action.[24]

Against a utopianized Christianity Marx's critique loses much of its force, since the motivation to transform existing conditions is given a priority of comparable importance to that which it had for Marx. It is only in relation to other expressions of Christianity that the Marxian critique becomes a suitable, and indeed much needed, tool of *religious* criticism.

Since he had no ambitions to reform religion, such a concession would have been unacceptable to Marx, for whom the criticism of religion was "the premise of all criticism."[25] Marx's atheism cannot be separated from his basic methodology. Thus in his materialist conception of history he developed the idea that history should be understood as the "self-creation" of humankind—demystifying Hegel's idealist philosophy by substituting human activity for absolute Spirit.[26]

But cannot the working of the divine purpose be perceived as unfolding in and through human endeavor? If it can, then belief in God does not destroy human freedom, and there exists no inherent incompatibility between historical materialism and Christian theism. Marx's reading of Christian theology was in fact a supernaturalist one, which in modern theology has become widely discredited. For example, Wolfhart Pannenberg, in his concept of "revelation as history," rejects the notion of "direct" revelation, and argues that revelation as direct unmediated theophany (i.e., through divine appearances) should be abandoned in favor of an understanding of revelation as "indirect." Here revelation takes place through the ordinary events of history, and thus does not overturn the natural order or historical process.[27] As with any scientific explanation, Marx's theory of history must be submitted to rational scrutiny. Theology itself is not concerned with providing a competing explanation of the detailed workings of the historical process, since the religious interpretation of events is a complementary one which addresses itself to the *meaning* of history.

This response to Marx's atheism differs from much of recent liberation theology, which has tended to ignore the atheism of Marxism and concentrate on utilizing Marxism as a suitable method for the scientific analysis of society. In this approach it has been influenced by the French Marxist, Louis Althusser, who makes a distinction between Marxism as a "science," and its "ideology." But this presupposes a division between the later "scientific" Marx and the earlier "humanist" Marx. Moreover, such an approach may avoid certain difficulties, but only at the expense of neglecting the problems that serious dialogue poses.[28]

It must be conceded, however, that although the perspective outlined above makes it possible for Christians consistently to affirm some of the central tenets of Marxian socialism, it still remains the case that atheism is integral to how Marxism defines itself. This, coupled with the need to be both critical of the deficiencies in Marxism and alert to the richness of the non-Marxist socialist tradition, makes the idea of a *Christian Marxism* problematic.

View of Human Nature

We now move on to consider the second issue that was noted, the objection that socialist utopianism is incompatible with the Christian doctrine of human nature.

The charges of utopianism and an inadequate anthropology have been recurring criticisms of recent liberation theology, and it will be instructive to consider the sharp attack upon liberation theology from the proponents of the influential tradition of "Christian Realism," stemming from the work of Reinhold Niebuhr. Despite his earlier Marxist sympathies, Niebuhr came to vehemently reject Marxism because of its utopianism, and in his Christian Realism he advocated reform within a continuing capitalist structure and support for the mixed economy and the welfare state as the appropriate response for Christian social ethics.[29]

In line with this tradition, Thomas Sanders criticizes liberation theology for its "soft" utopianism and "'moralistic' ideology in utopian form," which fail to take seriously the reality of sin or to appreciate the moral ambiguity in all political decisions. Rejecting the idea of revolutionary change, Sanders argues for a more piecemeal and pragmatic approach.[30] This closely echoed Niebuhr's scathing rejection of Marxism's utopianism:

> It sought to establish the kingdom of perfect brotherhood or perfect justice on earth. It completely failed to appreciate the possibility of corruption through self-interest in any structure of society....It prompted the illusion that the

"socialization" of property would radically alter human character. Men would cease to be selfish and would live in complete harmony with one another. This is the very root of the utopian illusions of Marxism.[31]

In the face of such criticism it is necessary to be clear about the claim which socialism is making about the future society. From reading Gustavo Gutiérrez it might be assumed that human nature will completely change on the other side of the revolution. Thus, speaking of the "creation of a new man," he writes: "That creation is the place of encounter between political liberation and the communion of all men with God. This communion implies liberation from sin, the ultimate root of all injustice, all exploitation, all dissidence among men [sic]."[32] But such an assertion is in danger of confusing the liberation from the *specific* forms of alienation and exploitation with which Marxism is concerned, with the elimination of all disharmony and strife that arises from the human condition. It is true that people will be *different* in the communist society of the future insofar as they are historical beings, and will benefit from the greatly increased opportunities for the development of their potentialities, but they will still be *human* and therefore remain subject to sin and finitude.

This widespread misconception of communism—shared by its opponents and advocates alike—requires explanation. In his account in the *Paris Manuscripts* of human alienation under the conditions of capitalist society, Marx refers to the workers' alienation from the product of their labor, from themselves, from their species-being (i.e., their essential characteristics as social individuals and members of the human species), and from other people. The worker's plight stands in contrast to the description Marx gives us of the unalienated individual in communist society. In his mature writings, although Marx's energies were given over to analyzing the capitalist mode of production and his reflections on the future were more limited, he frequently contrasted the "fragmented" and alienated individual of capitalist society with the "fully developed" or "social" individual of the future.[33]

It is clear therefore that although Marx did not expect a *total* transformation of human nature, he envisaged a new person to go with the new society. What Marx had in mind was the realization of the inherent human potentiality, which in alienated society had been suppressed. His conception of human nature had two components—an anthropological and a historical one. Thus in *Capital*, criticizing Jeremy Bentham, he writes:

To know what is useful for a dog, one must investigate the nature of dogs. This nature is not itself deducible from the principle of utility. Applying this to man, he that would judge all human acts, movements, relations, etc. according to the principle of utility would first have to deal with *human nature in general, and then with human nature as historically modified in each epoch.* Bentham does not trouble himself with this. With the driest naïvete he assumes that the modern petty bourgeois, especially the English petty bourgeois, is the normal man.[34] [My italics.]

The idea that human nature includes a historical component is uncontroversial, and merely asserts that human needs and characteristics are shaped by social conditions. Marx's claim goes further than this in saying that specific conditions make possible a *qualitatively* greater realization of the full potential of human beings. However, this should not be confused with the even stronger contention that certain basic human characteristics are not just modified but disappear altogether. Can we not assume Marx thought that, just as people in future communist society would still experience hunger, possess sexual drives, and desire affection, so human egotism and its manifestation in greed, jealousy, and pride would continue to exist? Although Marx thought that the structural manifestation of human egotism intrinsic to capitalism would be eliminated in the new social order, and that many of the social factors which encouraged individual egotism would not be present, this is not to say that human egotism would no longer exist. Is it not more likely that Marx took certain things for granted, and concentrated on the task in hand, namely, outlining the prospect of overcoming *social* forms of alienation. Thus, in Marx's most sustained comments on human nature and needs, which are to be found in the rather turgid section of *The German Ideology* attacking Max Stirner's book *The Ego and His Own*, he declares:

The communists have no intention of abolishing the fixedness of their desires and needs, an intention which Stirner, immersed in his world of fancy, ascribes to them and to all other men; they will only strive to achieve an organization of production and intercourse which will make possible the normal satisfaction of all needs, i.e., a satisfaction which is limited only by the needs themselves.[35]

It is only on the basis of his description in the *Paris Manuscripts* of communism as "the genuine solution of the antagonisms between man and nature and between man and man," that Marx might reasonably be charged with believing human egotism would somehow be eradicated. And then is it reasonable to assign to him a view only expressed in the course of work not intended for publication and written during his mid-twenties?[36] In any case, as I have indicated in Chapter 1 above (p. 26f), here it is communism more as a transcendent ideal that Marx is discussing. Nowhere else in his writings do we find speculation concerning the ending of all the ills of human nature. Gollwitzer mentions a remark by Engels in *The Origin of the Family* that the division of labor resulted in the emergence of the instincts of avarice, violence and egoism, but this fails to recognize that Engels' often speculative views sometimes diverged considerably from Marx's.[37]

The issue is of course still further complicated by the history of Marxism since Marx, not least by some of the inflated claims which have characterized the Leninist credo of Soviet orthodoxy. As Ruurd Veldhuis has argued, Niebuhr's critique of Marxism was deficient in not making these kinds of distinctions—there is no point in attacking Lenin or Stalin, and thinking we have thereby dealt with Marx.[38] The idea that communism involves a *total* transformation of human nature stands or falls on the textual evidence of Marx's own corpus, which provides no basis for such an argument.

Marx was in fact on a number of occasions quite specific about the difficulties with which communist society would be faced. He rightly stressed the stages of communist society, since as he made clear in his *Critique of the Gotha Programme*, the reorganization of the social relations of production under advanced conditions, with the imposition of democratic control, is but a first step on the way to the society of the future:

> What we have to deal with here is a communist society, not as it has *developed* on its own foundations, but, on the contrary, just as it *emerges* from capitalist society; which is thus in every respect, economically, morally, and intellectually, still stamped with the birth marks of the old society from whose womb it emerges.[39]

Under present conditions, the problems of underdevelopment and the growing ecological crisis would be a first priority. Moreover, the reeducation of human values implied in the transition from universal self-interest to social solidarity, from the ruthless exploitation of nature to respect for the earth's resources, from nationalism and militarism to internationalism and a commitment to peace, would undoubtedly need time before it could take root in society. Nevertheless, to hope for such a transformation of political, social, and moral conditions, is surely consistent not only with Marxist expectation but with Christian teaching. Such a transformation does not imply that humans are no longer human, but only the possibility of redemption achieving a substantial social expression through the opportunities created by historical development. To make the doctrine of original sin a reason for rejecting any prospect of the social and moral regeneration of mankind would be a travesty of the Christian message. For as Nicholas Lash reminds us: "To surrender the struggle for the transformation of patterns of human behavior and relationship, to cease to grapple with the practical problems—at once moral, social and ecclesial—of the organization of redemptive love, would be to surrender hope."[40]

Those who dismiss the Marxian utopia as naive and impossible are in danger of absolutizing the present—a position that must also be critically examined. Why should it be believed that capitalism is a permanent phenomenon? Why should it be thought that change is always piecemeal and evolutionary and never revolutionary? Why should major structural injustice be regarded as an abiding feature of human history? Why should the attempt to relate the Christian hope for the Kingdom of God to the movement and direction of history be so readily abandoned? Rubem Alves puts his case well when, in reply to Thomas Sanders' criticisms, he argues that Christian utopianism does not advance

> a belief in the possibility of a perfect society but rather the belief in the non-necessity of *this* imperfect order. It does not claim that it is possible to abolish sin, but it affirms that there is no reason for us to accept the rule of the sinful structures that now control our society.[41]

The attempt to defend Marx's utopia from the judgment that it was predicated upon a denial of fallen human nature, should not detract from the *legitimate* criticism that he was over-optimistic about the prospects for overcoming social alienation and the realization of human potential in a classless society. Although Marx carefully distinguished the different stages of communist society, and only envisaged a progressive disaliena-tion, he did not give sufficient consideration to how conflicts of interest that would continue to exist might be resolved, and had little to say about the form which the state should take. In *The Communist Manifesto*, he identified a first stage of communism where the proletariat using its "political supremacy" would "centralize all instruments of production in the hands of the state." This would give way to a second stage where "class distinctions have disappeared," and "the public power will lose its political character."[42] Since Marx understood the state as an instrument of class rule, once social classes were abolished there would be an identity of interest and the state would gradually disappear. The only clue he gives us to the nature of the state under communism is his endorsement of the system of direct democracy, with recall of delegates, practiced in the Paris Commune.[43]

As a response to the problems which the organization of future communist society raises, this approach was woefully inadequate. In failing to offer any sustained reflection upon a theory of the state in post-revolutionary society, Marx left some pressing questions unanswered. What would be the relationship of local democracy to the national and international level? How would the bureaucracy needed to coordinate production and services be controlled? Would not some form of state, however subordinate to democratic restraint, still be required, even at a higher stage of communism? There is in Marx's thinking more than a trace of Rousseauesque naïveté concerning the harmonious resolution of the problems of social organization. The Marxist historian E. P. Thompson perceptively comments:

> Marx's cryptic expressions of faith as to the dramatic consequences of revolution disarmed socialist theory, led to a gross oversimplification of process, a very serious under estimation of the difficulties of socialist institution making, a skepticism as to democratic values (which arose from a necessary critique of the democratic rhetoric of bourgeois politicians), an undue optimism as to the revolutionary transformation of human nature, and an inhibition of utopianism...[44]

Finitude and Evil

Attention must now be given to the way in which Marx so totally neglected existential anxiety, human mortality, and the problem of suffering and evil.

There exist other forms of self-alienation beside those arising in the social and economic realm, which are part of the human condition. Concern with the meaning of life will continue to be central in future communist society, and social cohesion and security will not thereby remove all anxiety. Indeed, Milan Machovec suggests that after the solution of economic problems, the "searching for the meaning of life" will become more and more crucial.[45]

Mortality was a subject on which Marx also had little to say, and what he did say was somewhat superficial, reading more like an attempt to evade the issue. In his *Paris Manuscripts* he writes: "Death appears as the harsh victory of the species over the particular individual and seems to contradict their unity; but the particular individual is only a determinate species-being and thus mortal."[46] Not much solace here—especially when in a nuclear age even the survival of the species is at issue! It is of course true that within Marxism the death of those engaged in the struggle for socialism has meaning as they contribute to the eventual achievement of a classless society. This has motivated noble acts of sacrifice, but it remains only a partial answer since it excludes the rest of humanity and even the meaning it can be thought to give to the death of socialists is rather nebulous. It would therefore seem that in the face of death—the ultimate in alienation—the Marxian utopia is silent.

Suffering and evil also raise acute difficulties. Reflecting on the circumstances in which people make their own history, Marx once wrote that "the tradition of all the dead generations weighs like a nightmare on the brain of the living."[47] But it is surely not just the traditions and ideas we inherit from our forbears which "weigh" upon us, but also the memory of their plight. Marxism too readily assigns mankind's prehistory to insignificance, as simply a necessary stage on the way to the future society of freedom. Marxism has nothing to say about the suffering of an innocent child, about the inquisitions, about the exploited masses who created the historical conditions of future abundance—save that they belong to the tragedy of history. But does the prospect of human freedom and fulfillment for future generations provide consolation for the victims and maimed of the past? Arguing for a reassessment of this issue by Marxists, Christian Lenhardt maintains: "The evils of prehistory may have been overcome, but they will linger on in the collective *anamnesis* of liberated mankind....To pretend that these ancestral shadows have no place in the sun-lit world of solidarity is to be unkind, inhuman." While not seeking a theological answer, stressing communist society's possession of the means of production bequeathed by previous generations, Lenhardt calls for "a more spiritual mode of appropriating the past," and a "solidarity of the living with the dead by virtue of a bond of inheritance."[48] The remembrance and solidarity of which Lenhardt speaks is certainly important, but is not *hope* also required? Confronting this dilemma squarely, Roger Garaudy asks himself:

> How could I possibly speak of a universal project for humanity and of a meaning that must be attributed to its history when millions of humans are excluded from its past, when so many slaves and soldiers have lived and died without their lives and deaths being meaningful? How could I reconcile myself to the thought that people in the future, too, will sacrifice their lives for the new world if I were not convinced that all these are included in this new reality and so survive that they are resurrected in it? Either my ideal of future socialism is an abstract idea which promises to the elect of the future a victory possibly gained through the millenia-long annihilation of the masses, or things so happen that my whole action is founded on a belief in the resurrection of the dead.[49]

Conclusion

Marx's excessive optimism regarding future socialist society and his failure to deal with what might be referred to as the "ultimate" questions suggests two possible responses: the abandonment altogether of the idea of a socialist political theology, in which case socialism's hopes for society would also be jettisoned, or for socialist political theology to attempt to introduce new elements into socialist theory, in the context of a critical solidarity with the socialist movement.

Adopting the latter approach, a number of observations can be made. Firstly, the inadequacy of Marx's thinking on the form of the state in future socialist society is widely recognized by socialists themselves—as the quotation from E. P. Thompson indicates. There is no reason to regard this as an insurmountable problem, but it clearly suggests the need for fundamental reflection upon such issues as the nature of democracy, the use of power, the role of institutions and the significance of cultural life and its relation to the socialist state. Political theology must contribute to the kind of rethinking and development of socialist ideas which this implies. A vision of the Kingdom of God which encourages reflection upon the future is a useful counter to the traditional reluctance of Marxism (despite its implicit utopianism) to proceed beyond the scientific analysis of the present. Indeed, the Christian utopia or millennium, if only in symbolic terms, has already begun the task of describing a future liberated society.

Secondly, although future socialist society would have overcome the contradictions of capitalism, it must be stressed that this does not mean that it would thereby be free from all contradictions. Development would continue (as Marx readily acknowledged), with conflict manifesting itself at an individual and structural level, since the dialectical process itself does not come to a halt. However, the combination of social, economic, and political freedoms that characterizes such a society is novel. Thus while Marx presented too sanguine a picture of the communist future, he was right in asserting that it would be qualitatively different. It is far from clear why this particular historical possibility should be so routinely dismissed by theologians. The belief that human beings possess certain fundamental characteristics does not lead us to expect a return to slavery or the capricious rule of absolute monarchs, since it is recognized that such evils can only exist in the context of definite social conditions. All Marx is saying is that once the productive forces have reached a high level of development, capitalist social relations lose their economic basis, and that a new more advanced and humane set of social relations become practicable.

Thirdly, regarding the failure of socialism to deal with the ultimate questions of life, political theology offers the insight that socialism is not sufficiently expansive in its utopianism, which has become too restricted in conceiving its hopes as exclusively directed toward society. The hope of the resurrection and the promise that every tear will be wiped away, as the Apocalypse of John has it, respond to questions which are beyond the scope of a materialist philosophy, but which a fully humanist socialism must wrestle with. Such a view may be considered tantamount to a rejection of Marxism, but as Harvey Cox perceptively asks: "Are Marxists ready to see the impulses of Marxism absorbed, if not now then sometime in the future, in a large humanism that will include insights from many different traditions?"[50]

Although a socialist political theology must therefore have a critical content, the significance of socialism's utopianism should not be obscured. As was concluded in Chapter 8 on Moltmann (p.158), the "eschatology of the resurrection" must not be allowed to detract from Christianity's own immanent utopian hopes, since the two complement one another and are not mutually exclusive. Nor must Marx's undue optimism impede the justifiable effort to create a political theology in union with socialist utopianism. Thus, in opposition to the unwarranted justification of the status quo in so-called "Christian Realism," the hope for a qualitatively new society can be affirmed.

Constructing a socialist political theology will require the development of a whole range of categories in which to express its content. Here Tillich's concepts of "kairos," "theonomy," "expectation," and "the demonic," albeit suitably modified, will deservedly find a place. For example, a political theology serious about socialism will await a decisive turning point in history, a kairos; indeed it will expect circumstances to arise where it may once again dare to announce such a kairos! However, aware that even the momentous achievements of future socialism will not remove all conflict, it must retain an emphasis upon the demonic, not in the sense of relapsing into a cyclical view of history but in the recognition that this society too will in turn manifest new distortions and contradictions that will need to be overcome. As well as needing such categories, the scope of this theology will need to be comprehensive, embracing as Moltmann has it, previous existential and cosmological theology. There will also need to be a willingness to engage in detailed social, economic, and political analysis, in order to inform the strategic decisions and commitments that will be necessary. Moreover, given that dialogue with Marxism will assume a central importance, the need for sustained interpretative work on Marxism will become essential. Set against the enormity of such an task, this book can only hope to serve as a prolegomenon.

The most exciting thing about the socialist political theology here proposed is that it would lead not only to a renewal of Christianity's original utopian impulse, but that it also holds out important possibilities for the renewal of socialism through its cultivation of a utopianism which has the power to motivate action. Writing amid the unstable conditions in South America, Gustavo Gutiérrez in his *A Theology of Liberation* maintains that although utopianism has in the past often been thought of as synonymous with illusion and unrealism, it is once again assuming a subversive quality and becoming "a driving force of history." Utopia, he writes, involves both the "denunciation" of existing dehumanization, and the "annunciation" of that which is not yet, "the forecast of a different order of things, a new society." Through this forward movement and projection utopia becomes "a dynamic and mobilizing factor in history."[51] Marxism as a tradition needs to rediscover its utopian dimension, since utopia and scientific analysis are interrelated and stand in need of each other if they are to be effective. As José Míguez Bonino maintains: "Utopia without political science is romantic, ineffective day-dreaming; science without a mobilizing dream is inhuman or merely functional."[52]

Once the productive forces have created the preconditions for socialism the process of transition will not be automatic. Utopianism will be needed to illuminate the pathway to the future, for it is only when humankind possesses the vision of this new society that it will have the determination and courage to create it. But, it might be asked, what hopes will inspire humankind once socialism has been achieved? Here too there is a vision, that of the transcendent fulfillment of the Kingdom of God, which not only addresses all ultimate questions and sorrows, but remains as a standard and incentive for yet further advancement beyond the first beginnings of the millennium of human freedom.

Notes

Introduction

1. See T. More, *Utopia*, trans. P. Turner (Harmondsworth: Penguin, 1965), p.27, and F. E. Manuel and F. P. Manuel, *Utopian Thought in the Western World* (Oxford: Blackwell, 1979), pp.1ff and 117ff.

2. This point is made by Karl Mannheim in *Ideology and Utopia: An Introduction to the Sociology of Knowledge* (London: Routledge, 1936; rep. 1979), pp.176f.

3. See E. Bloch, *The Principle of Hope*, Vol. 1 (Oxford: Blackwell, 1986). Also the brief but helpful discussion of Bloch's understanding of utopianism in B. Goodwin and K. Taylor, *The Politics of Utopia* (London: Hutchinson, 1982), pp.80f.

4. On utopianism in Judaism, along with Chapter 5 on Bloch in this volume, see J. Hertzler, *The History of Utopian Thought* (New York: Macmillan, 1923; rep. 1965), pp.7ff. On the classical utopia see Manuel and Manuel, *Utopian Thought*, pp.64ff and L. Mumford's "Utopia, the City and the Machine" in F.E. Manuel, ed., *Utopias and Utopian Thought* (London: Souvenir Press, 1973), pp.3-24.

5. See N. Cohn, *The Pursuit of the Millennium* (London: Paladin, 1970). On the influence of the classical tradition on the modern Western utopia see Manuel and Manuel, *Utopian Thought*, pp.93ff, and K. Kumar, *Utopia and Anti-Utopia in Modern Times* (Oxford: Blackwell, 1987), pp.5ff. While acknowledging classical and Christian influences, Kumar associates the origin of utopia with Renaissance Europe. Reinhold Niebuhr stresses the influence of Christian eschatology via the Franciscan-Joachimite tradition on Renaissance views of history and utopianism in *The Nature and Destiny of Man*, Vol. 2, *Human Destiny* (New York: Scribners, 1964), pp.160ff.

6. See Wayne Hudson's discussion in *The Marxist Philosophy of Ernst Bloch* (London: Macmillan, 1982), pp.49ff, and Mannheim, *Ideology and Utopia*, pp.173ff.

7. For a helpful discussion of the problems of definition see J. C. Davies, "The History of Utopia: the Chronology of Nowhere," in P. Alexander and R. Gill, eds., *Utopias*

(London: Duckworth, 1984), pp.1-17, and T. Kenyon, "Utopia in Reality: 'Ideal' Societies in Social and Political Theory," *History of Political Thought* III, no. 1 (January 1982): 123-55. Regarding some of the links between millenarianism and enlightenment ideas of utopia and progress see E. L. Tuveson, *Millennium and Utopia: A Study in the Background of the Idea of Progress* (New York: Harper and Row, 1964), and C. L. Becker, *The Heavenly City and the Eighteenth Century Philosophers* (New Haven: Yale University Press, 1932).

8. It should be noted that incorporation of the moral dimension excludes phenomena such as fascism and Stalinism, which whatever their pretensions to the contrary, have objectives which are the antithesis of utopia. Pace V. Geoghegan, *Marxism and Utopianism* (London: Methuen, 1987), p.4.

9. "Interpretations of History," *The Protestant Era,* abridged ed., trans. J. L. Adams (Chicago: University of Chicago Press, 1957), pp.16-31 (22).

10. See Z. Bauman, *Socialism: The Active Utopia* (London: Allen and Unwin, 1976), p.13. For Bauman's definition of utopia as "an image of future and better world" see p.17.

11. Ibid., p.47.

12. *Political Writings of William Morris*, edited with an introduction by A. L. Morton (London: Lawrence and Wishart, 1979), pp.228f. On Morris' utopianism see E. P. Thompson, *William Morris: Romantic to Revolutionary*, revised ed. (New York: Pantheon Books, 1976), and P. Anderson, *Arguments Within English Marxism* (London: Verso, 1980), ch. 6.

13. J. Weiss, *Jesus' Proclamation of the Kingdom of God* (1892; London: SCM, 1971), and A. Schweitzer, *The Quest of the Historical Jesus* (1906; London: A. & C. Black, 1910).

14. *Radical Christianity: A Reading of Recovery* (Cambridge: Polity Press, 1988), pp.1-88 (40).

15. R. Coste, *Marxist Analysis and Christian Faith*, trans. R. A. Couture (New York: Orbis, 1985), makes this fundamental error and runs the danger of simply contributing to the whole cold war mentality.

16. "The Church and Communism," *Religion in Life* 6, no. 3 (1937): 347-57 (347f). Nicholas Lash's impressive writing on Marx is such an exception. See especially *A Matter of Hope: A Theologian's Reflections on the Thought of Karl Marx* (London: Darton, Longman & Todd, 1981).

Chapter 1. Utopian Beginnings

1. See G. Lichtheim, *The Origins of Socialism* (London: Weidenfeld, 1969), pp.176ff and 165f.

2. M. Evans, *Karl Marx* (London: Allen and Unwin, 1975), pp.15ff, and D. McLellan, *Karl Marx: His Life and Thought* (London: Granada, 1976), pp.1-16 and 55ff.

3. In opposition to the historical school of law, under the influence of Saint-Simon, Gans emphasized the importance of reason in the development of law. In his *Critique of Hegel's Philosophy of Right: Introduction* Marx criticizes the historical school of law, "which justifies the infamy of today by that of yesterday." In an editor's note T. Bottomore refers to Gans in *Karl Marx: Early Writings* (London: Watts and Co., 1963), p.45 (hereinafter KMEW). See also D. McLellan, *Marx Before Marxism*, 2nd ed. (London: Macmillan, 1980), pp.50ff, and *Karl Marx*, pp.55ff.

4. McLellan, *Marx Before Marxism*, pp.130ff.

5. See Lichtheim, *Origins of Socialism*, pp.26ff and 39ff, and L. Kolakowski, *Main Currents in Marxism: Its Origins, Growth and Dissolution*, Vol. 1 (Oxford: Oxford University Press, 1981), ch.10. The more practical orientation of Louis Blanc contrasts with the utopian schema of other French socialists. (See Kolakowski, *Main Currents*, pp.216ff).

6. Lichtheim, *Origins of Socialism*, pp. 31ff and 39ff, and Kolakowski, *Main Currents*, pp.187ff and 198ff.

7. See I. Berlin, *Karl Marx: His Life and Environment*, 3rd ed. (London: Oxford University Press, 1963), pp.89-100, and Kolakowski, *Main Currents*, pp.218ff.

8. See McLellan, *Karl Marx*, p.128.

9. KMEW, pp.77, 152, 155f. These criticisms are mentioned below. For a discussion of Marx's relation to the utopian socialists, see Kolakowski, *Main Currents*, Vol. 1, pp.218ff and Berlin, *Karl Marx*, pp.82ff (esp. 97f).

10. K. Marx and F. Engels, *Collected Works* (London: Lawrence and Wishart, 1975-), Vol. 5, p.461, and *The German Ideology*, ed. C. J. Arthur (London: Lawrence and Wishart, 1977), pp. 56f.

11. *The Communist Manifesto*, introduction by A. J. P. Taylor (Harmondsworth: Penguin, 1967), pp.114ff (116).

12. Quoted by M. Solomon, "Marx and Bloch: Reflections on Utopia and Art," *Telos* 13 (1972): 68-85 (69).

13. Quoted by F. E. Manuel and F. P. Manuel, *Utopian Thought in the Western World* (Oxford: Blackwell, 1979), p.702.

14. Ibid., p.706.

15. Solomon, "Marx and Bloch," p.70.

16. KMEW, pp.72 and 69f.

17. Ibid., pp.103ff (115).

18. Marx made this claim in his introduction to the *Manuscripts*: "It is hardly necessary to assure the reader that my conclusions are the fruit of an entirely empirical analysis, based on a careful critical study of political economy" (see ibid., p.63).

19. See E. Kamenka, *The Ethical Foundations of Marxism*, 2nd ed. (London: Routledge, 1972), p.2.

20. KMEW, pp.120ff.

21. Ibid., p.122.

22. Ibid., pp.123 and 125f.

23. Ibid., pp.124f.

24. See ibid., pp.126 and 13. Also see McLellan, *Karl Marx*, p.111, and J. Maguire, *Marx's Paris Writings: An Analysis* (Dublin: Gill and Macmillan, 1972), p.11.

25. Ibid., p.127f.

26. Ibid., p.129.

27. Ibid., p.130.

28. "On James Mill," *Karl Marx: Early Texts*, ed. D. McLellan (Oxford: Blackwell, 1979), p.202.

29. Marx includes a brief discussion of species-life earlier on in his notes on James Mill, where he stresses humankind's communal nature (see ibid., pp.193f).

30. KMEW, p.152.

31. Ibid., p.154.

32. Ibid., p.155.

33. Ibid., pp.155f.

34. Ibid., pp.159-62.

35. Ibid., p.167.

36. Ibid., p.167.

37. Ibid., p.155. I am indebted to R. N. Berki's discussion of this passage in his *Insight and Vision: The Problem of Communism in Marx's Thought* (London: J. M. Dent and Sons, 1983), pp.51-57.

38. With a footnote to S. Lukes, "Alienation and Anomie," McLellan mentions Schiller's *Briefe* (see *Karl Marx*, pp.121f). Lichtheim also mentions Schiller in *A Short History of Socialism* (London: Fontana, pp.77f). M. Rader has a very good chapter on Marx's relation to the Romantic movement in *Marx's Interpretation of History* (New York: Oxford University Press, 1979), pp.137ff.

39. See Lichtheim, *The Origins of Socialism*, p.165.

40. Ibid., pp.10ff.

41. In his account Lichtheim indicates the importance of the moral dimension for the Saint Simonians and Pecqueur (see ibid., pp.51ff and 76ff). McLellan, discussing the *Paris Manuscripts*, maintains that Marx's moral judgments were inspired by Schulz, Pecqueur, Sismondi, and Buret (see *Karl Marx*, p.116).

42. *The Concept of Nature in Marx* (London: NLB, 1971), pp.128f. See also my discussion of Feuerbach in Chapter 2 (pp.36ff) and my critique of Ernest Mandel in Chapter 3 (p.62).

43. For a discussion of Hess and "true socialism" see Lichtheim, *The Origins of Socialism*, pp.178-84 (esp.183); also D. McLellan, *The Young Hegelians and Karl Marx* (London: Macmillan, 1969; rep. 1980), pp.158ff.

44. E.g., Daniel Bell and Sidney Hook.

Chapter 2. History and Utopia

1. H. Fleischer, *Marxism and History*, trans. E. Mosbacher (London: Penguin, 1973), pp.7ff.

2. See Marx's letter to his father reprinted in *Karl Marx: Early Texts* (hereinafter KMET), ed. D. McLellan (Oxford: Blackwell, 1979), pp.1ff. For the Hegelian background see J. Seigel, *Marx's Fate: The Shape of a Life* (Princeton: Princeton University Press, 1978), pp.65ff; I. Zeitlin, *Marxism: A Reexamination* (New York: Van Nostrand, 1967), pp.1ff; S. Avineri, *The Social and Political Thought of Karl Marx* (Cambridge: Cambridge University Press, 1970), pp.8ff; D. Mc-Lellan, *Marx Before Marxism*, 2nd ed. (London: Macmillan, 1980), pp.46ff; and *The Young Hegelians and Karl Marx* (1969; London: Macmillan, 1969; rep. 1980), pp.1ff.

3. See *Karl Marx: Selected Writings* (hereinafter KMSW), ed. D. McLellan (Oxford: Oxford University Press, 1977), pp.388ff. Marx's articles on the wood thefts and Moselle wine growers were published in October 1842 and January 1843, respectively. Terrell Carver maintains that in his journalistic writings Marx parts company with Hegel. However, he does not provide much evidence to support this contention, which misunderstands Marx's position at the time, and is contradicted by specific passages where Marx embraces Hegel's view of the state (*Marx's Social Theory* [Oxford: Oxford University Press, 1982], p.7). Regarding the Hegelian passages in these writings see McLellan, *Marx Before Marxism*, pp.90 and 101. The view that Marx remained a Hegelian throughout this period, but that his work with the *Rheinische Zeitung* was nevertheless influential for his later break with Hegel is argued by D. Howard and J. Seigel (see D. Howard, *The Development of the Marxian Dialectic* [Carbondale, Ill.: Southern Illinois University Press, 1972], pp.24ff, and Seigel, *Marx's Fate*, pp.91-94). Howard expresses it well when he writes: "The critique of the actions of the Landtag thus sows the seeds of doubt in Marx's mind concerning the Hegelian notion of the state which he was using as a paradigm to attack the proposed legislation of the Landtag" (p.47).

4. See Carver, *Marx's Social Theory*, pp.13ff and Avineri, *The Social and Political Thought*, pp.8ff.

5. Feuerbach's influence is often mistakenly attributed to *The Essence of Christianity* (1841), but should more properly be dated to 1843. Marx singles out these later writings in the *Paris Manuscripts* (KMET, p.158), and in a letter to Feuerbach in 1844 (KMET, p.184). On Feuerbach's influence see Seigel, *Marx's Fate*, pp.96-98; Avineri, *The Social and Political Thought*, pp.8ff; McLellan, *Marx Before Marxism*, pp.107ff, and *The Young Hegelians and Karl Marx*, pp.97ff.

6. Quotes taken from McLellan, *The Young Hegelians and Karl Marx*, pp.99 and 103.

7. KMET, p.62. For discussion of Marx's *Critique* see L. Dupré, *The Philosophical Foundations of Marxism* (New York: Harcourt, Brace and World, 1966), pp.87ff;

McLellan, *Marx Before Marxism*, pp.102ff; Seigel, *Marx's Fate*, pp.103ff; Avineri, *The Social and Political Thought*, pp.8ff. Feuerbach's significance lay in the way he provided the methodological key for the critique of Hegel. However, Marx's thought was already moving in the direction of a critical relation to Hegel, and Feuerbach's influence, though seminal, should not be stressed to the exclusion of other factors.

8. KMSW, p.389. The importance Engels attached to the 1843 *Critique* is evident from his comment years later that Marx arrived at the theory of class struggle and historical materialism in this work and the two articles written in the *Deutsch-Französische Jahrbücher* in 1844. See M. Rader, *Marx's Interpretation of History* (New York: Oxford University Press, 1979), pp.6f.

9. On Hess's influence see McLellan, *The Young Hegelians and Karl Marx*, pp.137ff, and *Karl Marx: His Life and Thought* (London: Granada, 1976), pp.55ff; and Seigel, *Marx's Fate*, pp.120ff.

10. In the *Paris Manuscripts* Marx singled out the writings of Engels and Hess as "the substantial and original German works," and quoted them in the main body of the text. Looking back years later in 1859, he praised Engels' article as a "brilliant sketch" (KMET, p.131 and KMSW, p.390). For Engels' influence on Marx see T. Carver, *Marx and Engels: The Intellectual Relationship* (Sussex: Harvester, 1983); McLellan, *Marx Before Marxism*, pp.163ff; Seigel, *Marx's Fate*, pp.120ff.

11. KMET, pp.128 and 123.

12. Quoted by L. Kolakowski, *Main Currents of Marxism: Its Origins, Growth and Dissolution*, Vol. 1 (Oxford: Oxford University Press, 1981), p.128.

13. See KMET, pp.156, 149, and 153f.

14. Ibid., p.163.

15. In the Postface to the Second Edition of *Capital: A Critique of Political Economy*, Vol. I, Marx discusses his relation to Hegel, and writes: "The mystification which the dialectic suffers in Hegel's hands by no means prevents him from being the first to present its general forms of motion in a comprehensive and conscious manner. With him it is standing on its head. It must be inverted, in order to discover the rational kernel within the mystical shell" (Harmondsworth: Penguin, 1976, p.103). In the *Paris Manuscripts* Marx refers to the relation of subject and predicate being inverted in Hegel (see KMET, p.174).

16. K. Marx and F. Engels, *Collected Works*, Vol. 4 (London: Lawrence and Wishart, 1975), p.119. *The Holy Family* was written with Engels, though he only contributed about fifteen pages. A valuable discussion of this work is given in L.Dupré, *The Philosophical Foundations*, pp.137ff.

17. KMSW, pp.134f.

18. Ibid., p.135.

19. Ibid., p.154. Marx's relation to French materialism is helpfully discussed in J. Lewis, *The Marxism of Marx* (London: Lawrence and Wishart, 1972), pp.76ff, and T. Sowell, *Marxism: Philosophy and Economics* (London: Allen and Unwin,

1985), pp.31ff. See also J. Maguire, *Marx's Paris Writings: An Analysis* (Dublin: Gill and Macmillan, 1972).

20. In 1867 Marx reread *The Holy Family* and his comment to Engels suggests its rejection of metaphysical materialism posed no difficulties for him: "I was pleasantly surprised to find that we do not need to be ashamed of this work, although the cult of Feuerbach produces a very humorous effect upon one now." Karl Marx and Friedrich Engels, *Correspondence 1864-95* (London: Lawrence and Wishart, 1936).

21. KMET, pp.167 and 159. In his section on Hegel's dialectic, Marx describes Feuerbach as "the only person to have a serious and critical relationship to the Hegelian dialectic and to have made real discoveries in this field" (see KMET, p.159). During 1844, Marx in fact wrote a letter to Feuerbach, in which he refers to his work as having "given a philosophical basis to socialism" (see KMET, pp.184ff).

22. KMET, p.60. On Marx's relation to Feuerbach, along with works previously mentioned in note 5 above, see F. Jakubowski, *Ideology and Superstructure in Historical Materialism*, trans. A. Booth (London: Allison and Busby, 1976), pp.21ff; I. Mészáros, *Marx's Theory of Alienation* (London: Merlin, rep. 1982), pp.232ff; and A. Oakley, *Marx's Critique of Political Economy*, Vol. 1 (London: Routledge, 1984), pp.92ff.

23. See esp. Jakubowski, *Ideology and Superstructure*, pp.21ff and Mészáros, *Marx's Theory*, pp.232ff.

24. Marx's critique of Feuerbach and emphasis on the "active side" was to some extent a return in the direction of Hegel. See H. Marcuse, *Reason and Revolution: Hegel and the Rise of Social Theory*, 2nd ed. (London: Routledge, rep. 1977), pp.271ff.

25. K. Marx and F. Engels, *Selected Works in One Volume* (London: Lawrence and Wishart, 1968), p.585.

26. KMSW, p.156.

27. Ibid., pp.156-58.

28. Ibid., pp.389f. Such scholars include Mészáros, *Marx's Theory*, pp.232ff.; R. Tucker, *Philosophy and Myth in Karl Marx* (Cambridge: Cambridge University Press, 1961), pp.165ff; and Avineri, *The Social and Political Thought*, pp.8ff. T. Bottomore strikes a better balance in his brief comment in *Karl Marx* (Oxford: Blackwell, 1979), pp.9f.

29. *The German Ideology*, ed. C. J. Arthur (London: Lawrence and Wishart, 1977), pp.39ff (42 and 69).

30. Ibid., pp.42f.

31. Ibid., p.46.

32. Ibid., p.53.

33. Ibid., p.47. See also p.58, where Marx writes that his materialist conception of history "does not explain practice from the idea but explains the formation of ideas from material practice."

34. Ibid., p.64.
35. Ibid., pp.94f.
36. KMSW, p.202. For discussion of Marx's relation to Proudhon see H. P. Adams, *Karl Marx: In His Earlier Writings* (London: Allen and Unwin, 1940), ch. 11, pp.183ff, and R. L. Hoffman, *Revolutionary Justice: The Social and Political Theory of P.J. Proudhon* (Urbana: University of Illinois Press, 1972), pp.82ff.
37. Concerning Proudhon's use of Hegel, the following quotation from Proudhon, which Hoffman cites, says it all: "I cannot judge the kinship between my metaphysics and the logic of Hegel, since I have never read Hegel; but I am persuaded that it is his logic that I am going to employ in my next work; now, this logic is only a particular case or, if you wish, the simplest case of my own." Letter to Bergmann, January 1845, see Hoffman, *Revolutionary Justice*, pp.93f.
38. Engels' comment is taken from his letter to J. Bloch which is printed in Marx and Engels, *Selected Works in One Volume*, p.683.
39. *The Poverty of Philosophy* (Moscow: Progress Publishers, 1975), pp.160 and 116f.
40. Ibid., p.117.
41. KMSW, p.389.
42. That Marx regarded forms of cooperation to be among the productive forces is well attested. Thus, in *The German Ideology* he writes: "A certain mode of production, or industrial stage, is always combined with a certain mode of cooperation, or social stage, and this mode of cooperation is itself a 'productive force'"(p.50). See also "Cooperation," *Capital*, Vol. 1, ch. 13. William Shaw is incorrect therefore when he includes work relations among the production relations in *Marx's Theory of History* (London: Hutchinson, 1978), pp.27ff.
43. John Plamenatz argues that the wide variety of possible property relations refutes Marx's claim concerning the role of production. See *Man and Society: A Critical Examination of Some Important Social and Political Theories from Machiavelli to Marx*, Vol. 2 (London: Longman, 1963), pp.281ff. However, this critique only applies to narrower interpretations of Marx's doctrine.
44. G. A. Cohen, *Karl Marx's Theory of History: A Defence* (Oxford: Clarendon, 1978), p.31.
45. Ibid., p.134.
46. Ibid., pp.136f.
47. Ibid., pp.142-46.
48. Ibid., p.158.
49. Ibid., p.160.
50. Ibid., pp.161-63. The dependence of the productive forces on the relations of production is also acknowledged by Shaw in his defense of productive force primacy (see *Marx's Theory of History*, p.64).
51. Ibid., pp.197ff (200). Cohen writes: "The 'endless nuances' of precapitalist class history resist theorization as sets of productive relations whose succession reflects a series of rises in the level of productive power."

52. Ibid., p.176. See J. Plamenatz, *Man and Society*, p.282.
53. Ibid., pp.177-79. Cohen does not mention nontechnological factors. However, new forms of cooperation, which should be included among the productive forces, were also important for capitalist development. This point is made by Richard Miller in "The Consistency of Historical Materialism," *Philosophy and Public Affairs* 4 (1975-76):390-409 (397ff).
54. The question of the scope of historical materialism is discussed by Cohen in an essay entitled "Restricted and Inclusive Historical Materialism" in *Marx En Perspective*, Textes réunis par Bernard Chavance (Paris, 1983), pp.53-76. Here Cohen helpfully argues for a more "restricted" interpretation of historical materialism. However, his view that Marx opted for a more "inclusive variant" has less to commend it, not least because he makes the case on the basis of Engels' speech at Marx's graveside! (See pp.63ff.)
55. In *The German Ideology* Marx writes of the productive forces (p.92): "These forces are only real forces in the intercourse and association of these individuals." For the quote from Fleischer see *Marxism and History*, p.55. See also J. McMurtry, *The Structure of Marx's World-View* (Princeton: Princeton University Press, 1978), p.39; Jakubowski, *Ideology and Superstructure*, p.33; and Lewis, *The Marxism of Marx*, pp. 173ff.
56. For helpful treatments of Marx's terminology in the Preface, see Rader, *Marx's Interpretation*, pp.14ff; Fleischer, *Marxism and History*, pp.106ff; McMurtry, *The Structure of Marx's World-View*, pp.157ff. Raymond Williams is also useful in this respect, and in showing how Marx was reacting to idealist thought ("Base and Superstructure in Marxist Cultural Theory," *New Left Review* 82 [1977]): 3-16.
57. KMSW, pp.389f.
58. *The German Ideology*, p.58, and *Theories of Surplus Value*, Pt. 1 (London: Lawrence and Wishart, 1969), p.285.
59. Ibid., p.59.
60. Marx and Engels, *Selected Works in One Volume*, p.682.
61. Marx and Engels, *Selected Works in Two Volumes*, Vol. II (Moscow: Progress Publishers, 1962), p.504.
62. KMSW, p.572.
63. The reference to "free spiritual production" is in *Theories of Surplus Value*, p.285. The reading of this passage is in dispute—see the discussion by S. S. Prawer, *Karl Marx and World Literature* (Oxford: Clarendon, 1976), pp.313ff. Regarding Marx's views on law, art, morality, etc., see Rader, *Marx's Interpretation*, pp.35ff.
64 E. P. Thompson, *The Poverty of Theory* (London: Merlin, 1978), p.79.
65. Referring to what he calls "the received notion of the base," Raymond Williams describes Marx's theory of history as being "more complicated and more contradictory than the developed metaphorical notion of 'the base' could possibly allow us to realise" ("Base and Superstructure in Marx's Cultural Theory," p.5).
66. See *The Poverty of Philosophy*, p.160. Marx describes "the human being

himself" as "the main productive force," in *Grundrisse: Foundations of a Critique of Political Economy,* trans. M. Nicolaus (Harmondsworth: Penguin, 1973), p.422.

67. See H.B. Acton, *The Illusion of the Epoch* (London: Cohen and West, 1955), pp.159ff and J. Plamenatz, *Man and Society,* pp.279ff.

68. Cohen, *Karl Marx's Theory,* pp.216ff. See Carver's discussion in *Marx's Social Theory,* pp. 27ff.

69. See Jakubowski, *Ideology and Superstructure,* pp.37ff. For Cohen's account and classification of the productive forces see ibid., pp.28ff.

70. In my discussion of Marx's historical writings I am indebted to I. Zeitlin, *Marxism: A Reexamination,* pp.121ff. Zeitlin draws attention to Engels' letter to Conrad Schmidt, where he comments: "If therefore [anyone] supposes that we deny any and every reaction, of the political, etc., reflexes of the economic movement upon the movement itself, he is simply tilting at windmills. He has only to look at Marx's *Eighteenth Brumaire,* which deals almost exclusively with the popular part played by political struggles and events, of course within their general dependence on economic conditions" (p.140).

71. Marx and Engels, *Selected Works in One Volume,* pp.96-99.

72. See McLellan, *Karl Marx,* p.304.

73. *Grundrisse,* p.278.

74. *Capital,* Vol. 1, p.93.

75. Rader, *Marx's Interpretation,* p.56. In my discussion of Marx's model of organic totality, I have drawn considerably on Rader's book. Discussing the merits of this model, Rader writes: "It preserves the concept of different degrees of dominance and subordination which is the core of the base-superstructure model, but avoids its mechanical and reductionist connotations" (p.77).

76. F. Engels, *Anti-Dühring* (Moscow: Progress Publishers, 1947), p.16.

77. I have drawn closely on Carver's discussion of these issues (*Marx and Engels,* esp. pp. 107ff and 125ff). The tendency to view Marx and Engels more or less as a composite personality has been widespread. For example, M.M. Bober writes: "In this essay Marx and Engels are treated like one personality. The two friends thought and worked together, and it would be impossible to dissever the thoughts of one from those of the other" (*Karl Marx's Interpretation of History* [Cambridge: Harvard University Press, 1962], 2nd ed., Preface).

78. Jakubowski, *Ideology and Superstructure,* pp.66ff.

79. For example, in the Preface to the First Edition, Marx writes: "It is a question of these laws themselves, of these tendencies working with iron necessity toward inevitable results" (from the translation of the Moore and Aveling German edition, London: Glaiser, 1912, p.xvii.). In the Penguin (1976) edition, it reads: "It is a question of these laws themselves, of these tendencies winning their way through and working themselves out with iron necessity" (p. 91).

80. McMurtry, *The Structure of Marx's World-View,* p.142.

81. L. Kolakowski, *Toward a Marxist Humanism* (New York: Grove Press, 1968), p.69.

Chapter 3. Future Communist Society

1. K. Marx and F. Engels, *Collected Works*, Vol. 40 (London: Lawrence and Wishart, 1983), p.217. "Grundrisse" is simply the German word for outlines.
2. *Grundrisse: Foundations of a Critique of Political Economy*, translated with a foreword by M. Nicolaus (Harmondsworth: Penguin, 1973), p.7; D. McLellan, *Marx's Grundrisse* (London: Granada, 1973), pp.14 and 24.
3. For a discussion of the relation of the *Grundrisse* to *Capital*, see McLellan, *Marx's Grundrisse*, pp.20-22, and *Karl Marx: His Life and Thought* (London: Granada, 1976; rep. 1983), pp.292ff. For a contrary view to McLellan see R. L. Meek, *Studies in the Labour Theory of Value*, 2nd ed. (London: Lawrence and Wishart, 1973), pp.viiiff.
4. See B. Ollman, *Alienation: Marx's Conception of Man in Capitalist Society*, 2nd ed. (Cambridge: Cambridge University Press, 1976), pp.xiff; J. Elliott, "Continuity and Change in the Evolution of Marx's Theory of Alienation: From the *Manuscripts* through the *Grundrisse* to *Capital*," *History of Political Economy* 11, no. 3 (Fall 1979): 317-62; J. Elliott, "The *Grundrisse* As Social Theory: Link Between Young Marx and Mature Marx," *Social Science Quarterly* 59 (1978): 239-56; and D. McLellan in "Marx and the Missing Link," *Encounter* 35 (November 1970): 35-45 (42).
5. See E. Mandel, *The Formation of the Economic Thought of Karl Marx*, 2nd imp. (London: NLB, 1977), chs. 3 and 6, and J. Seigel, *Marx's Fate: The Shape of a Life* (Princeton: Princeton University Press, 1978), ch.10.
6. In the account that follows I have not dealt with the differences between Volume 1 and Volumes 2 and 3 of *Capital* and the so-called transformation problem. For discussion of the various criticisms and defenses of Marx's theory of value see I. Steedman, et al., *The Value Controversy* (London: NLB, 1981), and B. Fine and L. Harris, "Controversial Issues in Marxist Economic Theory," *The Socialist Register*, 1976, pp.141-78.
7. *Grundrisse*, pp.136ff (140) and 196. For Marx, "market value equates itself with real value by means of its constant oscillations" (p.137).
8. Ibid., p.142.
9. Ibid., pp.203 and 214f.
10. Ibid., pp.253 and 856.
11. See ibid., pp.471ff and 497ff(503).
12. Ibid., pp.282ff.
13. Ibid., p.274.

14. Ibid., p.298.
15. Ibid., p.321.
16. Ibid., pp.324f.
17. Ibid., p.323.
18. For a discussion of Marx's understanding of exploitation see M. Howard and J. King, *The Political Economy of Marx*, 2nd ed. (London: Longman, 1985), p.48ff; L. Colletti, "Bernstein and the Marxism of the Second International," in *From Rousseau to Lenin* (London: NLB, 1972), pp.92ff; see also N. Geras on the illusory character of the wage form in his "Marx and The Critique of Political Economy," in R. Blackburn, ed., *Ideology in Social Science: Readings in Critical Social Theory* (Glasgow: Collins, 1979), pp.284-305 (pp.298ff).
19. *Grundrisse*, pp.510 and 324.
20. Ibid., pp.514f and 247f.
21. Ibid., p.464.
22. Ibid., p.652.
23. *Capital: A Critique of Political Economy*, Vol. 1 (Harmondsworth: Penguin, 1976), pp.320ff.
24. Ibid., p.680.
25. Ibid., p.280.
26. Ibid., pp.729f.
27. *Capital: A Critique of Political Economy*, Vol. 3 (Harmondsworth: Penguin, 1981), p.502. Also Vol. 1, pp.125ff.
28. *History and Class Consciousness* (London: Merlin, 1971), p.92.
29. This interpretation of Marx's theory of value is supported by Ollman, *Alienation*, pp.166ff; Howard and King, *The Political Economy of Marx*, pp.52ff; P. Walton and A. Gamble, *From Alienation to Surplus Value*, 2nd ed. (London: Sheed and Ward, 1976), pp.24ff; and Elliott, "Continuity and Change," pp.317-62.
30. Elliott, "Continuity and Change," p.339.
31. Mandel, *The Formation of the Economic Thought of Karl Marx*, pp.165ff (esp. 167 and 175).
32. *Marx's Fate: The Shape of a Life*, p.322; *Grundrisse*, pp.259ff; and *Capital*, Vol. 3, p.373.
33. David McLellan's translation in McLellan, ed., *Karl Marx: Selected Writings* (Oxford: Oxford University Press (hereinafter *KMSW*), p.515.
34. The *Grundrisse* adds a further aspect of alienation through its consideration of the workers' complete subordination to automatic machinery in the labor process. In the system of automatic machinery, "the workers themselves are cast merely as its conscious linkages." Unlike instruments which the worker animates, automation means that the workers activity "is determined and regulated on all sides by the movement of the machinery, and not the opposite" (pp.692f).
35. *Grundrisse*, p.308.
36. Ibid., p.453.

37. Ibid., p.454.
38. Ibid., pp.611f.
39. Ibid., p.243.
40. Ibid., p.455.
41. Ibid., pp.289 and 307.
42. Ibid., p.158.
43. Ibid., p.458.
44. Ibid., pp.307f and 458.
45. E.g., S. Hook and L. Althusser.
46. *Capital*, Vol. 1, p.716.
47. See McLellan's translation in *KMSW*, pp. 508f, 515, 518. (The Penguin edition of *Capital*, Vol. 1, includes the missing chapter as an appendix, pp.943ff.)
48. Quoting from McLellan's translation in *KMSW*, p.500. The indexes for the Penguin edition of *Capital* give numerous references to alienation, alien, etc.
49. Meek, *Studies in the Labour Theory of Value*, pp.xiff. See also D. McLellan, *Marx Before Marxism*, 2nd ed. (London: Macmillan, 1980), pp.217ff.
50. Elliott, "Continuity and Change," p.352.
51. Mandel, *The Formation of the Economic Thought of Karl Marx*, pp.161ff. Others who argue that Marx's conception of alienation differed in his later writings include Geras,"Marx and the Critique of Political Economy," p.289, and Nicolaus in his foreword to the *Grundrisse*, pp.50ff. See also the discussion in Chapter 1, p.28.
52. D. McLellan, ed., *Karl Marx: Early Texts* (Oxford: Blackwell, 1979), pp.138ff.
53. Ibid, pp.169ff; and Mandel, *The Formation of the Economic Thought of Karl Marx*, p.170.
54. For a discussion of Feuerbach's influence on Marx see Mészáros, *Marx's Theory of Alienation* (London: Merlin, 1982), pp.81ff, 219ff, and 232ff; and McLellan, *Marx Before Marxism*, pp.107ff. Also the discussion in Chapter 2 above, p.36f.
55. *Capital*, Vol. 1, pp. 283f. See also *Grundrisse*, p.243, where Marx uses the term "species-being."
56. McLellan, *Marx's Grundrisse*, p.78 and *Grundrisse*, p.158. McLellan's translation for this passage is clearer.
57. *Grundrisse*, p.832.
58. Ibid., p.325.
59. Ibid., p.708 and 711.
60. Ibid., pp. 704-6.
61. Ibid., pp.611f and 705.
62. I have taken this quote from the translation of the German, Moore and Aveling edition, *Capital: A Critical Analysis of Capitalist Production*, Vol. 1 (London: Glaisher, 1912), p.494 (p.618 in Penguin ed.).
63. *Capital*, Vol. 3, p.959.
64. See *KMSW*, pp.564ff (569).

65. A useful discussion of automation and communism is to be found in A. Gorz, *Paths to Paradise* (London: Pluto, 1985), especially ch. 4.

66. For a discussion of Marx's theory of fetishism see the following: Ollman, *Alienation*, pp.187ff and 195ff; G. Cohen, *Marx's Theory of History: A Defence* (Oxford: Clarendon, 1978), pp.115ff; Geras, "Marx and the Critique of Political Economy," pp.284ff; P. Sweezy, *The Theory of Capitalist Development* (New York: Monthly Review Press, 1942; rep. 1970), pp.34ff; Colletti, "Bernstein and the Marxism of the Second International," pp.82ff; I. Rubin, *Essays on Marx's Theory of Value* (translated from 3rd ed., Moscow, 1928) (Montréal: Black Rose Books, 1973), pp.5ff; and I. Fetscher, "The Young Marx and the Old Marx," in S. Avineri, ed., *Marx's Socialism* (New York: Lieber-Atherton, 1973), pp.36ff.

67. *Capital*, Vol. 1, pp.164f.

68. Ibid., p.167f. See also Geras, "Marx and the Critique of Political Economy," p.287.

69. Sweezy, *The Theory of Capitalist Development*, p.36.

70. Quoted by Ollman, *Alienation*, p.200. See also pp.197ff.

71. *Capital*, Vol. 3, p.516.

72. Ibid., pp.953ff. See also Ollman, *Alienation,* pp.197f and Colletti, "Bernstein and the Marxism of the Second International," pp.90f.

73. *Capital*, Vol. 1, p.165. In a footnote in *Capital*, Marx refers to the materialist starting point of the critique of religion as being the correct method: "It is, in reality, much easier to discover by analysis the earthly kernel of the misty creations of religion than to do the opposite, i.e., to develop from the actual, given relations of life the forms in which these have been apotheosized. The latter method is the only materialist, and therefore the only scientific one" (p.494). See also Cohen, *Marx's Theory of History*, pp.125ff, who writes that "Marx was bringing to the economic domain a form of diagnosis he had applied rather earlier to religion" (p.125).

74. Fetscher, "The Young Marx," p.54. In the *Grundrisse* passages discussing the alienating character of money clearly foreshadow Marx's treatment of fetishism in *Capital*. "The social character of activity, as well as the social form of the product, and the share of the individuals in production here appear as something alien and objective, confronting the individuals, not as their relation to one another, but as their subordination to relations which subsist independently of them....In exchange-value, the social connection between persons is transformed into a social relation between things..." (p.157).

75. *Capital*, Vol. 1, Appendix, p.1003.

76. See Geras, "Marx and the Critique of Political Economy," pp.291f.

77. *Capital*, Vol. 1, p.173.

78. *Capital*, Vol. 3, p.373.

79. Ibid., pp.969f. See also Ollman, *Alienation*, pp.197f.

80. Colletti, "Bernstein and the Marxism," p.91.

81. See Cohen, *Marx's Theory of History*, pp.330 and 334.

82. *Capital*, Vol. 3, p.517.

Chapter 4. Utopian Consciousness

1. Marx's four "laws of motion" of capitalism are summarized by J. Gillman as: "(1) the law of the falling rate of profit; (2) the law of the increasing severity of the cyclical crisis; (3) the law of concentration and centralization of capital; (4) the law of the increasing misery of the working class." *The Falling Rate of Profit: Marx's Law and Its Significance to Twentieth-Century Capitalism* (London: Dennis Dobson, 1957), p.1. See also R. L. Meek's discussion of the laws in the section on "Marxist Economics" in his *Economics and Ideology and Other Essays: Studies in the Development of Economic Thought* (London: Chapman and Hall, 1967).

2. *Grundrisse: Foundations of a Critique of Political Economy*, trans. M. Nicolaus (Harmondsworth: Penguin, 1973), pp.745ff (763). See p.389 for Marx's definition of constant and variable capital.

3. Ibid., pp.333ff (340).

4. Ibid., p.435. Rosdolsky draws attention to the importance of this relative decline in living labor, and quotes Marx's *Theories of Surplus Value*, Pt. 3 (London: Lawrence and Wishart, 1972), p.241: "although the worker is exploited more than, or just as much as before...the portion of capital which is exchanged for living labor declines relatively." See *The Making of Marx's "Capital"* (London: Pluto, 1977), p.380; he takes up this question again on pp.409ff.

5. Ibid., pp.749f.

6. Ibid., p.750.

7. *Capital: A Critique of Political Economy*, Vol. 3, trans. D. Fernbach (Harmondsworth: Penguin, 1981), pp.317ff.

8. Ibid., pp.318f.

9. Ibid., p.329.

10. Ibid., p.336.

11. Ibid., p.333.

12. Ibid., pp.339ff. Marx supplements these five points with a discussion of share capital. Counteracting influences are also dealt with in the *Grundrisse* (see pp.750f).

13. Ibid., p.346.

14. Ibid., p.347.

15. Ibid., pp.349ff (esp. 359ff).

16. Ibid., pp.359ff (367).

17. Ibid., pp.355f.

18. Ibid., p.368.

19. Scholars citing evidence of a profits squeeze include Walton and Gamble, *Capitalism in Crisis: Inflation and the State* (London: Macmillan, 1976), pp.137ff, and E. Mandel, *The Second Slump* (London: Verso, 1977), pp.22-25. Ron Smith gives an instructive review of some of the international evidence in S. Aaronovitch

and R. Smith, *The Political Economy of British Capitalism: A Marxist Analysis* (London: McGraw-Hill, 1981), pp.179ff.

20. New York: Monthly Review Press, 1971, p.100ff(102).
21. *Four Lectures On Marxism* (New York: Monthly Review Press, 1981), pp.46-54.
22. Ibid., p.50f.
23. "The Theory of the Falling Rate of Profit," *New Left Review* 84 (March/April 1974):55-82 (60).
24. Ibid., p.63.
25. M. Blaug, "Technical Change and Marxian Economics," in David Horowitz, ed., *Marx and Modern Economics* (New York: Monthly Review Press, 1968), p.242.
26. Capital, Vol. 3, pp.163ff.
27. *Studies on the Left* 7, no.1 (1968): 22-49.
28. Ibid., p.23.
29. Ibid., pp.23f.
30. Ibid., p.36.
31. Ibid., pp.44-46. He also quotes Marx on p.42.
32. "The Unknown Marx," *New Left Review* 48 (March/April 1968): 41-61 (59). See also "The Crisis of Late Capitalism" in G. Fisher, ed., *The Revival of American Socialism* (Oxford: Oxford University Press, 1971), pp.3-21.
33. On Marx's use of the work of bourgeois historians for his understanding of classes see T. Bottomore and M. Rubel, *Karl Marx: Selected Writings* (Harmondsworth: Penguin, 1961), pp.19ff. Discussing Marx's *Critique of Hegel's Philosophy of Right: Introduction*, where we find the first references to the role of the proletariat, David McLellan stresses the importance of Marx's study of the French Revolution and contact with French socialist intellectuals, maintaining that "Marx's sudden espousal of the proletarian cause can be directly attributed (as can that of other early German communists such as Weitling and Hess) to his first-hand contacts with socialist intellectuals in France (see *Karl Marx: His Life and Thought* [London: Granada, 1976], p.97).
34. See his essay in Fisher, ed., *The Revival of American Socialism*, and his "Comment on Paul Walton's Paper," in P. Walton and S. Hall, eds., *Situating Marx* (London: Chaucer, 1972), pp.37-43 (41-43).
35. "The *Grundrisse* in the Context of Marx's Work as a Whole," in Walton and Hall, eds., *Situating Marx*, pp.7-14 (13f).
36. "From Alienation to Surplus Value: Developments in the Dialectic of Labour," in ibid., pp.15-36 (33-35).
37. *Critical Theory of Society*, trans. John Cumming (New York: Herder, 1971), p.114.
38. A. Oakley, *Marx's Critique of Political Economy*, Vol. 1 (London: Routledge, 1984), p.196. See also J. Elliott, "Marx's *Grundrisse*: Vision of Capitalism's Creative Destruction," *Journal of Post-Keynesian Economics*, pp.148-69 (166).
39. Penguin edition, introduction by A. J. P. Taylor, 1967, p.93.
40. Marx's theory of immiserization has received much critical attention. Three of

the most helpful discussions are in E. Mandel, *The Formation of the Economic Thought of Karl Marx* (London: NLB, 1977), pp.147ff; Rosdolsky, *The Making of Marx's "Capital,"* pp.282ff; and Meek, "Marxist Economics," pp.113ff.

41. *Grundrisse*, p.287.
42. *Capital: A Critique of Political Economy*, Vol. 1, trans. B. Fowkes (Harmondsworth: Penguin, 1976) p.275. See Rosdolsky, *The Making of Marx's "Capital,"* p.283.
43. See ibid., pp.768f.
44. See *Theories of Surplus Value*, Pt. 2 (London: Lawrence and Wishart, 1972), p.439. Also Rosdolsky, *The Making of Marx's "Capital,"* p.286ff, and Walton and Gamble, *Capitalism in Crisis*, p.124.
45. Rosdolsky, *The Making of Marx's "Capital,"* pp.377f and D. Yaffe, "The Crisis of Profitability: a Critique of the Glyn-Sutcliffe Thesis," *New Left Review* 80 (1973): 45-62 (48).
46. *Capital*, Vol. 1, p.799. See Mandel, *The Formation of the Economic Thought*, p.150.
47. *Theories of Surplus Value*, Pt. 3 (London: Lawrence and Wishart, 1972), p.312.
48. Quoted in Mandel, *The Formation of the Economic Thought*, p.147; also Rosdolsky, *The Making of Marx's "Capital,"* p.289.
49. *Capital*, Vol. 1, pp.768f.
50. See G. Williams, "18 Brumaire: Karl Marx and Defeat," in B. Matthews, ed., *Marx: A Hundred Years On* (London: Lawrence and Wishart, 1973), pp.11-37; and D. McLellan, *The Thought of Karl Marx*, 2nd ed. (London: Macmillan, 1980), pp.226ff.
51. See McLellan, *The Thought of Karl Marx*, p.227, where he writes: "In the *Grundrisse* the impression is given that capitalism has a very long way to go before it exhausts its capacities to exploit the enormous possibilities of automated machinery." Although Marx referred dramatically to the crisis of 1857 as "the deluge," this does not necessarily mean he regarded it as the final crisis, as Oakley suggests in *Marx's Critique*, pp.189ff. Rosdolsky also equates "the deluge" with revolution; see *The Making of Marx's "Capital,"* pp.7f.
52. *Grundrisse*, p.708.
53. Ibid., p.750.
54. Ibid., p.543.
55. *Situating Marx*, p.13.
56. David McLellan suggests this in a comment on the *Grundrisse*, where he confuses Marx's predictions for future communist society with conditions within capitalism at an advanced stage of development: "Marx is often credited with a simplistic view of a revolution inevitably breaking out as a result of a depression in workers' living standards. In the *Grundrisse*, however, he talks of capital's historical vocation being fulfilled only when there will be shorter working hours for the whole of society, when capitalism has exhausted its ability to pay what Marx calls

"surplus wages," and when machines have replaced human labor whenever possible—in other words when there will be no more workers in the current sense of the term." On the following page he continues: "The very factors often cited to disprove Marx's analysis—the growth of technology and automation, the rise in working class living standards and scientific competence, the emergence of leisure and indeed the virtual disappearance of the "working class" in its original primitive form—are actually viewed by Marx as necessary preconditions for his revolution" (ibid., pp. 12f).

57. The role of crises in generating revolutionary consciousness is stressed by J. Elliott, who, unlike Oakley, recognizes the important differences with the *Manifesto*. See "Marx's *Grundrisse*," p.160.

58. *Grundrisse*, p.750.

59. See J. Seigel, *Marx's Fate: The Shape of a Life* (Princeton: Princeton University Press, 1978), pp.314-16.

60. *Grundrisse*, pp.748f.

61. Ibid., p.749. See also pp.415ff.

62. Ibid., pp.700 and 704ff.

63. Ibid., pp.415ff, 749, 704ff.

64. Ibid., p.706.

65. Ibid., pp.705f.

66. Ibid., p.701.

67. Marx discusses this question in the context of criticizing Adam Smith in *Capital*, Vol. 1, pp. 611f. See Elliott, "Marx's *Grundrisse*, pp.165f.

68. *Capital*, Vol. 3, p.373.

69. *Capital*, Vol. 1, p.99.

70. Ibid., p.92.

71. See D. McLellan, *Karl Marx: Selected Writings* (Oxford: Oxford University Press, 1977), pp.564ff.

72. Ibid., pp.539ff. It should be noted that Marx's attitude to the Commune was complex and by no means uncritical. See S. Avineri, *The Social and Political Thought of Karl Marx* (Cambridge: Cambridge University Press, 1970), pp.239ff.

73. "Marx's Vision of Communism: A Reconstruction," *Critique*, Summer 1977, pp.4-41 (8).

74. *Grundrisse*, p. 463.

75. C.f. J. Elliott, "Continuity and Change in the Evolution of Marx's Theory of Alienation: from the *Manuscripts* through the *Grundrisse* to *Capital*," *History of Political Economy* 11, no.3 (Fall 1979): 317-62 (326ff).

76. See further, C. Johnson, "The Problem of Reformism and Marx's Theory of Fetishism," *New Left Review* 119 (January-February 1980): 68-96.

77. See Jack Lindsay's discussion of Gramsci in his *The Crisis in Marxism* (U.K.: Moonraker Press, 1981); and P. Sweezy and C. Bettleheim, *On the Transition to Socialism* (New York: Monthly Review Press, 1971), pp.107ff.

78. Quoted from the translation of the German Moore and Aveling edition, *Capital: A Critical Analysis of Capitalist Production* (London: Glaisher, 1912), p.494 (p.618 in Penguin ed.).

79. Lindsay, *The Crisis in Marxism*, pp.139-43.

80. While the *Paris Manuscripts* stress the importance of harmony with the world of nature, in later writings Marx's unrestrained optimism about automation, etc., tended to eclipse ecological considerations. On ecological questions R. Bahro's *The Alternative In Eastern Europe* (London: NLB, 1978) is a valuable corrective.

81. *Capital*, Vol. 3, pp.571f.

Chapter 5. Bloch's Messianic Marxism

1. For biographical information see W. Hudson, *The Marxist Philosophy of Ernst Bloch* (London: Macmillan, 1982), pp.5ff; the translators' introduction in *The Principle of Hope* (hereinafter *PH*), trans. N. Plaice, S. Plaice, and P. Knight (Oxford: Blackwell, 1986), pp.xixff; J. Moltmann's introduction to E. Bloch, *Man On His Own* (anthology), trans. E. B. Ashton (New York: Herder, 1970), pp.19-29; J. Bentley, *Between Marx and Christ* (London: Verso, 1982), pp.79ff; D. Gross "Ernst Bloch: The Dialectics of Hope," in D. Howard and K. Klare, *The Unknown Dimension* (London/New York: Basic Books, 1972), pp.107ff; and M. Lowy, "Interview with Ernst Bloch," *New German Critique* 9 (1976): 35-45.

2. See *Atheism in Christianity*, trans. J. T. Swann (New York: Herder, 1972), pp.268f; also Hudson, *The Marxist Philosophy*, p.56.

3. E. Bloch, *On Karl Marx* (anthology), trans. J. Maxwell (New York: Herder, 1971), pp.21 and 23 (*PH*, 1358f).

4. See ibid., pp.22f (*PH*, 1358f).

5. Ibid., pp.18-20 (*PH*, 1355-57).

6. Ibid., p.88 (*PH*, 274).

7. Ibid., p.21 (*PH*, 1358).

8. Ibid., pp.76f (*PH*, 264f).

9. Ibid., p.36 (*PH*, 1370).

10. See ibid., pp.16-45, esp. 44f (*PH*, 1354ff, esp. 1375f), and ibid., p.172; *Atheism in Christianity*, pp.270ff; *A Philosophy of the Future*, trans. J. Cumming (New York: Herder, 1970), pp.96 and 138. Also Hudson, *The Marxist Philosophy*, pp.99ff and 202ff, and Gross, "Ernst Bloch," pp.121ff.

11. See *On Karl Marx*, pp.30ff (*PH*, 1365ff); *PH*, pp.205ff; and *Atheism in Christianity*, pp. 268f.

12. *On Karl Marx*, pp.171f.

13. See ibid., p.139. Also pp.39ff (*PH*, 1371ff).

14. Ibid., p.33 (*PH*, 1367).

15. *Man On His Own*, p.118 (*PH*, 496).
16. Ibid., p.119 (*PH*, 497).
17. *Atheism in Christianity*, p.100.
18. Ibid., p.103.
19. *Man On His Own*, p.126 (*PH*, 502f).
20. Ibid., p.131 (*PH*, 507).
21. Ibid., p.130 (*PH*, 506).
22. Ibid., pp.133f (*PH*, 509).
23. Ibid., p.135 (*PH*, 510).
24. Ibid., p.137 (*PH*, 512).
25. *Atheism in Christianity*, p.52.
26. Ibid., pp.51ff.
27. Ibid., pp.38ff and 42ff.
28. On setting utopian hopes "on their feet" see *On Karl Marx*, pp.23ff (*PH*, 1359ff), and the discussion by Hudson, *The Marxist Philosophy*, pp.55 and 63. Regarding the importance of vital and elemental drives, etc. see K. Mannheim, *Ideology and Utopia: An Introduction the Sociology of Knowledge* (London: Routledge, 1936; rep. 1979), pp. 190ff, and P. Tillich, *The Socialist Decision*, trans. F. Sherman (New York: Harper, 1977), pp.132-37.
29. *Atheism in Christianity*, pp.58-63.
30. Ibid., p.210. Also see *Man On His Own*, pp.209ff (*PH*, 1284ff), and Hudson, *The Marxist Philosophy*, p.185.
31. *Man On His Own*, p.219ff (*PH*, 1293ff).
32. *Atheism in Christianity*, p.239.
33. Ibid., p.69. See also ibid., p.9, and *Man On His Own*, pp.147ff (*PH*, 1189ff).
34. *Man On His Own*, pp.169f (*PH*, 1233f). For the term "meta-religion" see pp.163 and 213 (*PH*, 1201 and 1288).
35. Ibid., p.223 (*PH*, 1296).
36. See P. Tillich's discussion of the "polarity of freedom and destiny" in his *Systematic Theology* (London: SCM, 1978), Vol. I, pp.182-86; J. Moltmann in *Religion, Revolution and the Future* (New York: Scribners, 1969), pp.63ff.
37. *Atheism in Christianity*, p.272.
38. M. Solomon, "Marx and Bloch: Reflections on Utopia and Art," *Telos*, pp.68-85.
39. B. Ollman, "Marx's Vision of Communism: A Reconstruction," *Critique* 8 (Summer 1977): 4-41 (9).
40. Mannheim, *Ideology and Utopia*, pp.215f.

Chapter 6. Tillich's Religious Socialism

1. See John R. Stumme, *Socialism in Theological Perspective: A Study of Paul Tillich*

1918-33 (Missoula, MT: Scholars Press, 1978), pp.16ff, also Stumme's introduction to P. Tillich, *The Socialist Decision*, trans. F. Sherman (New York: Harper and Row, 1977), p.x. I am greatly indebted to Stumme's impressive and original work on Tillich's religious socialism.

2. In C. W. Kegley and R. W. Bretall, eds., *The Theology of Paul Tillich* (New York: Macmillan, 1952), p.7.

3. Ibid., pp.7f and 12.

4. See Stumme, *Socialism in Theological Perspective*, pp.19-21 (esp. note 34); Adams' introduction in P. Tillich, *Political Expectation* (New York: Harper and Row, 1971), p.vi; W.Pauck and M. Pauck, *Paul Tillich: His Life and Thought*, Vol. 1, *Life* (London: Collins, 1977), pp.51f.

5. *On the Boundary*, introduction by J. Heywood Thomas (London: Collins, 1967), p.5. Tillich indicates that he was in some measure prepared for his decisive break with idealism through his earlier reading of Kierkegaard and the writings of Schelling's second period. His reading of Nietzsche during the war also made a strong impression upon him (pp.83f and 53). See also Kegley and Bretall, eds., *The Theology of Paul Tillich*, p.11, and Pauck and Pauck, *Paul Tillich*, p. 52.

6. In his "Autobiographical Reflections" Tillich writes that shortly after the war began he realized that "the unity of the first four weeks was an illusion, that the nation was split into classes, and that the industrial masses considered the Church as an unquestioned ally of the ruling groups." Kegley and Bretall, eds., *The Theology of Paul Tillich*, p.12. See also *On the Boundary*, pp.32f.

7. *The Religious Situation*, trans. 1926 ed. (Cleveland: Meridan, 1956), p.112.

8. See *On the Boundary*, pp.32f, and J. Heywood Thomas, *Paul Tillich: An Appraisal* (London: SCM, 1963), p.162. Theodor Siegfried refers to members of the younger generation who wished to go beyond the limited goal of political and economic reform advocated by Harnack, Troeltsch, and others, and sought instead to enter into critical solidarity with the socialist movement. See "The Significance of Tillich's Theology for the German Situation," in Kegley and Bretall, eds., *The Theology of Paul Tillich*, pp.70f.

9. See *On the Boundary*, p.32.

10. J. Fisher, "The Politicizing of Paul Tillich: The First Phase," in J. J. Carey, ed., *Tillich Studies* (Tallahassee, FL: North American Paul Tillich Society, 1975), pp.27-38.

11. Ibid., p.29.

12. Stumme, *Socialism in Theological Perspective*, pp.23f.

13. Tillich's reply has been translated and published in "Answer to an Inquiry of the Protestant Consistory of Brandenburg," trans. J. L. Adams, *Metanoia* 3, pt. 10 (September 1971): 9-12. Also see discussion by Pauck and Pauck, *Paul Tillich*, pp.68f; Stumme, *Socialism in Theological Perspective*, pp.25ff; and J. Fisher, "The Politicizing of Paul Tillich," pp.33-35.

14. Fisher, "The Politicizing of Paul Tillich," p.35.
15. Stumme, *Socialism in Theological Perspective*, pp.32ff; Pauck and Pauck, *Paul Tillich*, pp.70ff.
16. P. Tillich, "Kairos," *The Protestant Era*, abridged ed. (Chicago: University of Chicago, 1957), p.33 and the introduction, p.xv.
17. See Tillich's comments, ibid., p.xv, and Stumme, *Socialism in Theological Perspective*, p.33.
18 See Stumme, *Socialism in Theological Perspective*, p.35.; Pauck and Pauck, *Paul Tillich*, p.70ff. The Paucks say that Rüstow was a historian and economist (p.71).
19. See Stumme, *Socialism in Theological Perspective*, pp.34 and 29ff.
20. See Pauck and Pauck, *Paul Tillich*, p.70, and E. Busch, *Karl Barth: His Life from Letters and Autobiographical Texts* (London: SCM, 1976), pp.109-12.
21. Adams' introduction in P. Tillich, *Political Expectation*, p.xv.
22. "Religious Socialism," *Political Expectation*, pp.40-57 (41).
23. *On the Boundary*, p.21. See also Stumme, *Socialism in Theoretical Perspective*, p.41, esp. note 157.
24. For Tillich's relation to the young socialists and the *Neue Blätter* see Stumme, *Socialism in Theoretical Perspective*, pp.39ff.
25. See ibid., pp.31 and 44ff; Pauck and Pauck, *Paul Tillich*, pp.57-65 and 110ff.
26. See Chapter 7 below (pp. 130 and 208, note 30).
27. *The Protestant Era*, p.213.
28. *What is Religion?* trans. with introduction by J. L. Adams (New York: Harper and Row, 1969 [1973]), p.161.
29. Ibid., p.142. Tillich links the 1919 and 1922 essays together in his introduction to *The Protestant Era*.
30. Ibid., p.148.
31. Ibid., pp.162f.
32. *Political Expectation*, p.47.
33. Here I am entirely reliant upon Stumme, *Socialism in Theoretical Perspective*, pp.71ff (esp. 73 and 77). The essay in question is "Klassenkampf und Religiöser Sozialismus" (1929).
34. "Religious Socialism," *Political Expectation*, p.42.
35. *The Protestant Era*, p.59.
36. Ibid., pp.161-81 (162).
37. Ibid., p.163.
38. Ibid., p.166.
39. See *On the Boundary*, pp.74f.
40. Ibid., p.74.
41. See D. Bonhoeffer, *Ethics*, ed. E. Bethge (London: SCM, 1978).
42. "Religious Socialism," *Political Expectation*, p.57. In his 1923 essay "Basic Principles of Religious Socialism," Tillich argues that religion always has a dual relation to socialism; it involves both affirmation and radical criticism. The

requirements of what Tillich called the "*reservatum religiosum*" excluded the possibility of an unqualified identification of religion and culture, or of the Gospel and any given political reality. This religious withdrawal is the positive side of the Lutheran position. However, the "No" of the "*reservatum religiosum*" must be combined with the "Yes" of the "*obligatum religiosum,*" which acknowledges the relation of religion to culture and politics. See *Political Expectation*, pp.58-88 (64).

43. *The Religious Situation*, pp.90 and 116.
44. "Basic Principles of Religious Socialism," *Political Expectation*, pp.58-61.
45. See "Religious Socialism," pp.40f.
46. "Tillich's Doctrine of Religious Socialism," Kegley and Bretall, eds., *The Theology of Paul Tillich*, p.318.
47. *Communism and the Theologians* (London: SCM, 1958), p.197.
48. *The Socialist Decision*, p.xxxvi.
49. *The Protestant Era.*, p. xiii.
50. J. L. Adams, "Tillich's Interpretation of History," in Kegley and Bretall, eds., *The Theology of Paul Tillich*, p.308, and Tillich's introduction to *The Protestant Era*, pp.xiiff.
51. *The Protestant Era*, pp.42ff (43). See also the comments by Tillich in the introduction, p.xii, and his 1946 essay, "Religion and Secular Culture," pp.55ff. The concepts of autonomy and heteronomy were employed by Kant, but "theonomy" was Tillich's own term.
52. Concerning the relation to Tillich's theology of culture and philosophy of religion see his essays of 1919 and 1922 in *What Is Religion?* esp. pp.151ff and 163ff (164).
53. *The Protestant Era*, pp.45 and 47.
54. See "Tillich's Doctrine of Religious Socialism," *The Theology of Paul Tillich*, p.314.
55. See *On the Boundary*, pp.78f, and Tillich's reply to Heimann in Kegley and Bretall, eds., *The Theology of Paul Tillich*, p.345.
56. *The Protestant Era*, pp.46f.
57. Ibid., pp.35-38.
58. Ibid., pp.39-42.
59. Ibid., pp.42 and 47.
60. Ibid., p.48. In his *Perspectives on Nineteenth and Twentieth Century Theology*, ed. C. Braaten (London: SCM, 1967), Tillich refers to the difference between Marx and the Jewish prophets as being the emphasis on the "vertical line" (pp.189-91).
61. *The Protestant Era*, p.49. Tillich's critical comments on pp.49f prefigure his more detailed discussion of socialism in *The Socialist Decision*. Note especially his remarks on socialism's dependence on bourgeois presuppositions.
62. Ibid., pp.xvi-ii.
63. This essay appeared in *The Interpretation of History*, trans. N. A. Rasetzki and E. L. Talmey (New York: Scribners, 1936), pp.77-122 (85).

64. Ibid., p.81.

65. Ibid., pp.84f.

66. Ibid., pp.119ff. In his "Basic Principles of Religious Socialism" of 1923, Tillich argues that religion must oppose the demonic and not the secular. In the struggle against old sacramental demonries (the fixation of the holy upon objects), there is a danger of a loss of sacred import, resulting in an empty autonomy. The demonic then reappears in new naturalistic demonic creations which occupy the empty space. Religious socialism as a movement directs itself against both "sacramental and natural demonries." By natural demonries Tillich particularly had in mind destructive forms of nationalism. He also condemned capitalism as bearing the "unmistakable stamp of the demonic." *Political Expectation*, pp.58ff, esp. 66-68 and 77.

67. See *On the Boundary*.

68. "Religious Socialism," *Political Expectation*, pp.50f.

69. This essay also appears in *The Interpretation of History*, pp.219ff (234).

70. "Kairos," *The Protestant Era*, p.38.

71. See Tillich's lecture "Religion and Secular Culture," ibid., pp.59f. This criticism is made by John Heywood Thomas in *Paul Tillich: An Appraisal*, pp.169f.

72. "Kairos and Logos" appeared in his *The Interpretation of History*, pp.123ff (see esp. 131, 147, and 151). See also Eduard Heimann's treatment of this issue and Tillich's comments in Kegley and Bretall, eds., *The Theology of Paul Tillich*, pp.316f and 345f.

73. In 1934, Tillich criticized Hirsch's work in the form of an open letter, a translation of which is included in J. L. Adams, R. Shinn, and W. Pauck, eds., *The Thought of Paul Tillich* (San Francisco: Harper and Row, 1985), pp.353ff. Although this text does not particularly add anything to Tillich's previous writings on religious socialism, as an *application* of his ideas it is something of a *tour de force*. Tillich's exchange with Hirsch is discussed in W. F. Bense, "Tillich's *Kairos* and Hitler's Seizure of Power: The Tillich Hirsch Exchange of 1934-35," in Carey, ed., *Tillich Studies*, pp.39-50. More critical in tone is Louis Midgley's wide-ranging treatment of the issues raised by this exchange in his article "Ultimate Concern and Politics: A Critical Examination of Paul Tillich's Political Theology," *The Western Political Quarterly* 20 (March 1967): 31-50. For Tillich's personal relationship with Hirsch see Pauck and Pauck, *Paul Tillich*.

74. In the 1919 essay Tillich writes: "What was essentially intended in the theological system of ethics can only be realized by means of a theology of culture applying not only to ethics but to all functions of culture. Not a theological system of ethics, but a theology of culture." See *What is Religion?* pp.159ff.

75. *The Courage to Be* (London: Collins, 1977; orig. pub. 1952), and *Love, Power, and Justice: Ontological Analyses and Ethical Applications* (London: Oxford University Press, 1977; orig. pub. 1954).

76. *The Alternative Future: A Vision of Christian Marxism* (Harmondsworth: Penguin,

1976), p.90. For a critical treatment of Garaudy's work see R. B. Norris, *God, Marx, and the Future: Dialogue with Roger Garaudy* (Philadelphia: Fortress Press, 1974).

77. See J. Moltmann's discussion of Christian hope in "Ernst Bloch and Hope Without Faith," *The Experiment Hope* (London: SCM, 1975), esp. pp.34f.

78. *The Interpretation of History*, pp.243ff and 272ff.

79. Ibid., p.280.

80. Ibid., p.250.

81. Ibid., pp.280 and 276-78.

82. Ibid., p.270.

83. *The Protestant Era*, p.33.

84. Stumme, *Socialism in Theological Perspective*, pp.237f; C. Braaten, *Christ and Counter Christ* (Philadelphia: Fortress Press, 1972), pp.54-56.

85. *The Interpretation of History*, pp.282 and 276-78.

Chapter 7. Rethinking Socialism

1. For some of the background to this period see J. Braunthal, *History of the International*, Vol. 2, 1914-43, trans. J. Clark (London: Nelson, 1967), and C. Harman, *The Lost Revolution: Germany 1918-23* (London: Bookmarks, 1982).

2. *The Socialist Decision*, trans. F. Sherman with introduction by J. R. Stumme (New York: Harper and Row, 1977), p.xxxvi.

3. Ibid., p.xxv. Tillich's comment was made in a conversation with J. L. Adams. (See F. Sherman, "Tillich's Social Thought: New Perspectives," *The Christian Century* 93 [February 1976]: 168.).

4. Ibid., p.xxxi.

5. Ibid., p.2. Tillich's political analysis in *The Socialist Decision* is considered in articles by W. Weisskopf and D. McCann in J. L. Adams, R. Shinn, and W. Pauck, eds., *The Thought of Paul Tillich* (San Francisco: Harper and Row, 1985). Also, Louis Midgley includes an excellent treatment of Tillich's discussion of the roots of political thought, which draws upon some of Tillich's unpublished material, in his article "Ultimate Concern and Politics: A Critical Examination of Paul Tillich's Political Theology," *The Western Political Quarterly* 20 (March 1967): 31-50.

6. Ibid., p.3.

7. Ibid., p.4, and pp.13ff for discussion of "powers of origin."

8. Ibid., pp.4-6.

9. See *On the Boundary* (London: Collins, 1967), pp.84ff. Here, discussing "existential thinking," Tillich indicates his indebtedness to Marx, and refers to his coming under the influence of Kierkegaard's "aggressive dialectics." In his "Autobiographical Reflections," in C. W. Kegley and R. W. Bretall, eds., *The*

Theology of Paul Tillich (New York: Macmillan, 1952), p.14, regarding Heidegger's existentialism, Tillich tells us: "I resisted, I tried to learn, I accepted the new way of thinking more than the answers it gave." In his "Open Letter to Emanuel Hirsch" (1934), published in Adams et al., eds., *The Thought of Paul Tillich*, p.368, he writes: "Heidegger must be criticized from the standpoint of existential philosophical thinking. He has concealed the concrete historical limitation of his concepts by his abstract use of the concept of historicity."

10. *The Socialist Decision*, pp.13, 15, 19, 23ff. Guy Hammond writes: "It would seem that this distinction between the father as origin and the father as liberating demand reflects Tillich's effort to come to grips with Freud's analysis of the primal father (and the repressive superego) while at the same time affirming a potentially more positive role for a father figure." "Tillich and the Frankfurt Debates about Patriarchy and the Family," in J.J. Carey, ed., *Theonomy and Autonomy: Studies in Paul Tillich's Engagement with Modern Culture* (Macon, GA: Mercer University Press, 1984), pp.89-110 (97f).

11. *The Courage to Be* (London: Collins, 1977; orig. pub. 1952), pp.84ff.

12. *The Socialist Decision*, pp.18ff.

13. Ibid., pp.23f. Tillich's discussion here resembles closely his earlier writings on theonomy and the demonic, the warning concerning a new paganism being very similar to his discussion of new "natural demonries" which erupt in empty autonomy. See especially the passage on the demonic in Tillich's 1923 essay "Basic Principles of Religious Socialism," *Political Expectation*, edited and introduced by J. L. Adams (New York: Harper and Row, 1971), pp.58-88 (66ff).

14. *The Socialist Decision*, pp.47f.

15. Ibid., pp.49-51.

16. Ibid., pp.25, 27ff, and 42ff.

17. Ibid., pp.66ff.

18. Ibid., pp.97ff.

19. Ibid., pp.100f.

20. Ibid., pp.102ff, and 106ff. On pp.131f Tillich explicitly dissociates himself from any belief in a future period of complete harmony. See also his discussion of "belief-ful realism" in *The Religious Situation*, trans. 1926 ed. (Cleveland: Meridan, 1956), p.116.

21. Ibid., p.104.

22. Ibid., pp.110-12.

23. Ibid., pp. 69ff.

24. Ibid., pp.130ff.

25. Ibid., pp.71ff.

26. Ibid., pp.132ff.

27. Ibid., pp.75ff.

28. Ibid., pp.137ff.

29. Ibid., pp.79ff and 144ff.

30. On Tillich's relation to the Frankfurt School see R. Stone, *Paul Tillich's Radical*

Social Thought (Atlanta: John Knox Press, 1980), pp.63ff; J. R. Stumme, *Socialism in Theological Perspective: A Study of Paul Tillich 1918-33* (Missoula, MT: Scholars Press, 1978), pp.44ff; T. O'Keeffe, "Paul Tillich's Marxism," *Social Research* 48, no.3 (1981): 472-99; and articles by O'Keeffe and Hammond in Carey, ed., *Theonomy and Autonomy*. For a history of the Frankfurt School see M. Jay, *The Dialectical Imagination: A History of the Frankfurt School and the Institute of Social Research 1923-50* (London: Heinemann, 1973).

31. J. P. Mayer and S. Landshut, who discovered and published the *Paris Manuscripts* in 1932, were both contributors to the *Neue Blätter*, with which Tillich was also involved. (See J. Stumme's introduction to *The Socialist Decision*, pp.xviii-ix.) Tillich refers to the recent rediscovery of Marx's early writings in a footnote to a passage discussing the significance of the "young Marx." (See *The Socialist Decision*, pp.125 and 175.)

32. G. Lukács' *History and Class Consciousness* was first published in 1923. For an excellent commentary on Lukács' idea of reification and its relation to Marx's work on fetishism in *Capital* see G. H. Parkinson, *Georg Lukács* (London: Routledge, 1977), pp.54-62. Franklin Sherman discusses his translation of *Verdinglichung* in a note at the beginning of *The Socialist Decision*, p.xxviii. Parkinson translates *Verdinglichung* as reification and *Vergegenständlichung* as objectification, and points out that Lukács himself—as he later admitted—incorrectly equated these terms in his *History and Class Consciousness*.

33. *The Religious Situation*, pp.105ff.

34. *One-Dimensional Man: Studies in the Ideology of Advanced Industrial Society* (Boston: Beacon Press, 1964).

35. *The Socialist Decision*, pp.61ff.

36. Ibid., pp.127ff.

37. Ibid., p.146.

38. *Perspectives on Nineteenth and Twentieth Century Theology*, ed. C. Braaten (London: SCM, 1967) , p.189.

39. "Marxism and Christian Socialism," *The Protestant Era*, unabridged ed. (London: Nisbet, 1951), pp.277-85 (278). Also "Christianity and Marxism," *Political Expectation*, pp.89-96.

40. In his 1930 essay "Religious Socialism," Tillich expressed a remarkable degree of skepticism with regard to Marx's economic theory: "The agreement of religious socialism with Marx's sociological analysis of capitalism does not as a matter of course imply its assent to his economic theory. Religious socialism takes no position whatsoever with respect to this theory...." *Political Expectation*, pp.40-57 (49). This should not be taken to mean that Tillich had no interest in economic issues—his thinking in this area had been stimulated by his friends, the economists E. Heimann and A. Löwe, who had participated in "the Kairos Circle." For Tillich's treatment of the inner conflict in socialist economics see *The Socialist Decision*, pp.89ff and 153ff. (Roger Shinn is mistaken when he suggests this work included

no discussion of economics in his "Tillich as Interpreter and Disturber of Contemporary Civilization," in Adams et al., eds., *The Thought of Paul Tillich*, p.53.)

41. For Bloch's discussion of the "warm" and "cold" stream in Marxism see *The Principle of Hope*, Vol. 1 (Oxford: Blackwell, 1986), pp.205ff.

42. *The Socialist Decision*, pp.102-4.

43. See ibid., pp.64, 107, and 121. On p.64 Tillich writes: "The struggle against utopian socialism is based on the inseparable connection between socialism and the proletariat that Marx has demonstrated." For Tillich's theological critique of utopianism see especially *On the Boundary*, pp.74ff.

44. *Religion in Life* 6, no. 3 (1937): 347-57 (352).

45. See *On the Boundary*, p.77.

46. Quoted by Stumme, *Socialism in Theological Perspective*, p.188.

47. *Political Expectation*, pp.125-80 (169, 177, and 179).

48. *The Socialist Decision*, p.79.

49. *Political Expectation*, p.170.

50. See "Marxism and Christian Socialism," *The Protestant Era*, unabridged ed., pp.281f, and "Christianity and Marxism," *Political Expectation*, p.91.

51. *The Children of Light and the Children of Darkness* (London: Nisbet, 1945), p.66.

52. Linked with his treatment of historical materialism in *The Socialist Decision*, Tillich stressed the role of ideology as "false consciousness." As an apologia for the existing structures of capitalism, the ideology of the bourgeoisie needed to be subjected to the criticism implied in the expectation of the emergence of a new order of society. He regarded the refutation of the bourgeois belief in harmony as "the most significant and most effective accomplishment of the Marxist theory of ideology." Nor does the criticism stop here. When socialism adopts its version of the bourgeois belief in harmony, the theory of ideology should also be directed against socialism itself. (p.116-18). In "The Protestant Principle and the Proletarian Situation" (1931), Tillich linked ideology with the Protestant principle, arguing that both are concerned with exposing the concealment of the true human situation. See *The Protestant Era*, abridged ed. (Chicago: University of Chicago Press, 1957), pp.161-81 (165ff). Stumme gives a lengthy account of Tillich's view of ideology, pp.139ff. See also T. O'Keeffe's excellent "Ideology and the Protestant Principle," *Journal of the American Academy of Religion* 50, no.2 (1983): 283-305.

53. *The Socialist Decision*, pp.113f.

54. Ibid., pp. 115ff.

55. The essay was entitled "Die Religiose und Philosophische Welterbindung des Sozialismus." I have made use of Stumme's discussion, *Socialism in Theological Perspective*, pp.126ff and 164.

56. Ibid., pp. 118ff and pp.xxxiii-iv. Tillich associated "ethical socialism" with the younger generation who experienced the Russian Revolution.

57. *The Protestant Era*, abridged ed., p.173. In "Religious Socialism" (1930), he makes the connection with eschatology, writing that religious socialism "regards

the unity of the socialist dialectic, a unity of expectation and demand of that which is to come, as a conceptual unity and at the same time as a concrete and contemporary transformation of the Christian eschatological tension." *Political Expectation*, pp.40-57 (50).

58. Tillich is regarded as one of the foremost theologians of the present century, but interest in his work has tended to concentrate on his later work, and especially his *Systematic Theology*. However, since the 1970s there has been a greater interest in his earlier work. R. Bulman refers to these developments in "Theonomy and Technology: A Study in Tillich's Theology and Culture," in J. J. Carey, ed., *Kairos and Logos: Studies in the Roots and Implications of Tillich's Theology* (Macon, GA: Mercer University Press, 1984), pp.213-31.

59. See J.L. Adams' introduction in Tillich's *Political Expectation*, pp. ixff. Also Tillich's critique of Heidegger and Sartre in "The Political Meaning of Utopia," *Political Expectation*, pp.135ff and 146.

60. *Christians and the Great Economic Debate* (London: SCM, 1977), p.133.

61. "Man and Society in Religious Socialism," *Christianity and Society* 8, pt.4 (1943): 10-21 (21); "Beyond Religious Socialism: How I Changed My Mind in the Last Ten Years," *The Christian Century*, June 15, 1949, pp.732-33; Kegley and Bretall, eds., *The Theology of Paul Tillich*, p. 13; "Rejoinder," *The Journal of Religion* 46 (January 1966): 189-91; *Political Expectation*, pp.xix-xx.

62. On Tillich's political activity in the United States see Stone, *Paul Tillich's Radical Social Thought*, pp.97ff; for his relationship to the fellowship of Christian Socialists see ibid., pp.91 and 129.

63. Ibid., p.67.

Chapter 8. Eschatology and Politics

1. Moltmann's foreword in M. D. Meeks, *Origins of the Theology of Hope* (Philadelphia: Fortress, 1974), pp.ixff. Further autobiographical reflections can be found in *Experiences of God* (London, SCM, 1980), pp.6ff. See also Moltmann's comments on his experience as a prisoner of war in his essay "Dostoevsky and the Hope of Prisoners," *The Experiment Hope* (London: SCM, 1975), pp.85-100.

2. On Moltmann's relation to Barth see *Experiences of God*, pp.10f. Moltmann mentions his indebtedness to his Göttingen teachers in his foreword in Meeks, *Origins*, p.xi, and also in *The Crucified God: The Cross as the Foundation and Criticism of Christian Theology*, trans. R. A. Wilson and J. Bowden (London: SCM, 1974), p.1. Moltmann's theological development is carefully documented by Meeks, *Origins*. See also R. Bauckham, *Moltmann: Messianic Theology in the Making* (Hants.: Marshall Morgan and Scott, 1987), pp.3ff; C. Morse, *The Logic of Promise in Moltmann's Theology* (Philadelphia: Fortress, 1979), pp.1ff.

3. See especially "Ernst Bloch and Hope Without Faith," *The Experiment Hope*,

pp.30-43. Moltmann first read Bloch's *Das Prinzip Hoffnung* while on holiday in Switzerland. Recalling the experience, he writes: "The beauty of the Swiss mountains passed me by unnoticed." When he began writing *Theology of Hope*, he tells us, "suddenly all the different threads of biblical theology, and the theology of the apostolate, hope for the kingdom of God and the philosophy of hope all came together, like a pattern for a tapestry, where everything matched" (*Experiences of God*, p.11). On Moltmann's use of Bloch see Bauckham, *Moltmann*, pp.7ff; G. O'Collins, "The Principle and Theology of Hope," *Scottish Journal of Theology* 21 (1968): 129-44; G. C. Chapman, Jr., "Jürgen Moltmann and the Christian Dialogue with Marxism," *Journal of Ecumenical Studies* 18, no.3 (Summer 1981): 435-50; and F. Fiorenza, "Dialectical Theology and Hope," *Heythrop Journal* 9 (1968): 143-63, 384-99 and 10 (1969):26-42.

4. See "Hope and History," *Religion, Revolution and the Future* (New York: Scribners, 1969), pp.200-20 (218); *Experiences of God*, p.14; and "Political Theology," *The Experiment Hope*, pp.101-18. Also see Meeks discussion, in *Origins*, pp.129ff.

5. *Theology of Hope: On the Ground and the Implications of a Christian Eschatology*, trans. J. W. Leitch (London: SCM, 1967), p.16.

6. Ibid., pp.40f. Moltmann maintains that revelation must be understood in terms of promise and expectation, and is critical of the transcendental eschatology that lies behind Barth's doctrine of the self-revelation of God, and Bultmann's existentialism. He also rejects the idea of history as the indirect self-revelation of God, as presented in the theology of Pannenberg and others. In contrast to these views of revelation, which still show the influence of Greek thought, Moltmann writes: "the revelation of the risen Christ is not a form of the epiphany of the eternal present, but necessitates a view of revelation as apocalypse of the promised future of the truth" (pp. 42ff [84]).

7. Ibid., pp.95ff (107). The law too is intimately related to promise, since promise creates an interval for obedience, and requires directions for the filling out of this interval (pp.120ff).

8. Ibid., p.125.

9. Ibid., pp.133ff.

10. Ibid., pp.139ff.

11. See ibid., pp.172ff, 182ff, and 190ff.

12. Ibid., pp.168ff (172) and p.211. On the influence of Hegel on Moltmann's understanding of cross and resurrection see Meeks, *Origins*, pp.35ff, and Bauckham, *Moltmann*, pp.35f.

13. Ibid., pp.199-201.

14. Ibid., p.229.

15. Ibid., p.224.

16. Ibid., pp.304ff (326). For an excellent discussion of this chapter see F. Kerr, "Eschatology as Politics," *New Blackfriars* 49 (1967): 343-51. Kerr highlights

Moltmann's indebtedness to Hegel in his analysis of modern industrial society—
especially Hegel's *Philosophy of Law.*

17. Ibid., pp.103 and 88.
18. Ibid., p.103.
19. Cf. R. Alves, *A Theology of Human Hope* (New York: Abbey Press, 1969; rep. 1975), pp.65ff.
20. Ibid., p.65.
21. Gerald O'Collins mentions Moltmann's arbitrary use of scripture, and points out that *Theology of Hope* contains no references to John's Gospel. See "Spes Quaerens Intellectum," *Interpretation* 22 (1968): 36-52 (48). See also R. Wilburn, "Some Questions on Moltmann's Theology of Hope," *Religion in Life* 38 (Winter 1969): 578-95. Wilburn comments that Moltmann "would be forced to classify John's theology as another instance of the Greek corruption of Christian eschatology by 'the epiphany of the eternal present'" (p. 587).
22. *The Crucified God,* p.4, also pp.1ff and 65ff.
23. Ibid., p.317.
24. Ibid., pp.85f.
25. Ibid., p.88.
26. Ibid., p.98.
27. Ibid., pp.112ff (121ff).
28. Ibid., pp.126ff.
29. Ibid., pp.128ff (129). This clash between Jesus and the law is taken up in primitive interpretations of the cross and resurrection. For example, the Pauline discussion of "the end of the law" in Romans chapter ten (p.133).
30. Ibid., pp.136ff.
31. Ibid., pp.145ff (147).
32. Ibid., pp.240f. See also Moltmann's comments on his views in *The Crucified God* in *The Trinity and the Kingdom of God: The Doctrine of God,* trans. M. Kohl (London: SCM, 1981), p.160.
33. Ibid., pp.151f and 200-7.
34. Ibid., p.248.
35. Ibid., p.243.
36. Ibid., p.244.
37. *Theology of Hope,* p.169.
38. *The Crucified God,* pp.246-49. See also p.217.
39. Ibid., pp.160ff. Moltmann's twofold approach to understanding the cross, i.e., from the "historical" and then "eschatological" perspective, which structures chapters 4 and 5, is also discussed on pp.113 and 184.
40. Ibid., p.176.
41. Ibid., p.153.
42. Ibid., pp.144f.
43. Ibid., p.327.

44. Ibid., p.195.

45. Ibid., pp.321ff (328-29).

46. Ibid., p.25.

47. Ibid., pp.329ff.

48. See E. Käsemann, *Essays on New Testament Themes* (London: SCM, 1964), pp.15ff, and *New Testament Questions of Today* (London: SCM, 1969), pp.23ff (esp. 64).

49. For a useful treatment of this issue which cites much of the relevant literature see G. Gutiérrez, *A Theology of Liberation* (London: SCM, 1974), pp.225ff. It should be noted that Moltmann, unlike Brandon, does not attempt to make a case that Jesus was a political revolutionary. See S. Brandon, *Jesus and the Zealots* (Manchester: Manchester University Press, 1967). For a critique of Brandon see M. Hengel, *Christ and Power* (Philadelphia: Fortress Press, 1977).

50. J. Míguez Bonino, *Revolutionary Theology Comes of Age* (London: SPCK, 1975), pp.144-50, and E. Dussell, "Domination-Liberation: A New Approach," *Concilium* 6, no. 10 (June 1974): 34-56 (pp.52f).

51. See *The Trinity and the Kingdom of God*, and *God in Creation: An Ecological Doctrine of Creation* (London: SCM, 1985).

52. Míguez Bonino, *Revolutionary Theology*, pp.150 and 147. Dussell writes of Moltmann's work: "Hope extends as far as an historical change in the pattern of life, but not to a radical renewal of the present system with a view to an historical liberation movement as a true sign of eschatological advance. Without this concrete mediation their hopes reaffirm the *status quo* and constitute a false dream." ("Domination-Liberation," p.53.)

53. In "An Open Letter to José Míguez Bonino," *Christianity and Crisis*, March 29, 1976, pp.57-63. Here I am thinking particularly of Moltmann's comment: "It is more important to live and to work in and with the people than to relish the classless society in the correct theories" (p.61).

54. Cf. Morse, *The Logic of Promise*, p.121 and Bauckham, *Moltmann*, p.106.

55. *The Church in the Power of the Spirit: A Contribution to Messianic Ecclesiology*, trans. M. Kohl (London: SCM, 1977), pp.50ff. For a discussion of Moltmann's understanding of the Trinity in *The Crucified God* and his later writings see Bauckham, *Moltmann*, pp.91ff; R. Bauckham, "Jürgen Moltmann," in P. Toon and J. D. Spiceland, *One God in Trinity* (London: Bagster, 1980), pp.111-32; Morse, *The Logic of Promise*, pp.119ff; and R. Olson, "Trinity and Eschatology: The Historical Being of God in Jürgen Moltmann and Wolfhart Pannenberg," *Scottish Journal of Theology* 36 (1983): 213-27.

56. *The Trinity and the Kingdom of God*, pp.160f.

57. "Theology as Eschatology," in F. Herzog, ed., *The Future of Hope* (New York: Herder, 1970), pp.1-50 (1ff).

58. "Hope and History," *Religion, Revolution, and the Future*, pp.200-20 (204-6).

59. Ibid., pp.204-6 and "Theology as Eschatology," in Herzog, ed., *The Future of Hope*, pp.46-48.
60. "Methods in Eschatology," *The Future of Creation* (London: SCM, 1979), pp.41-48.
61. "The Future as a New Paradigm of Transcendence," ibid., pp.1-17 (esp. 9 and 11).
62. "Theology as Eschatology," in Herzog, ed., *The Future of Hope*, pp.9ff, and "Trends in Eschatology," *The Future of Creation*, pp.18-40 (29f).
63. "What is 'New' in Christianity," *Religion, Revolution, and the Future*, pp.3-18 (16f), and "Theology as Eschatology," in Herzog, ed., *The Future of Hope*, p.13. See also "Hope and History," *Religion, Revolution, and the Future*, p.210.
64. "Theology as Eschatology," in Herzog, ed., *The Future of Hope*, pp.15f.
65. "What is 'New' in Christianity," *Religion, Revolution, and the Future*, p.9.
66. Alves, *A Theology of Human Hope*, pp.61 and 65. Some of the ambiguities in the account of the relation between the "new" and the "old" in Moltmann's eschatology are highlighted in Brian Walsh's article, "Theology of Hope and the Doctrine of Creation: An Appraisal of Jürgen Moltmann," *Evangelical Quarterly* 59 (1987): 53-76.
67. E.g., *The Crucified God*, p.318, and "The Revolution of Freedom," *Religion, Revolution, and the Future*, p.70.
68. "Theology as Eschatology," in Herzog, ed., *The Future of Hope*, pp.10-11, 20, and 24.
69. "Hope and History," *Religion, Revolution, and the Future*, pp.212f.
70. "The Universal and Immediate Presence of God," in Herzog, ed., *The Future of Hope*, pp.81-109. In the critique of Moltmann's doctrine of God, Gilkey's work is seminal. See also his *Reaping the Whirlwind: A Christian Interpretation of History* (New York: Seabury Press, 1976), pp.226-38; and "The Contribution of Culture to the Reign of God," in M. Muckenhirn, ed., *The Future as the Presence of Shared Hope* (New York: Sheed and Ward, 1968), pp.34-58. For further discussion of Moltmann's doctrine of God see Meeks, *Origins*, pp.80ff; Morse, *The Logic of Promise*, pp.111ff; and D. Vree, *On Synthesizing Marxism and Christianity* (New York: Wiley, 1976), pp.90ff. In his latest book Moltmann again affirms his notion of the future as the mode of God's being. (See *God in Creation: An Ecological Doctrine of Creation*, pp.132ff.)
71. E.g., "Theology as Eschatology," in Herzog, ed., *The Future of Hope*, p.13.
72. See L. Gilkey, "The Universal and Immediate Presence of God," in Herzog, ed., *The Future of Hope*, p.83, and Vree, *On Synthesizing Marxism*, pp.90ff.
73. L. Weeks, III, "Can Saint Thomas' *Summa Theologiae* Speak to Moltmann's *Theology of Hope*," *The Thomist* 33, no.2 (April 1969): 215-28.
74. "Hope and Confidence: A Conversation with Ernst Bloch," *Religion, Revolution, and the Future*, pp.148-76 (161 and 164). See also "Ernst Bloch and Hope Without Faith," *The Experiment Hope*, pp.30-43.
75. Ibid., pp.161 and 165ff.

76. Ibid., pp.159ff.
77. Ibid., pp.159ff (158).
78. Moltmann, *Man: Christian Anthropology in the Conflicts of the Present*, trans. J. Sturdy (London: SPCK, 1974), p.47ff (esp. 54-56).
79. *Theology and Joy*, trans. R. Ulrich (London: SCM, 1973), p.73.
80. E.g., *The Crucified God*, pp.332f.
81. "The Principle and Theology of Hope," p.143. Also of interest is Clarke Chapman's reference to a letter he received from Moltmann, where Moltmann comments: "I discovered that not so much his neomarxism but his Jewish messianism brought me into fellowship with Ernst Bloch" ("Jürgen Moltmann," p.438).

Chapter 9. Political Theology and Socialist Utopianism

1. E. Busch, *Karl Barth: His Life from Letters and Autobiographical Texts* (London: SCM, 1976), pp.109ff.
2. J. Macquarrie, *Existentialism* (Harmondsworth: Penguin, 1973), pp.240ff (251). In his *Systematic Theology*, Vol. 1 (London: SCM, 1978), p.163, Tillich explains why he uses the word "ontology" and not "metaphysics." Macquarrie uses the two words almost interchangeably.
3. *Systematic Theology*, Vol. 1, pp.100ff.
4. On "process" theology see the collection of essays from a wide range of authors edited by E. Cousins, *Process Theology: Basic Writings* (New York: Newman Press, 1971). Here "futurist" theology refers to developments in theology associated with W. Pannenberg and J. Moltmann. See C. Braaten and R. Jenson, *The Futurist Option* (New York, Newman Press, 1970).
5. K. Rahner, "Marxist Utopianism and Christian Hope," in R. Garaudy, *From Anathema to Dialogue: The Challenge of Marxist-Christian Cooperation* (London: Collins, 1967), p.17.
6. On the historical background see T. Ling, *Karl Marx and Religion: In Europe and India* (London: Macmillan, 1980). For the importance of Bauer see D. McLellan, *The Young Hegelians and Karl Marx* (London: Macmillan, 1969 [1980]), pp.69ff, 78ff and 96, and K. L. Clarkson and D. J. Hawkin, "Marx on Religion: The Influence of Bruno Bauer and Ludwig Feuerbach on His Thought and Its Implications for the Marxist-Christian Dialogue," *Scottish Journal of Theology* 31 (1978): 533-55.
7. L. Feuerbach, *The Essence of Christianity* (New York: Harper, 1957), pp.29-31. See also pp.213f.
8. Ibid., p.26. For Feuerbach on religious alienation see especially pp.230f.
9. Ibid., p.184.
10. See L. Kolakowski, *Main Currents in Marxism: Its Origins, Growth and Dissolu-*

tion, Vol. 1 (Oxford: Oxford University Press, 1978), pp.116ff, and Clarkson and Hawkin, "Marx on Religion," p.544.

11. K. Marx and F. Engels, *On Religion* (Moscow: Progress Publishers, 1975), p.38. For a discussion of Marx's critique, see D. McLellan, *Marxism and Religion: A Description and Assessment of the Marxist Critique of Christianity* (London: Macmillan, 1987); N. Lash, *A Matter of Hope: A Theologian's Reflections on the Thought of Karl Marx* (London: Darton, Longman & Todd, 1981); and H. Gollwitzer, *The Christian Faith and the Marxist Criticism of Religion*, trans. D. Cairns (Edinburgh, St. Andrew Press, 1970).

12. Ibid., pp.14f (I have omitted the Greek from the text).

13. Ibid., p.39.

14. Ibid., pp.38f.

15. Ibid., p.39. For an account of the various instances of the description of religion as opium prior to Marx see Gollwitzer, *The Christian Faith*, pp.15ff.

16. Ibid., p.39.

17. Ibid., p.46.

18. K. Marx and F. Engels, *The German Ideology*, ed. C. J. Arthur (London: Lawrence and Wishart, 1977), pp.58 and 50 (Marx's *Theses on Feuerbach* are printed on pp.121ff).

19. K. Marx, *Capital: A Critique of Political Economy*, Vol. 1, trans. B. Fowkes (Harmondsworth: Penguin, 1976), p.172.

20. Lash, *A Matter of Hope*, p.168.

21. J. Míguez Bonino, *Revolutionary Theology Comes of Age* (London: SPCK, 1975), p.166.

22. Marx and Engels, *On Religion*, p.39.

23. See E. Bloch, *Atheism in Christianity*, trans. J. T. Swann (New York: Herder, 1972), p.62, where after quoting Marx, Bloch concludes: "There is 'sigh' there, and 'protest' too, against the bad conditions of the day; it is clearly not just a question of putting to sleep."

24. E. Bloch, *Man on His Own*, trans. E. B. Ashton (New York: Herder, 1970), pp.161 and 152. See also Chapter 5, this volume.

25. Marx and Engels, *On Religion*, p.38.

26. D. McLellan, trans. and ed., *Karl Marx: Early Texts* (Oxford: Blackwell, 1979), pp.157ff.

27. "Dogmatic Theses on the Concept of Revelation" in W. Pannenberg, ed., *Revelation As History* (London: Sheed and Ward, 1979 [1969]), pp.123-58.

28. See L. Althusser, *For Marx*, trans. B. Brewster (London: Verso, 1979). For Althusser's influence on liberation theology see P. Hebblethwaite, *The Christian-Marxist Dialogue and Beyond: Beginnings, Present Status, and Beyond* (London: Darton, Longman & Todd, 1977), pp.50-52.

29. See R. Niebuhr, "Biblical Faith and Socialism: A Critical Appraisal" in W. Leibrecht, *Essays in Honour of Paul Tillich* (London: SCM, 1958), pp.44-57. Also

essays by Bennett and Schlesinger in C. W. Kegley and R. W. Bretall, eds., *Reinhold Niebuhr: His Religious, Social, and Political Thought* (New York: Macmillan, 1956).

30. T. Sanders, "The Theology of Liberation: Christian Utopianism," *Christianity and Crisis*, September 17, 1973, pp.167-73 (167f). This debate is discussed in the foreword by W. H. Lazerath in Míguez Bonino, *Revolutionary Theology*, p.vii, and by J.Míguez Bonino in *Toward a Christian Political Ethics* (London: SCM, 1983), pp.89f.

31. Niebuhr, "Biblical Faith and Socialism," pp.51-53.

32. G. Gutiérrez, *A Theology of Liberation* (London: SCM, 1974), p.237.

33. See Chapters 1, 3, and 4 in this volume.

34. *Capital*, Vol. 1, pp.758f.

35. K. Marx and F. Engels, *Collected Works*, Vol. 5 (London: Lawrence and Wishart, 1975-), p.256. On Marx's understanding of human nature see the excellent discussion in N. Geras, *Marx and Human Nature: Refutation of a Legend* (London: Verso, 1983).

36. McLellan, *Karl Marx: Early Texts*, p.148. Here I give McLellan's translation rather than Bottomore's used in Chapter 1 (p.26). Cf. with treatment of this matter by Gollwitzer, *The Christian Faith*, pp.73f.

37. See Chapters 1 and 2 in this volume; see also Gollwitzer, *The Christian Faith*, pp.123f.

38. *Realism Versus Utopianism? Reinhold Niebuhr's Christian Realism and the Relevance of Utopian Thought for Social Ethics* (The Netherlands: van Gorcum, 1975), pp.78f.

39. K. Marx and F. Engels, *Selected Works in One Volume* (London: Lawrence and Wishart, 1968), p.319. Another such text can be found in Marx's review of the achievement of the Paris Commune. "The working class," he writes, "know that in order to work out their own emancipation, and along with it that higher form to which present society is irresistibly tending by its own economical agencies, they will have to pass through long struggles, through a series of historic processes, transforming circumstances and men" (p.291).

40. Lash, *A Matter of Hope*, p.278. I cannot, however, concur with Lash's treatment of Marx's anthropology. Lash asks of Marx: "What grounds do we have for supposing that human beings will undergo that *moral* transformation which would abolish the 'externality' of one man's egotism to the needs of another?" (p.266). Similarly he maintains Marx "was unwarrantedly optimistic in his conviction that transformation of structures and circumstances would lead, not simply to a corresponding transformation of consciousness (i.e., language and mental attitude), but to a *moral* transformation: a transformation of patterns of behavior and relationship, such that human egotism would have been irreversibly uprooted and 'abolished'" (p.408 in "All Shall Be Well: Christian and Marxist Hope," *New Blackfriars* 63 (1982): 404-15).

41. R. Alves, "Christian Realism: Ideology of the Establishment," *Christianity and Crisis*, September 17, 1973, pp.173-76 (175).

42. K. Marx and F. Engels, *The Communist Manifesto*, Introduction by A. J. P. Taylor (Harmondsworth: Penguin, 1967), pp.104f.

43. Marx and Engels, *Selected Works in One Volume*, p.288.

44. E.P. Thompson, *The Poverty of Theory and Other Essays* (London: Merlin, 1978), p.157.

45. Mentioned by J. Moltmann in *Religion, Revolution, and the Future* (New York: Scribners, 1969), p.64.

46. McLellan, *Karl Marx: Early Texts*, p.151.

47. Marx and Engels, *Selected Works in One Volume*, p.96.

48. "Anamnestic Solidarity: The Proletariat and its *Manes*," *Telos* 25 (1975): 133-54 (138 and 151f).

49. Quoted in McLellan, *Marxism and Religion*, pp.170f.

50. "The Marxist-Christian Dialogue: What Next?" in H. Aptheker, ed., *Marxism and Christianity* (New York: Humanities Press, 1968), pp.15-28 (24).

51. Gutiérrez, *A Theology of Liberation*, pp.232ff (Gutiérrez adopts the terminology of utopia as "denunciation" and "annunciation" from Freire). Although written from a critical perspective, a useful review of utopian motifs in recent political theology can be found in Alfredo Fierro's, *The Militant Gospel: An Analysis of Contemporary Political Theologies* (London: SCM, 1977), pp.257ff.

52. J. Míguez Bonino, *Christians and Marxists: The Mutual Challenge to Revolution* (London: Hodder and Stoughton, 1976), p.127.

Selected Bibliography

The following list of books and articles is a selection from the materials I have consulted. For other works cited see the notes for individual chapters.

I. Marx and Engels

Engels, F. *Anti-Dühring* (Moscow: Progress Publishers, 1947).

Marx, K. *Capital: A Critique of Political Economy*, Vols. 1-3 (Harmondsworth: Penguin, 1976-81).

———. *Early Texts*, ed. D. McLellan (Oxford: Blackwell, 1979).

———. Early Writings, ed. T. Bottomore (London: Watts and Co., 1963).

———. *Grundrisse: Foundations of a Critique of Political Economy*, trans. and foreword by M. Nicolaus (Harmondsworth: Penguin, 1973).

———. *Marx's Grundrisse*, ed. D. McLellan (London: Grenada, 1973).

———. *The Poverty of Philosophy* (Moscow: Progress Publishers, 1975).

———. *Selected Writings*, ed. D. McLellan (Oxford: Oxford University Press, 1977).

———. *Selected Writings in Sociology and Social Philosophy*, ed. T. Bottomore and M. Rubel (Harmondsworth: Penguin, 1961).

———. *Theories of Surplus Value*, Pts. 1-3 (London: Lawrence and Wishart, 1969-72).

Marx, K. and F. Engels. *Collected Works* (London: Lawrence and Wishart, 1975-).

———. *The Communist Manifesto*, introduction by A. J. P. Taylor (Harmondsworth: Penguin, 1967).

———. *The German Ideology*, ed. C. J. Arthur (London: Lawrence and Wishart, 1977).

———. *On Religion* (Moscow: Progress Publishers, 1975).

———. *Selected Works in One Volume* (London: Lawrence and Wishart, 1968).

2. Marxism

Acton, H. B. *The Illusion of the Epoch* (London: Cohen and West, 1955).

Adams, H. P. *Karl Marx: In His Earlier Writings* (London: Allen and Unwin, 1940).

Althusser, L. *For Marx*, trans. B. Brewster (London: Verso, 1979).

Anderson, P. *Arguments Within English Marxism* (London: Verso, 1980).

Avineri, S. *The Social and Political Thought of Karl Marx* (Cambridge: Cambridge University Press, 1970).

Avineri, S. ed. *Marx's Socialism* (New York: Lieber-Atherton, 1973).

Berlin, I. *Karl Marx: His Life and Environment*, 3rd ed. (London: Oxford University Press, 1963).

Blackburn, R. ed. *Ideology in Social Science: Readings in Critical Social Theory* (Glasgow: Collins, 1979).

Bober, M. M. *Karl Marx's Interpretation of History*, 2nd ed. (Cambridge: Harvard University Press, 1962).

Bottomore, T. *Karl Marx* (Oxford: Blackwell, 1979).

Braunthal, J. *History of the International*, Vol. 2, 1914-43, trans. John Clark (London: Nelson, 1967).

Carver, T. *Marx and Engels: The Intellectual Relationship* (Sussex: Harvester, 1983).

———. *Marx's Social Theory* (Oxford: Oxford University Press, 1982).

Cohen, G. A. *Karl Marx's Theory of History: A Defence* (Oxford, Clarendon, 1978).

———. "Restricted and Inclusive Historical Materialism," in *Marx En Perspective*, Textes réunis par Bernard Chavance (Paris, 1983), pp.53-76.

Colletti, L. *From Rousseau to Lenin* (London: NLB, 1972).

Dupré, L. *The Philosophical Foundations of Marxism* (New York: Harcourt, Brace and World, 1966).

Elliott, J. "Continuity and change in the evolution of Marx's Theory of Alienation: from the *Manuscripts* through the *Grundrisse* to *Capital*," *History of Political Economy* 11:3 (Fall 1979):317-62.

———. "The *Grundrisse* as Social Theory: Link Between Young Marx and Mature Marx," *Social Science Quarterly* 59 (1978):239-56.

———. "Marx's *Grundrisse:* Vision of Capitalism's Creative Destruction," *Journal of Post Keynesian Economics* 1:2 (1978-79):148-69.

Evans, M. *Karl Marx* (London: Allen and Unwin, 1975).

Fine, B. and L. Harris. "Controversial Issues in Marxist Economic Theory," *The Socialist Register* (1976):141-78.

Fleischer, H. *Marxism and History*, trans. E. Mosbacher (London: Penguin, 1973).

Geras, N. *Literature of Revolution: Essays on Marxism* (London: Verso, 1986).

———. *Marx and Human Nature: Refutation of a Legend* (London: Verso, 1983).

Gillman, J. *The Falling Rate of Profit: Marx's Law and its Significance to Twentieth-Century Capitalism* (London: Dennis Dobson, 1957).

Harman, C. *The Lost Revolution: Germany 1918-23* (London: Bookmarks, 1982).

Hodgson, G. "The Theory of the Falling Rate of Profit," *New Left Review* 84 (March/April 1974):55-82.

Hoffman, R. L. *Revolutionary Justice: The Social and Political Theory of P.J. Proudhon* (Urbana: University of Illinois Press, 1972).

Horowitz, D., ed. *Marx and Modern Economics* (New York: Monthly Review Press, 1968).

Howard, D. *The Development of the Marxian Dialectic* (Springfield, IL: Southern Illinois University Press, 1972).

Howard, D. and K. Klare. *The Unknown Dimension: European Marxism Since Lenin* (New York: Basic Books, 1972).

Howard, M. and J. King, *The Political Economy of Marx*, 2nd ed. (London: Longman, 1985).

Jakubowski, F. *Ideology and Superstructure in Historical Materialism*, trans. A. Booth (London: Allison and Busby, 1976).

Jay, M. *The Dialectical Imagination: A History of the Frankfurt School and the Institute of Social Research 1923-50* (London: Heinemann, 1973).

Johnson, C. "The Problem of Reformism and Marx's Theory of Fetishism," *New Left Review* 119 (January-February 1980):68-96.

Kolakowski, L. *Main Currents in Marxism: Its Origins, Growth and Dissolution*, Vol. 1 (Oxford: Oxford University Press, 1981).

———. *Toward a Marxist Humanism* (New York: Grove Press, 1968).

Lewis, J. *The Marxism of Marx* (London: Lawrence and Wishart, 1972).

Lichtheim, G. *A Short History of Socialism* (London: Fontana, 1983).

Lindsay, J. *The Crisis in Marxism* (UK: Moonraker Press, 1981).

Lukács, G. *History and Class Consciousness* (London: Merlin, 1971).

McLellan, D. *Karl Marx: His Life and Thought* (London: Granada, 1976).

———. *The Young Hegelians and Karl Marx* (London: Macmillan, 1969; rep. 1980).

McMurtry, J. *The Structure of Marx's World-View* (Princeton: Princeton University Press, 1978).

Maguire, J. *Marx's Paris Writings: An Analysis* (Dublin: Gill and Macmillan, 1972).

Mandel, E. *The Formation of the Economic Thought of Karl Marx*, 2nd imp. (London: NLB, 1977).

Marcuse, H. *One-Dimensional Man: Studies in the Ideology of Advanced Industrial Society* (Boston: Beacon Press, 1964).

———. *Reason and Revolution: Hegel and the Rise of Social Theory*, 2nd ed. (London: Routledge, rep. 1977).

Matthews, B., ed. *Marx: A Hundred Years On* (London: Lawrence and Wishart, 1973).

Meek, R. L. *Economics and Ideology and Other Essays: Studies in the Development of Economic Thought* (London: Chapman and Hall, 1967).

———. *Studies in the Labour Theory of Value*, 2nd ed. (London: Lawrence and Wishart, 1973).

Mészáros, I. *Marx's Theory of Alienation* (London: Merlin, rep. 1982).

Miller, R. "The Consistency of Historical Materialism," *Philosophy and Public Affairs* 4 (1975-76):390-409.

Nicolaus, M. "The Crisis of Late Capitalism," in G. Fisher, ed., *The Revival of American Socialism* (New York: Oxford University Press, 1971), pp. 3-21.

———. "Proletariat and Middle Class in Marx: Hegelian Choreography and the Capitalist Dialectic," *Studies on the Left* 7, no.1 (1968):22-49.

———. "The Unknown Marx," *New Left Review* 48 (March-April 1968):41-61.

Novack, G. *Humanism and Socialism* (New York: Pathfinder Press, 1973).

Oakley, A. *Marx's Critique of Political Economy: Intellectual Sources and Evolution*, 2 Vols. (London: Routledge, 1984-85).

Ollman, B. *Alienation: Marx's Conception of Man in Capitalist Society*, 2nd ed. (Cambridge: Cambridge University Press, 1976).

Parkinson, G. *George Lukács* (London: Routledge, 1977).

Plamenatz, J. *Man and Society: A Critical Examination of Some Important Social and Political Theories from Machiavelli to Marx*, Vol. 2 (London: Longman, 1963).

Prawer, S. S. *Karl Marx and World Literature* (Oxford: Clarendon, 1976).

Rader, M. *Marx's Interpretation of History* (New York: Oxford University Press, 1979).

Rosdolsky, R. *The Making of Marx's 'Capital'* (London: Pluto, 1977).

Rubin, I. *Essays on Marx's Theory of Value*, trans. from 3rd ed. Moscow, 1928 (Montréal: Black Rose Books, 1973).

Schmidt, A. *The Concept of Nature in Marx* (London: NLB, 1971).

Seigel, J. *Marx's Fate: The Shape of a Life* (Princeton: Princeton University Press, 1978).

Shaw, W. *Marx's Theory of History* (London: Hutchinson, 1978).

Sowell, T. *Marxism: Philosophy and Economics* (London: Allen and Unwin, 1985).

Steedman, I. et al. *The Value Controversy* (London: NLB, 1981).

Sweezy, P. *Four Lectures on Marxism* (New York: Monthly Review Press, 1981).

———. *The Theory of Capitalist Development* (London/New York: Monthly Review Press, 1942; rep. 1970).

Sweezy, P. and C. Bettleheim. *On the Transition to Socialism* (New York: Monthly Review Press, 1971).

Thompson, E. P. *The Poverty of Theory and Other Essays* (London: Merlin, 1978).

Walton, P. and A. Gamble. *Capitalism in Crisis: Inflation and the State* (London: Macmillan, 1976).

———. *From Alienation to Surplus Value*, 2nd ed. (London: Sheed and Ward, 1976).

Walton, P. and S. Hall. *Situating Marx* (London: Chaucer, 1972).

Wellmer, A. *Critical Theory of Society*, trans. John Cumming (New York: Herder, 1971).

Williams, R. "Base and Superstructure in Marxist Cultural Theory," *New Left Review* 82 (1977):3-16.

Yaffe, D. "The Crisis of Profitability: A Critique of the Glyn Sutcliffe Thesis," *New Left Review* 80 (1973):45-62.

Zeitlin, I. *Marxism: A Reexamination* (New York: Van Nostrand, 1967).

3. Marxism and Utopianism

Adamiak, R. "The 'Withering Away' of the State: A Reconsideration," *The Journal of Politics* 32 (1970):3-18.

Avineri, S. "Marx's Vision of Future Society and the Problems of Utopianism," *Dissent* 20 (Summer 1973):323-31.

Bahro, R. *The Alternative in Eastern Europe* (London: NLB, 1978).

Bauman, Z. *Socialism: The Active Utopia* (London: Allen and Unwin, 1976).

Berki, R. N. *Insight and Vision: The Problem of Communism in Marx's Thought* (London: J.M. Dent and Sons, 1983).

Burke, L. et al., eds. *Marxism and the Good Society* (Cambridge: Cambridge University Press, 1981).

Fetscher, I. "Concepts of the Communist Society of the Future," in his *Marx and Marxism* (New York: Herder, 1971), pp.182-203.

Geoghegan, V. *Marxism and Utopianism* (London: Methuen, 1987).

Gorz, A. *Paths to Paradise* (London: Pluto, 1985).

Harris, A. "Utopian Elements in Marx's Thought," *Ethics* 60, pt. 2 (January 1950):79-99.

Jameson, F. "Introduction/Prospectus: To Consider the Relationship of Marxism to Utopian Thought," *The Minnesota Review* 6 (1976):53-58.

Kamenka, E. *The Ethical Foundations of Marxism*, 2nd ed. (London: Routledge, 1972).

Kolakowski, L. "The Death of Utopia Reconsidered," in S. McCurrin, *The Tanner Lectures on Human Values* IV (Cambridge: Cambridge University Press, 1983), pp. 229-47.

Lichtheim, G. *The Origins of Socialism* (London: Weidenfeld, 1969).

Lukes, S. "Marxism and Utopianism," in P. Alexander and R. Gill, eds., *Utopias* (London: Duckworth, 1984), pp.153-67.

McLellan, D. "Marx's View of Unalienated Society," *Review of Politics* 31 (1969):459-65.

Mannheim, K. *Ideology and Utopia: An Introduction the Sociology of Knowledge* (London: Routledge, 1936; rep. 1979).

Marcuse, H. *Five Lectures: Psychoanalysis, Politics, Utopia* (Boston: Beacon Press, 1970).

Moore, S. *Marx on the Choice Between Socialism and Communism* (Cambridge: Harvard University Press, 1980).

——. "Utopian Themes in Marx and Mao: A Critique for Modern Revisionists," *Monthly Review* (June 1969):33-44.

Morris, W. *Political Writings of William Morris*, ed. A. L. Morton (London: Lawrence and Wishart, 1979).

Ollman, B. "Marx's Vision of Communism: A Reconstruction," *Critique* No. 8 (Summer 1977):4-41.

Solomon, M. "Marx and Bloch: Reflections on Utopia and Art," *Telos* No. 13 (1972):68-85.

Suvin, D. "'Utopian' and 'Scientific': Two Attributes for Socialism from Engels," *The Minnesota Review* 6 (1976):59-70.

Thompson, E. P. *William Morris: Romantic to Revolutionary*, rev. ed. (New York: Pantheon Books, 1976).

Tucker, R. *Philosophy and Myth in Karl Marx* (Cambridge: Cambridge University Press, 1961).

4. Marxism and Religion

Aptheker, H. ed. *Marxism and Christianity* (New York: Humanities Press, 1968).

Clarkson, K. L. and D. J. Hawkin. "Marx on Religion: The influence of Bruno Bauer and Ludwig Feuerbach on his thought and its implications for the Marxist-Christian Dialogue," *Scottish Journal of Theology* 31 (1978):533-55.

Coste, R. *Marxist Analysis and Christian Faith*, trans. R. A. Couture (New York: Orbis, 1985).

Fetscher, I. "Changes in the Marxist Critique of Religion," in his *Marx and Marxism* (New York: Herder, 1971), pp.252-73.

Garaudy, R. *The Alternative Future: A Vision of Christian Marxism* (Harmondsworth: Penguin, 1976).

——. *From Anathema to Dialogue: The Challenge of Marxist-Christian Cooperation* (London: Collins, 1967).

Gollwitzer, H. *The Christian Faith and the Marxist Criticism of Religion*, trans. D. Cairns (Edinburgh: St. Andrew Press, 1970).

Hebblethwaite, P. *The Christian-Marxist Dialogue and Beyond: Beginnings, Present Status, and Beyond* (London: Darton, Longman & Todd, 1977).

Kee, A. *Marxism and the Failure of Liberation Theology* (London: SCM, 1990).

Lash, N. *A Matter of Hope: A Theologian's Reflections on the Thought of Karl Marx* (London: Darton, Longman & Todd, 1981).

——. "All Shall Be Well: Christian and Marxist Hope," *New Blackfriars* 63 (1982):404-15.

Lenhardt, C. "Anamnestic Solidarity: The Proletariat and its Manes," *Telos* 25 (1975):133-54.

Ling, T. *Karl Marx and Religion: In Europe and India* (London: Macmillan, 1980).

Lobkowicz, N. "Marx's Attitude Toward Religion," in N. Lobkowicz, ed., *Marx and the Western World* (Great Bend, IN/London: Notre Dame University Press, 1967), pp.303-35. Also articles by Adams and Fessard.

Lochman, J. *Church in a Marxist Society: A Czechoslovak View* (London: SCM, 1970).

McLellan, D. *Marxism and Religion: A Description and Assessment of the Marxist Critique of Christianity* (London: Macmillan, 1987).

Míguez Bonino, J. *Christians and Marxists: The Mutual Challenge to Revolution* (London: Hodder and Stoughton, 1976).

Norris, R. B. *God, Marx, and the Future: Dialogue with Roger Garaudy* (Philadelphia: Fortress Press, 1974).

Oggletree, T., ed. *Openings for Christian-Marxist Dialogue* (Nashville: Abingdon, 1969).

Vree, D. *On Synthesizing Marxism and Christianity* (New York: Wiley, 1976).

5. Utopianism

Becker, C. L. *The Heavenly City and the Eighteenth Century Philosophers* (New Haven and London: Yale University Press, 1932).

Cohn, N. *The Pursuit of the Millennium* (London: Paladin, 1970).

Davies, J. C. "The History of Utopia: the Chronology of Nowhere," in P. Alexander and R. Gill, eds., *Utopias* (London: Duckworth, 1984), pp.1-17.

Goodwin, B. and K. Taylor. *The Politics of Utopia* (London: Hutchinson, 1982).

Harrison, J. "Millennium and Utopia," in P. Alexander and R. Gill, eds., *Utopias* (London: Duckworth, 1984), pp.61-66.

Hertzler, J. *The History of Utopian Thought* (New York: Macmillan, 1923; rep. 1965).

Horsburgh, H. "The Relevance of the Utopian," *Ethics* 67 (1957):127-38.

Kenyon, T. "Utopia in Reality: 'Ideal' Societies in Social and Political Theory," *History of Political Thought* III, no. 1 (January 1982):123-55.

Kumar, K. *Utopia and Anti-Utopia in Modern Times* (Oxford: Blackwell, 1987).

Levitas, R. *The Concept of Utopia* (New York/London: Philip Allan, 1990).

Mannheim, K. *Ideology and Utopia: An Introduction the Sociology of Knowledge* (London: Routledge, 1936; rep. 1979).

Manuel, F. E., ed. *Utopias and Utopian Thought* (London: Souvenir Press, 1973).

Manuel, F. E. and F. P. Manuel. *Utopian Thought in the Western World* (Oxford: Blackwell, 1979).

More, T. *Utopia*, trans. P. Turner (Harmondsworth: Penguin, 1965).

Tuveson, E. L. *Millennium and Utopia: A Study in the Background of the Idea of Progress* (New York: Harper and Row, 1964).

6. Bloch

Primary Sources

Atheism in Christianity, trans. J. T. Swann (New York: Herder, 1972).
"Man as Possibility," *Cross Currents* 18 (1968):273-83.
Man On His Own, trans. E. B. Ashton (New York: Herder, 1970).
On Karl Marx, trans. J. Maxwell (New York: Herder, 1971).
A Philosophy of the Future, trans. J. Cumming (New York: Herder, 1970).
The Principle of Hope, trans. N. Plaice, et al. (Oxford: Blackwell, 1986).

Secondary Sources

Bentley, J. *Between Marx and Christ* (London: Verso, 1982).
Gross, D. "Ernst Bloch: The Dialectics of Hope," in D. Howard and K. Klare, *The Unknown Dimension* (London/New York: Basic Books, 1972), pp.107-30.
———. "Marxism and Utopia: Ernst Bloch," in B. Grahl and P. Piccone, eds., *Towards a New Marxism* (St. Louis: Telos Press, 1973), pp.85-100.
Hudson, W. *The Marxist Philosophy of Ernst Bloch* (London: Macmillan, 1982).
Kellner, D. and H. O'Hara, "Utopia and Marxism in Ernst Bloch," *New German Critique* No.9 (1976):11-34.
Lowy, M. "Interview with Ernst Bloch," *New German Critique* No. 9 (1976):35-45.
Raulet, G. "Critique of Religion and Religion as Critique: The Secularized Hope of Ernst Bloch," *New German Critique* No. 9 (1976):71-85.
Rühle, J. "The Philosopher of Hope: Ernst Bloch," in L. Labedz, ed., *Revisionism: Essays on the History of Marxist Ideas* (London: Allen and Unwin, 1962), pp.166-78.
Solomon, M. "Marx and Bloch: Reflections on Utopia and Art," *Telos* No. 13 (1972):68-85.

7. Tillich

Primary Sources

"Answer to an Inquiry of the Protestant Consistory of Brandenburg," trans. J. L. Adams, *Metanoia* 3, pt. 10 (September 1971):9-12.
"Autobiograhical Reflections," in C.W. Kegley and R.W. Bretall, eds., *The Theology of Paul Tillich* (New York: Macmillan, 1952), pp.3-21.
"Beyond Religious Socialism: How I changed my mind in the last ten years," *The Christian Century,* June 15, 1949, pp.732-33.
"The Church and Communism," *Religion in Life* 6, no. 3 (1937):347-57.
The Courage to Be (London: Collins, 1977). Originally published 1952.

The Interpretation of History, trans. N. A. Rasetzki and E. L. Talmey (New York: Scribners, 1936).

Love, Power, and Justice: Ontological Analyses and Ethical Applications (London: Oxford University Press, 1954; rep. 1977).

"Man and Society in Religious Socialism," *Christianity and Society* 8, pt. 4 (1943):10-21.

"Marx's View of History: A Study in the History of the Philosophy of History," in S. Diamond, ed., *Culture in History* (New York: Columbia University Press, 1960), pp.631-41.

On the Boundary, introduction by J. Heywood Thomas (London: Collins, 1967).

"Open Letter to Emanuel Hirsch" (1934), in J. L. Adams et al., eds., *The Thought of Paul Tillich* (San Francisco: Harper and Row, 1985), pp.353-88.

Perspectives on Nineteenth and Twentieth Century Theology, ed. C. Braaten (London: SCM, 1967).

Political Expectation, J. L. Adams, ed. (New York: Harper and Row, 1971).

The Protestant Era, abridged ed., trans. J. L. Adams (Chicago: University of Chicago Press, 1957).

The Protestant Era, unabridged ed., trans. J. L. Adams with introduction by R. Daubney (London: Nisbet, 1951).

"Rejoinder," *The Journal of Religion* 46 (January 1966):189-91.

The Religious Situation, trans. 1926 ed. (Cleveland: Meridan, 1956).

The Socialist Decision, trans. F. Sherman (New York: Harper and Row, 1977).

Systematic Theology, 3 Vols. (London: SCM, 1978-).

What is Religion? trans. with introduction by J. L. Adams (New York: Harper and Row, 1969; rep. 1973).

Secondary Sources

Adams, J. L., R. Shinn, and W. Pauck, eds. *The Thought of Paul Tillich* (San Francisco: Harper and Row, 1985).

Bense, W. F. "Tillich's Kairos and Hitler's Seizure of Power: The Tillich-Hirsch Exchange of 1934/5," in John J. Carey, ed., *Tillich Studies* (Tallahassee: North American Paul Tillich Society, 1975), pp.39-50.

Bulman, R. "Theonomy and Technology: A Study in Tillich's Theology of Culture," in John J. Carey, ed., *Kairos and Logos: Studies in the Roots and Implications of Tillich's Theology*. Papers from the North American Paul Tillich Society (Macon, GA: Mercer University Press, 1984), pp.213-31.

Fisher, J. "The Politicizing of Paul Tillich: The First Phase," in John J. Carey, ed., *Tillich Studies* (Tallahassee: North American Paul Tillich Society, 1975),pp.27-38.

Fitch, R. "The Social Philosophy of Paul Tillich," *Religion in Life*, 27 (1958):247-56.

Hammond, G. "Tillich and the Frankfurt Debates about Patriarchy and the Family," in John J. Carey, ed., *Theonomy and Autonomy: Studies in Paul Tillich's Engage-*

ment with *Modern Culture* (Macon, GA: Mercer University Press, 1984), pp.89-110.

Heywood Thomas, J. *Paul Tillich: An Appraisal* (London: SCM, 1963).

Kegley, C. W. and R. W. Bretall, eds. *The Theology of Paul Tillich* (New York: Macmillan, 1952).

Midgley, L. "Ultimate Concern and Politics: A Critical Examination of Paul Tillich's Political Theology," *The Western Political Quarterly* 20 (March 1967):31-50.

O'Keeffe, T. "Ideology and the Protestant Principle," *Journal of the American Academy of Religion* 51, no.2 (1983):283-305.

————. "Paul Tillich's Marxism," *Social Research* 48, no.3 (1981):472-99.

Pauck, W. and M. *Paul Tillich: His Life and Thought*, Vol. 1, *Life* (London: Collins, 1977).

Sabatino, C. "An Interpretation of the Significance of Theonomy Within Tillich's Theology," *Encounter* 45 (Winter 1984):23-38.

Sherman, F. "Tillich's Social Thought: New Perspectives," *The Christian Century* 93 (February 1976):168-72.

Stone, R. *Paul Tillich's Radical Social Thought* (Atlanta: John Knox Press, 1980).

Stumme, J. R. *Socialism in Theological Perspective: A Study of Paul Tillich. 1918-33* (Missoula, MT: Scholars Press, 1978).

8. Moltmann

Primary Sources

The Church in the Power of the Spirit: A Contribution to Messianic Ecclesiology, trans. M. Kohl (London: SCM, 1977).

The Crucified God: The Cross as the Foundation and Criticism of Christian Theology, trans. R. A. Wilson and J. Bowden (London: SCM, 1974).

Experiences of God (London: SCM, 1980).

The Experiment Hope (London: SCM, 1975).

The Future of Creation (London: SCM, 1979).

God in Creation: An Ecological Doctrine of Creation (London: SCM, 1985).

Man: Christian Anthropology in the Conflicts of the Present, trans. J. Sturdy (London: SPCK, 1974).

"An Open Letter to José Míguez Bonino," *Christianity and Crisis*, March 29, 1976, pp.57-63.

Religion, Revolution, and the Future (New York: Scribners, 1969).

Theology and Joy, trans. R. Ulrich (London: SCM, 1973).

"Theology as Eschatology," in F. Herzog, ed., *The Future of Hope* (New York: Herder, 1970), pp.1-50 .

Theology of Hope: On the Ground and the Implications of a Christian Eschatology, trans. J. W. Leitch (London: SCM, 1967).

The Trinity and the Kingdom of God: The Doctrine of God, trans. M. Kohl (London: SCM, 1981).

Secondary Sources

Alves, R. *A Theology of Human Hope* (New York: Abbey Press, 1969; rep. 1975).

Attfield, D. "Can God be Crucified? A Discussion of J. Moltmann," *Scottish Journal of Theology* 30 (1977):47-57.

Bauckham, R. "Jürgen Moltmann," in P. Toon and J. D. Spiceland, *One God in Trinity* (London: Bagster, 1980), pp.111-32.

———. *Moltmann: Messianic Theology in the Making* (Hants: Marshall Morgan and Scott, 1987).

Capps, W., ed. *The Future of Hope* (Philadelphia: Fortress Press, 1970).

Clarke Chapman, Jr. "Jürgen Moltmann and the Christian Dialogue with Marxism," *Journal of Ecumenical Studies* 18:3 (Summer 1981):435-50.

Fiorenza, F. "Dialectical Theology and Hope," *Heythrop Journal* 9 (1968):143-63, 384-99 and 10 (1969):26-42.

Gilkey, L. "The Contribution of Culture to the Reign of God," in M. Muckenhirn, ed., *The Future as the Presence of Shared Hope* (New York: Sheed and Ward, 1968), pp.34-58.

———. *Reaping the Whirlwind: A Christian Interpretation of History* (New York: Seabury Press, 1976).

———. "The Universal and Immediate Presence of God," in F. Herzog, ed., *The Future of Hope* (New York: Herder, 1970), pp.81-109.

Kerr, F. "Eschatology as Politics," *New Blackfriars* 49 (1967):343-51.

Meeks, M. D. *Origins of the Theology of Hope* (Philadelphia: Fortress Press, 1974).

Míguez Bonino, J. *Revolutionary Theology Comes of Age* (London: SPCK, 1975).

Morse, C. *The Logic of Promise in Moltmann's Theology* (Philadelphia: Fortress Press, 1979).

O'Collins, G. "The Principle and Theology of Hope," *Scottish Journal of Theology* 21 (1968):129-44.

———. "Spes Quaerens Intellectum," *Interpretation* 22 (1968):36-52.

Olson, R. "Trinity and Eschatology: The Historical Being of God in Jürgen Moltmann and Wolfhart Pannenberg," *Scottish Journal of Theology* 36 (1983):213-27.

Walsh, B. "Theology of Hope and the Doctrine of Creation: An Appraisal of Jürgen Moltmann," *Evangelical Quarterly* 59 (1987):53-76.

Weeks, L. III, "Can Saint Thomas' Summa Theologiae Speak to Moltmann's Theology of Hope," *The Thomist* 33, no.2 (April 1969):215-28.

Wilburn, R. "Some Questions on Moltmann's Theology of Hope," *Religion in Life* 38 (Winter 1969):578-95.

9. *Miscellaneous Theology*

Alves, R. "Christian Realism: Ideology of the Establishment," *Christianity and Crisis,* September 17, 1973, pp.173-76.

Bonhoeffer, D. *Ethics,* ed. E. Bethge (London: SCM, 1978).

Braaten, C. *Christ and Counter Christ* (Philadelphia: Fortress Press, 1972).

Braaten, C. and R. Jenson. *The Futurist Option* (New York: Newman Press, 1970).

Brandon, S. *Jesus and the Zealots* (Manchester: Manchester University Press, 1967).

Busch, E. *Karl Barth: His Life from Letters and Autobiographical Texts* (London: SCM, 1976).

Cadorrette, C. *From the Heart of the People: The Theology of Gustavo Gutiérrez* (Oak Park, IL: Meyer Stone, 1988).

Cobb, J.B. *Process Theology as Political Theology* (Manchester: Manchester University Press, 1982).

Cousins, E. *Process Theology: Basic Writings* (New York: Newman Press, 1971).

Durkin, K. *Reinhold Niebuhr* (London: Geoffrey Chapman, 1989).

Dussell, E. "Domination Liberation: A New Approach," *Concilium* 6, no. 10 (June 1974):34-56.

Feuerbach, L. *The Essence of Christianity* (New York: Harper, 1957).

Fierro, A. *The Militant Gospel: An Analysis of Contemporary Political Theologies* (London: SCM, 1977).

Gutiérrez, G. *A Theology of Liberation* (London: SCM, 1974).

Hengel, M. *Christ and Power* (Philadelphia: Fortress Press, 1977).

Käsemann, E. *Essays on New Testament Themes* (London: SCM, 1964).

——. *New Testament Questions of Today* (London: SCM, 1969).

Kegley, C. W. and R. W. Bretall, eds. *Reinhold Niebuhr: His Religious, Social, and Political Thought* (New York: Macmillan, 1956).

Macquarrie, J. *Existentialism* (Harmondsworth: Penguin, 1973).

Míguez Bonino, J. *Toward a Christian Political Ethics* (London: SCM, 1983).

Niebuhr, R. "Biblical Faith and Socialism: A Critical Appraisal," in W. Leibrecht, *Essays in Honour of Paul Tillich* (London: SCM, 1958), pp.44-57.

——. *The Children of Light and the Children of Darkness* (London: Nisbet, 1945).

——. *The Nature and Destiny of Man,* Vol. 2, *Human Destiny* (New York: Scribners, 1964).

Pannenberg, W., ed. *Revelation as History* (London: Sheed and Ward, 1969; rep. 1979).

Rowland, C. *Radical Christianity: A Reading of Recovery* (Cambridge: Polity Press, 1988).

Sanders, T. "The Theology of Liberation: Christian Utopianism," *Christianity and Crisis,* September 17, 1973, pp.167-73.

Schweitzer, A. *The Quest of the Historical Jesus E. T.* (London: A. & C. Black, 1910). Originally published 1906.

Veldhuis, R. *Realism Versus Utopianism? Reinhold Niebuhr's Christian Realism and the Relevance of Utopian Thought for Social Ethics* (The Netherlands: van Gorcum, 1975).

Weiss, J. *Jesus' Proclamation of the Kingdom of God E. T.* (London: SCM, 1971). Originally published 1892.

West, C. *Communism and the Theologians* (London: SCM, 1958).

Wogaman, P. *Christians and the Great Economic Debate* (London: SCM, 1977).

Index